The Funniest Man in London

The Life and Times of H.G. Pélissier (1874–1913)

Forgotten satirist and composer, founder of *The Follies*

Praise for *The Funniest Man in London*

H.G. Pélissier is among the master spirits of the Edwardian age, as writer, producer, composer and performer, hugely successful and influential, his early demise on the eve of WW1 fuelled by run-ins with the Lord Chamberlain's office and wilful hedonism seems to have consigned him to the rubbish bin of theatrical history. In Anthony Binns's biography, he lives again in all his comic glory, a man in many ways ahead of his time, now he can take his proper place in the pantheon of great British entertainers, an example and an inspiration.

Simon Callow – writer, actor & director

Anthony Binns's forensic detail about H.G. Pélissier's Follies in 'The Funniest Man in London', is a fascinating exploration into the history and evolution of British popular culture. Such material is often overlooked by academic historiography, yet this volume provides invaluable fresh insight into the ways in which high art and popular performance forms were blended during the early years of the twentieth century. This book is an exciting and timely contribution to our understanding of contemporary culture.

Dr Tony Lidington – author of *Don't Forget the Pierrots!* (*the complete history of British seaside pierrot troupes and concert parties*, Routledge, 2022)

H.G Pélissier was a man ahead of his time. He battled the censors and made the world laugh at pious, nay-saying officialdom. We could do with an H.G.P. today.

Quentin Letts – journalist & theatre critic

If you are about to read this book, I envy you. It's well worth the trip!

Barry Cryer – writer & comedian

The Funniest Man in London

The Life and Times of H.G. Pélissier (1874–1913)
Forgotten satirist and composer,
founder of *The Follies*

Anthony Binns

Edgerton Publishing Services
Pett, East Sussex

First published in Great Britain in 2022 by
Edgerton Publishing Services
Jasmine Cottage, Elms Lane, Pett, Hastings, East Sussex TN35 4JD
Tel. +44 (0) 1424 813003
Email penfold@eps-edge.co.uk

ISBN: 978-0-9933203-8-5

A CIP catalogue record for this book is available from the British Library.

Typeset in Zanzibar and Garamond by Edgerton Publishing Services.

Printed and bound in Great Britain by Ashford Colour Press, Gosport, UK.

Every effort has been made to trace and acknowledge ownership of copyright of the illustrations used in this book. The publisher will be pleased to make suitable arrangements to clear permission with any copyright holders whom it has not been possible to contact.

Cover design by Jaudy Pélissier and Laura Gonzalez.

The photograph on the back cover is taken from the painting of H.G. Pélissier by Sir John Collier.

To my dear wife Jane and all our family for their patience, encouragement and support and to Jaudy & all the Pélissiers for theirs.

And Li Po also died drunk.
He tried to embrace a moon
In the Yellow River.

Ezra Pound (from *Lustra*, 1916)

People think of history in the long term, but history, in fact, is a very sudden thing.

Philip Roth (from *American Pastoral*, 1997)

The Censor needs a censor humour!

H.G. Pélissier (1909)

Contents

Preface

Jaudy Pélissier

As a child I would stare at an oil painting of a smiling fat clown and notice that light would sparkle from the diamond ring on his little finger whenever it caught the sunlight. He had a chubby face and wore a black outfit with white pompoms down the front. As I learned later, the clown was in fact a pierrot, my grandfather Harry Gabriel Pélissier, a satirist, composer and impresario, sitting for his portrait by the society artist, Sir John Collier. The wayward son of a Franco-German diamond merchant, he was a man whom my writer/film director father, Anthony Pélissier, never knew and seldom mentioned.

When my stepmother, the actress Ursula Howells died, I inherited the painting, the gold ring (now *sans* diamond), his leather-bound musical manuscripts and a battered old leather briefcase. This contained a treasure trove of theatrical programmes, cuttings and photographs, as well as the moving love letters my grandfather had written to my grandmother, the actress Fay Compton. I would periodically root around the box, stare blankly at the silent manuscripts and say that one day I must do something with it. As to what exactly, I had no idea.

In March 2016, Anthony Binns sent me an article to be published in *The Call Boy*, the journal of the British Music Hall Society. It was called: 'H. G. Pélissier: The Birth of Modern Comedy'. This turned out to be the start of a wondrous unlocking of the life of a man whose theatrical, satirical and musical achievements had disappeared between the cracks of British theatre history; partly because of his untimely death on the eve of the First World War, but also because he is impossible to categorise – a pioneer who moved from seaside Pierrot to symphonic conductor, from the satirical to the romantic and, quite exceptionally, from the somewhat *outré* world of music hall into the glamorous mainstream of the West End.

Harry Pélissier was the founder of *The Follies* – the very first to use that title in the anglophone world and two decades before Florenz Ziegfeld. Under his guiding hand, they became a highly successful performing troupe that specialised in musical satire and for whom he composed over 60 songs, published both in the United Kingdom and in the USA. Their West End home was the Apollo Theatre on Shaftesbury Avenue, where the great and the good came to laugh and where he enjoyed the honour of occasionally having material banned by the Lord Chamberlain for being subversive; often with an absurdist and licentious humour that in its way uniquely prefigured the 'Swinging Sixties'.

Known as Harry, he was a larger-than-life figure, both physically and metaphorically, a man whose constant state of creative inventiveness led to considerable wealth. With homes in Hampstead and Pall Mall, fast cars and an insatiable taste for *cuvée* champagne, brandy and cigars, he lived life at 100 miles per hour. Little wonder that he died of cirrhosis of the liver aged 39 and left my grandmother a widowed mother at only 19.

I never heard Fay talk about Harry, but I'm in no doubt that, despite the controversy that surrounded their marriage and the 20-year age difference between them, it was a genuine romance. Fay married four times but it is only Harry's letters and mementos that she kept, letters that remained unread for over 100 years and which not only explain a shared sense of humour but also how much Harry treasured and needed her. As the letters prove, their relationship started as a secret correspondence when Fay was 15 and at boarding school. Certainly, Compton Mackenzie, her novelist brother, had no idea and in his memoirs claimed that it was he who had introduced the pair when he was working as a librettist for Harry.

My father would be amazed by what Anthony Binns's forensic research into this theatrical family has revealed; in particular Anthony's insights into the personality of the father he never knew. Fay was not at all maternal; as a beautiful young actress she was more interested in her own career and conveniently sent him off to boarding school aged five. No wonder he ran away from Charterhouse at 15. After a short spell as an actor, he became a writer/director and, in 1938, with his great friend, the actor John Mills, he produced *The Pélissier Follies of 1938*. It was not a success, more of an attempt by a young man to connect with a father he never knew. *The Follies*, by definition, was Harry Pélissier; he was the magic ingredient that made it work and so any other recreation was doomed to failure.

'The funniest man in London' was how the elderly poet Robert Graves described Harry to me in the 1970s. He was one of a handful of people I met who had seen my grandfather and *The Follies* at the Apollo. At the time, having no real sense of who he was, I gave this remark only the briefest of teenage acknowledgements, but, as I remember that reflective smile of the poet, I realised that after more than 60 years Harry Pélissier and *The Follies* still clearly made a lasting impression. Thanks to Anthony Binns's commitment to shine a torch on a forgotten maverick and genius, it is possible to understand why. I will be forever grateful for the theatrical adventure he has taken me on and the opportunity to share his story with you.

Jaudy G. Pélissier
January 2022

Acknowledgements

Many thanks for the warm and gracious support, encouragement and assistance of Jaudy Pélissier and his family, without whom this work would not have been possible. Thanks also to: the Victoria and Albert Museum for access to their uncatalogued archive on H.G. Pélissier; to the Society for Theatre research for their financial assistance; to the British Library for the kind assistance of their staff; to Professor Leonard Conolly, former President of the Shaw Society, for alerting me to the *New York Sun* review of *The Follies* and to Shaw's introduction to *The Shewing-Up of Blanco Posnet*; and to Professor Steve Nicholson for clrifying the personnel and titles at the Lord Chamberlain's office, particularly in regard to Chapter 7. Thanks also to David Roper at Heavy Entertainment for editorial assistance. Above all, many thanks to my patient wife, Jane, for the hours we spent apart as I researched and wrote.

Anthony Binns
May 2022

The Website

The Pélissier's Follies website **www.pelissiersfollies.com** gives a simple overview of the life of H.G. Pélissier, Fay Compton and The Follies. On the site you can also sample some of Harry's music. These include those original sound recordings of 1909–10 as listed in Appendix C as well as a selection of modern interpretations recorded by the author at Heavy Entertainment Studios, Wardour Street in 2019. Via the website, we would also welcome any additional information that may be forthcoming from readers of this book, in particular any descendants or family associates of *The Follies* cast members.

1

The Mystery

Figure 1. H.G. Pélissier, 1911

'A satiric genius'

You may never have heard of Harry Gabriel Pélissier before. Which is something of a mystery for, in his day, he was a celebrated star of the West End stage, as much a national figure as Marie Lloyd or Dan Leno, Oscar Wilde or Charlie Chaplin. He was a favourite comedian of King Edward VII and of other leading social and literary figures such as G.K. Chesterton and Hilaire Belloc and even a begrudging J.M. Barrie. George Bernard Shaw visited him backstage in his dressing room after a matinée performance at the Apollo,[1] and indeed, he was often compared with that distinguished playwright. The *Tatler* once claimed that 'from Shaw to Pélissier is not a great jump'.[2] The novelist E. Nesbit, author of *The Railway Children* and a founder member of the Fabian Society, referred to him as 'a satiric genius'.[3]

H.G. Pélissier was the creator of the satirical musical comedy troupe *The Follies* and the very first to use this name as a company title in the anglophone world, over a decade before Ziegfeld borrowed the term from him or Sondheim found the inspiration for his musical theatre classic. As a satirist he was the scourge of major politicians, including the Prime Minister Herbert Asquith, the First Sea Lord Winston Churchill and the Chancellor Lloyd George. And his bold defiance of the strict regime of theatre censorship under the Lord Chamberlain very nearly led to its demise over half a century before that office was finally abolished in 1968. In *The New York Times*, the critic Alfred Hauber pronounced his troupe, *The Follies*, to be 'the funniest people in London',[4] while in *The Dictionary of National Biography 1912–1921* he is described as 'the leading satirist of his day'.[5] He was also the first seaside entertainer and player of the music halls to make a sustained impact with his own shows in the West End. Thus, he breached the polarized class divide that constituted the formation of contrasting audiences in popular and mainstream theatres. In so doing, he quite uniquely drew together a following of working and middle class, as well as aristocratic and intellectual, composition.

Furthermore, H.G. Pélissier was arguably the creator of what we would today recognise as the modern comedy sketch, involving parody, topical humour, a concise narrative, satire, comic names and quickfire wit. His style was laced with wild improvisation and a sharp sense of the absurd, which, being far ahead of its time, bears more resemblance to the humour of *The Goon Show, Beyond the Fringe* and *Monty Python's Flying Circus* and indeed current stand-up comedy than it did to his fellow contemporaries in variety and music hall. Added to this, he was a pioneer in the formation of contemporary revue and the modern musical. His considerable skills as a pianist and composer drew on a whole range of styles from American cakewalk and ragtime to operetta and music hall in a way that was quite unprecedented for the time.

Once *The Follies* had made their West End debut in 1904, they were rarely out of the national papers for the next decade. *The Times* declared them to be 'a feast of sly wit [. . .] There is nothing else like it in London'.[6] *The Daily Telegraph* wrote of 'this brilliant little company [. . .] as unique as it is amusing'.[7] For Ignotus in the *Spectator*, they possessed 'superhuman cleverness', proving that 'laughter, and even absurdity, may join forces with good sense',[8] while Max Beerbohm wrote of their 'sober and solid satire' and 'wild, fantastic humour'.[9] For over a decade, they received regular reviews, even lengthy articles and interviews, in *Vanity Fair, Queen, Punch, The Observer, Pall Mall Gazette, Daily Mail* and a whole range of provincial newspapers and society or cultural magazines. They even received the ultimate accolade of a command performance before the Royal Family at Sandringham on the occasion of the Queen's birthday,[10] and for their unprecedented five-hundredth appearance at the Apollo on Shaftesbury Avenue, Prime Minister Asquith himself was in attendance.[11]

So why, one wonders, should H.G. Pélissier and *The Follies* have fallen so mysteriously out of the collective public memory? When Humphrey Carpenter, in what Jonathan Miller describes as the 'definitive' account of the satirical boom of the 1960s entitled *That Was Satire That Was*,[12] writes of the young Peter Cook's first encounters with satire, he mentions a great deal about Paris and Berlin. He waxes lyrical on *Le Chat Noir* in Montmartre, on Brecht and Weill and Werner Finck at The Catacombs. John Wells is quoted as saying: "I lived in Germany for a year in the 1950s [. . .] and I used to go to a lot of satirical night-clubs – and so did Peter Cook. There was direct influence of those. Peter went to Berlin and saw satirical night-clubs. I was absolutely amazed by it – no-one had seen them in England.[13]

At the time, this was true. The heavy hand of the Lord Chamberlain's censorship was still asserting its firm control over stage performances of all kinds. However, just such a satirical company and venue had once existed in London, approximately half a century before. Naturally, this was rather too far in the past for Cook and Wells to have shared the pleasure, but nevertheless it had once existed. Their principal location was at the Apollo Theatre on Shaftesbury Avenue, and their name was *The Follies*. And yet, they receive not a single mention in Carpenter's otherwise 'definitive' account. It is almost as though Pélissier and *The Follies* had never happened. And, for sure, it is quite probable, indeed understandable, natural even, that this later satirical generation had never heard of Pélissier. In many ways, it seems to be the case of a history that has been air-brushed out or unaccountably overlooked. After Pélissier's untimely demise in 1913, his work was certainly overshadowed by the advent of the Great War and the new fashion for silent cinema and big-band dance halls. But why, one wonders, should he have been overlooked quite so completely? Even in the more academic sphere, in the foremost theatrical and musical histories of the early twentieth century, H.G. Pélissier is little more than a footnote. Admittedly, he is given two columns in the *Dictionary of National Biography 1912–1921*,[14] but you will not find him mentioned in the *Twentieth Century Digest* of that publication[15] nor in *Who Was Who*,[16] while in the *Oxford Handbook of Musical Theatre*, he is merely granted a passing phrase as a 'bon vivant' precursor to Charcot in the realm of musical revue.[17]

'What is it?'

It is the summer of 1907. A poster appears throughout the streets of London, on billboards and at railway stations, and it causes a minor public sensation (see Figure 2). It displays the image of a mysterious fish-like creature with a long nose and drooping hands, dressed in a neck scarf and a pair of chequered pyjamas. The creature is kicking a tiny clown through the air while another clown looks on in astonishment and yet another sits exhausted. The caption reads 'DON'T WORRY ABOUT THIS. COME AND SEE THE FOLLIES'. In his 1910 memoir *Pure Folly*, Fitzroy Gardner recalls it thus:

> This weird gazeeka-like animal was examined and compared with ancient prints by Arthur Diosy, the well-known authority on Japan, who reported as follows:- 'The figure

Figure 2. 'Tengee Monster' – The Follies poster of 1907

probably represents a Tengee, a Japanese mythical being, similar to the ancient Greek harpy which is partly bird and partly human'.[18]

The *Sketch* reported: 'It illustrates the growing taste for what may be called "What-is-it?" advertising, for it arouses what is perhaps our greatest small failing – curiosity'.[19] In fact, the mysterious creature is entirely imaginary, part of a surreal design for the sell-out West End burlesque, *The Follies*, at Terry's Theatre on The Strand. A flavour of their anarchic humour is reflected in a companion poster to the afore mentioned, which advises the audience not to come along after all as the show is already sold out. Indeed, it warns prospective customers that there is a queue for tickets with 'hundreds turned away' (see Figure 3).[20]

One might also note in passing how the political influence of *The Follies* at the time is illustrated by the mimicry of this very poster in the national press, for it was widely referenced in publications from *Punch* to *The Daily Dispatch* in cartoons that lampoon national political Figures such as Churchill, Horridge and Byles.

Those who ignore the suggestion and do indeed turn up at the Palace or Terry's or the Apollo or at any of the many other metropolitan and provincial venues that constitute H.G. Pélissier's touring programme will behold an almost baby-faced, jovial figure, over six feet tall in height and weighing fifteen stone. He is dressed from head to foot in an incongruous pierrot outfit, complete with beauty spot and kiss curl. As the audience file into the packed auditorium, they are no doubt celebrity-spotting, often hoping for a seat in the front of the stalls

Figure 3. 'Hundreds Turned Away Nightly!' – The Follies poster 1906

in order to be caught in a verbal exchange with the Maestro and thus become a part of the improvisation. Today, we might think with hindsight that this smiling fellow, with his mop of foppish dark hair and sharp, mesmerising blue eyes, resembles a young Fatty Arbuckle or James Corden.

The keenly anticipated performance begins. One minute, our star pierrot is seated howling and barking[21] at a grand piano, especially constructed with a keyboard on both sides, to which he would race from one to the other dressed in his signature black and white costume; the next, he is leaping and twirling about the stage in an ankle-length dress impersonating Maud Allan's *Salomé*.[22] He is accompanied by his regular troupe of players, each with a myriad of character and costume changes. During the course of the evening, several Hamlets appear at once before finally William Shakespeare pops up to shoot them all dead.[23] There is an orchestra comprised entirely of vocal impersonations of instruments,[24] Peter Pan appears as a burglar in Wendy's bedroom,[25] a toothbrush falls in love with a sponge,[26] and, in one of his most celebrated sketches, not a word of the original script is actually spoken as the entire set collapses amid canon fire and hysterical screaming.[27] Pure Dada! The mystery of what exactly you might experience in the unpredictable, improvised, anarchic, constantly updated and topical satire of *The Follies* shows was surely one of their most appealing features.

Pélissier's mercurial personality also represents something of an enigma. For such a large man, he was elegantly light on his feet and his manically improvised dance routines were a regular feature of his shows. While single-mindedly ambitious and confident, he could also be self-deprecating and painfully self-conscious of his weight and appearance. Though he was generally regarded as generous, at least in gifts and favours, if not in salaries to his staff, he could also be ruthless with colleagues when he felt it necessary. Like many theatrical contemporaries of his time, he was antagonistic towards the suffragette movement, and yet he gave equal, if not greater, opportunity and prominence to female performers; not something that could be said of all producers and impresarios of the time, nor even of today. Ferociously active and hard-working, with a piano (that he would famously play well into the night) in every room at his large suburban house in Finchley, he was also given to introspective bouts of depression. In this, Compton Mackenzie, his brother-in-law and one-time collaborator, likened him to the comedian Tony Hancock, with whom he similarly associated the unique quality and charisma of his comic style.[28]

So, too, do his very origins present something of a mystery. Though it is clear that his father, Jean Frederic Antoine, was a naturalized migrant from Hanau in Germany, the actual circumstances of the family migration are a matter of speculation. Pélissier writes of his father's 'political activism' in his satirical and often flippantly unreliable memoirs,[29] yet it is difficult to discern the truth from the fantasy in such a wildly rich imagination. Despite his foreign ancestry, H.G. Pélissier always presents himself as a quintessential Englishman in his tastes, his tailoring, his attitudes and even in his urbane eccentricity. As a composer of comic songs, he bears comparison with, and may well have been an influence upon, Noel Coward and, as a composer of romantic ballads, his now forgotten works rival in beauty and poignancy those of his near contemporaries, Jerome Kern and Ivor Novello, both of whom he prefigures in his fusion of popular styles. He was even invited to perform one of his more classical pieces, a musical setting of William Davenant's 'Awake!', at the Henry Wood promenade concerts of 1901 and 1902.[30] Yet he appears to have had no formal musical training as such. Rather, it seems that he was self-taught, both at the piano and at composition. Still, he managed to produce a daily turnover of pieces in the fevered atmosphere of the West End, with over sixty works published on both sides of the Atlantic, becoming a very wealthy man in the process.

H.G. Pélissier also collaborated with some of the finest talents in the musical theatre of the age. To some, like Arthur Wimperis, who went on to a glittering career as the lyricist of *The Arcadians* and a string of successful musical revues and even a Hollywood career,[31] he gave a first start in the business. As a musician-performer, his piano parodies of classical composers such as Wagner and Tchaikovsky prefigure the comic works of Victor Borge and Dudley Moore; and yet he was also capable of stunningly beautiful, jazz-influenced ballads.

Together with his pioneering idea of a linked theme of comic sketches and songs, these compositions would pave the way for English musical revue and the development of the full-blown modern musical as we know it. In this way, Pélissier would go on to enjoy an unprecedented sell-out run of over five hundred shows at the Apollo in London's West End; and yet he had no theatrical training, neither as a comedian nor as a writer or impresario. Surprisingly too, though distinctly middle class in background, he was drawn from the very outset to the low-brow world of the music hall, variety and concert party. This youngest son of a comfortably off diamond merchant gave up the financial security that was readily available to him by way of the family business. Instead, he decided to perform concert parties at English seaside resorts with a troupe of minstrels, in his early years eking out a meagre existence while residing peripatetically in modest lodging houses and hotels.

In fact, *The Follies* immediately stood out from their rivals as being entirely different, unique even. In the process, H.G. Pélissier became a self-made millionaire (by contemporary standards) and a notorious socialite and *bon vivant*. He enjoyed a wildly libertarian lifestyle in the heady world of Edwardian Mayfair and Soho, as well as being a frequent visitor to the English coastal resorts and across the Channel to Paris. In the company of a troupe of clubbable friends, headed by the self-styled bohemian, his biographer Fitzroy Gardner, his hard-drinking, cigar-smoking and promiscuous, if ambivalent, sexuality became legendary. Thus, it was to widespread public astonishment that, at the age of thirty-seven, he married into the highly distinguished and respectable Compton-Bateman theatrical dynasty, taking as his bride his latest leading lady, the seventeen-year-old Fay Compton. Their union turned out to be tragically short-lived however, for after just two short years in which Fay became the mother of their only child, Harry met an untimely death through cirrhosis of the liver. In fact, the circumstances of their romance are themselves something of a mystery, for there are contradictory accounts from various family members as to exactly when and how Fay and Harry met and fell in love. However, what now seems clear from their personal correspondence, held in the Pélissier family archive, is that Harry and Fay had secretly known each other for some years prior to their marriage, even from Fay's schooldays. When announced, their marriage was to cause an irreparable breach between Harry Pélissier and Compton Mackenzie, Fay's brother and Harry's one time collaborator. The role of Fay's mother, the stern and rather forbidding matriarch that was Virginia Compton, seems also to require some explanation, for it was she, rather than Fay, who nursed the dying Harry Pélissier at the family home in Nevern Square. And she also arguably appears to have gained most from Harry's substantial legacy.

It is also intriguing that this whole affair seems to have provided inspiration to J. M. Barrie, (with whom Pélissier had something of a running feud throughout his career) for his play *Mary Rose*, which was perhaps his second most popular and celebrated work after *Peter Pan*. Written in 1920 especially for Harry's young widow Fay Compton, it was she who triumphantly created its eponymous heroine in performance. On close examination, the cryptic title of *Rosemary*, Fay Compton's autobiographical memoir of 1925, reads to us now as an inverted reference to the leading character of Barrie's play – the ghostly little girl who would never have the chance to grow up.

A mystery indeed, or rather web of mysteries that intertwine into one – the life and times that were H.G. 'Harry' Pélissier. It is a mystery upon which the wealth of documents in the Victoria and Albert Museum and in the British Library and in the private collection of the Pélissier family can perhaps begin to shed some light and at the same time help to resolve an even greater mystery. Whatever happened to British satirical revue in the first half of the twentieth century? And how and why exactly did this pioneering figure of musical comedy come to be so completely forgotten?

2

The Alien

Figure 4. J.F.A. Pélissier: Harry's father c.1870

'Cryptic warnings'

In September 1848, the young Jean Frederic Antoine Pélissier arrived at the Port of London.[1] This was not his first visit to England, but this time it would appear that he planned to stay. He was a bachelor, just twenty years of age, and he was leaving behind his homeland of the Electorate of Hesse-Cassel, in Germany, in a state of violent revolutionary turmoil. The London that Jean Frederic encountered was at that time the biggest city in the world, the hub of a vast Empire with mercantile and banking links across the globe. Little wonder that it would have represented an attractive location to the foot-loose young entrepreneur. With an ever-expanding population of close to two and a quarter million,[2] it must have seemed an awesome and exciting prospect, a city of boundless possibilities in complete contrast to Hanau, the small provincial German town of, at most, a few thousand that he had left behind. Perhaps he spoke sufficient English, learnt in his business dealings and previous visits, with which to manage his affairs, but, nevertheless, this was a journey into a dark and forbidding metropolis, a notorious epicentre of poverty and crime, disease and carnality, as well as of potential advancement and wealth. It would be daunting enough for a native-born Englishman, but for a relatively fresh-faced young foreigner it was surely fraught with risk.

We may never know what exactly may have impelled him to undertake such a journey. However, one possibility is that the young Jean Frederic had found himself caught up in the bitter factional fighting that was then engulfing the continent. His native Hanau was still in the throes of a tumultuous political upheaval, which had just seen the formation of Germany's first ever democratically elected assembly, the Frankfurt Parliament convened, on 18 March of that year. The old reactionary regime of the Hapsburg Empire was beginning to crumble and Germany was inching its way towards unification.[3] Karl Marx himself had made the same journey, a political exile, arriving in London the previous year. He was soon to publish his *Communist Manifesto* and, having been expelled from his native land, he settled in England, where he remained until his death in 1883. Indeed, London was a city full of émigrés, exiles and refugees from all over Europe. By 1901 there were reported to be 27,400 Germans and 11,300 French men and women resident in the capital, according to the census of that year,[4] the majority having travelled in search of work or having fled from persecution. In some cases, Jean Frederic would have found himself in illustrious company. Prince Metternich, the Austrian Chancellor thrown out by those self-same revolutionaries who were wreaking havoc throughout the continent, had found refuge in Eaton Square, Belgravia; while at the other end of the political spectrum, the failed Hungarian liberator Louis Kossuth had made his home in Chepstow Villas, Notting Hill. In 1886, the anarchist Prince Kropotkin found his way to London, fresh from a French prison at Clairvaux.[5] Strange neighbours indeed; London an open and inviting city to those who could endure or exploit its harsh realities.

We have no evidence that Jean Frederic himself was engaged in political activity. Apart from, that is, one ambivalent, almost whimsical, reference by his son Harry, in *Potted Pélissier*, the randomly anecdotal and absurdist 'autobiography' of 1913, in which he states the following:

> [. . .] it was apparent even to my infant perceptions that a threatening cloud hung over our family life. My father was by profession a political refugee and lived in a constant atmosphere of doubt and apprehension. There was one dark, sinister figure always looming in the background of our domesticity. I never heard his name but have a vague recollection that he was a *lord* of some kind, connected I believe, with *land*. Periodically, mysterious strangers would come secretly to our door and hand my father cryptic warnings writ on bluish paper. These were always the signal for a family conclave, for whispered advice and frenzied packings, and invariably ended in a midnight rush for safety. Then in our new quarters, life would resume its quiet, until my father's enemies again got wind of him, which it generally took them about three months to do.[6]

He is clearly making light of their seemingly precarious existence by way of the comic confla-tion of an evicting landlord with the world of political intrigue. As so often with H.G. Pélis-sier's writings, it is almost impossible to tell just how serious he is actually being. Like so many comedians, he tended to hide himself behind a wall of jest, so that one can hardly distinguish where he is being facetious and playful, and where he is presenting the truth. However, it is quite possible that Jean Frederic and his family did live in the shadow of danger, given his background and the fact that they did move address on several occasions – from Bedford Square in Bloomsbury[7] to Elm House[8] and then to another address in Finchley at Redburn House.[9] On the other hand, it is possible that Harry was merely having a little fun with his mildly exotic origins when he spoke of a 'sinister figure' and 'frenzied packings'.[10]

After a brief spell of partnership in the diamond trade, Harry's father set up his own inde-pendent business at 63 Berwick Street in the heart of Soho.[11] It is worth pausing here a moment to consider what that area was like in the second half of the nineteenth century. In his introduction to Joseph Conrad's *The Secret Agent*, Michael Newton describes it thus:

> Soho [. . .] was the apotheosis of Bohemian London, a bolthole for refugees, prosti-tutes and Anarchists. In Charles Booth's analysis of the district in 1898, what most characterized it was the starkly heterogeneous mix of its denizens, from the well-to-do to the nearly destitute.[12]

London had become 'the headquarters of the Continental movement' according to an Italian anarchist at his London trial in 1894.[13] Governments had become keenly aware of the threat of terrorist attacks across the globe. President McKinley had been assassinated in America, and a French President, an Italian King and an Austrian Empress had all recently suffered the same fate. These anarchist *attentats* spawned a new breed of literature. The Rosetti sisters wrote *A Girl Among the Anarchists*[14] under the pseudonym of Isabel Meredith, while Henry James created the conspiratorial Hyacinth Robinson in *The Princess Casamassima*.[15] Most famously of all, Joseph Conrad's *The Secret Agent* located its principal protagonist, the anarchist Verloc, in the very heart of Soho.[16] The Metropolitan Guide of 1893 refers to the area as 'Soho French District'.[17] One can easily imagine it as a shadowy den of intrigue where 'warn-ings writ on bluish paper' and 'frenzied packings' might be an everyday occurrence.

All of these murky goings-on were being played out at a time when the rival European Empires were engaged in what Rudyard Kipling had dubbed the 'Great Game' of interna-tional intrigue, as so vividly depicted in his novel *Kim*. Bismarck's Prussia had led the way in such techniques through the extraordinary master-spy William Stieber, who at various points was working for the Germans and Russians and even 'started to influence the Russian com-munity in London, working on potential double agents and assassins and instituted what we would call "counter-intelligence"'.[18] London, and Soho in particular, was awash with such activity. So even if Harry's suspicions of his father are more fantastical than real, the possi-bility was certainly there, particularly given, as we shall see, that another illustrious Pélissier, Jean Frederic's grand-uncle, was for a while the French Ambassador to London. The mere presence of these dark underworld figures and the social make-up and texture of the area must have coloured Pélissier's imagination and heightened his awareness of 'aliens' and 'foreignness'. In time, this would prove to be a pivotal subject for his satire, particularly with regard to one of his most notorious sketches. This was a sketch and a subject matter that was to embroil him in direct conflict with the Lord Chamberlain and result in a national scandal.[19]

'The best of Germans'

However, there were many other causes that might have spurred Jean Frederic's departure from Germany in 1848. He may well have been himself the victim of reactionary prejudice and persecution in his native Hesse-Cassel. The family name of Pélissier was French in origin and at that time prejudice against the French would have been at its height. As recently as 1813, Napoleon had overwhelmed the city in the Battle of Hanau and had ordered its defences to be destroyed. The French and Walloon inhabitants of the area were essentially outsiders. Jean Frederic's ancestors had fled Paris and its surrounding regions as Huguenot Protestant refugees in the late sixteenth century. Along with their co-religionists from the Netherlands, the sympathetic Count Philip Ludwig II had encouraged the Huguenots to settle in the region south of Frankfurt. Apart from his religious affinity, the Count would also have had an eye to the advanced technical skills of these exiles as expert goldsmiths and jewellers. As in Antwerp, further to the north, a thriving centre in these crafts and trades was to develop around Hanau and Frankfurt. Thus, the Pélissiers were not only foreign in origin but most probably part of the comfortably off bourgeoisie that would have attracted the resentment of local radical revolutionaries in 1848. At the same time, conscious of their refugee origins, many of the Huguenot immigrants are on record as having displayed a fierce loyalty to their German hosts and in particular to the Hohenzollern monarchy and aristocracy that had welcomed them. Charles Ancillon in his history of French refugees published in 1690 praised them for their industry and loyalty,[20] while Chancellor Bismarck was later to single them out as 'the best of Germans'.[21] However, in 1848 this very economic status and loyalty to the Elector would have placed them in perilous conflict with the revolutionaries.

Yet another possibility is that Jean Frederic was fleeing from the cholera epidemic that was sweeping through Germany at the time; the irony being that, within just a few months of his arrival, London itself was gripped in the deadliest outbreak of the disease that it was ever to witness. Throughout the course of 1848 and 1849, it was to claim 53,000 lives in England.[22] And there is a further irony in that the disease appears to have arrived from Germany. As John Snow was to write in his 1855 edition of *On the Mode of Communication of Cholera*:

> The first case of Asiatic cholera in London, in the Autumn of 1848, was that of a seaman named John Harnold, who had newly arrived by the Elbe steamer from Hamburg (Germany), where the disease was prevailing. He left the vessel, and went to live at

No.8, New Lane, Gainsford Street, Horsleydown. He was seized with cholera on the 22nd September, and died in a few hours.[23]

Had John Harnold travelled on the very same ship as Jean Frederic Antoine Pélissier? We are unlikely ever to know, but as the disease spread from the Continent to London Bridge and thence to Lambeth and Southwark and north of the river to Soho and Broad Street, it almost certainly would have influenced Harry Pélissier's father in his decision to locate on the edge of the city in Bedford Square and then, when financially able, to remove his family entirely to the suburbs on the outskirts of London as so many of the middle classes then did.

Whatever the reason, and there are several possibilities, the twenty-year-old Jean Frederic took flight in September of 1848, for that is when his naturalisation papers (of some six years later) state his arrival in England.[24] On 11 August 1854, he was granted British nationality. There to vouch for and give witness to his 'respectability and loyalty' are four equally respectable signatories: Mr William Gregory, a tailor of Vernon Place, Bloomsbury; Mr Septimus Furse, a carver and gilder of St Pancras; Mr Benjamin Aaron Woolf, a jeweller resident in Oxford Street in the parish of St Giles; and Mr Frederick Smith of St Paul's Churchyard, hotel keeper of the St Paul's Hotel. He is stated as being resident at the highly respectable Number 2, South Crescent, Bedford Square, Middlesex. This was in fact, in the ownership of another jeweller, Jacob Woolf (perhaps a relative of the Benjamin Aaron Woolf who had vouched for his naturalisation) and together they formed the diamond trading business of Woolf and Pélissier at 63 Berwick Street, Soho. The young émigré was now situated a stone's throw from the newly founded University College, London and the fashionable streets of Fitzrovia and Bloomsbury, the British Museum and the bustling West End. More importantly perhaps, a stroll through Holborn and Clerkenwell would have taken him to Hatton Garden, the very centre of the British jewellery trade.

Another of Harry's colourful ancestors was a certain Aimable-Jean-Jacques Pélissier, 1st Duc de Malakoff (1764–1864). Not all the Pélissiers made the enforced exodus from France to Germany or England. One branch of the family had remained in Normandy. The progeny of a comfortably well-off artisan family (his father worked at the local gunpowder mill), Aimable-Jean-Jacques was born and raised in Maromme in northern France. He was educated and trained at military academies in La Flèche and Saint-Cyr, where he was commissioned as an artillery officer in 1815. Thus, he narrowly avoided the irony of bombarding in 1813 the city of Hanau, where his cousins resided! Rising rapidly through the ranks to Brigadier-General, he went on to distinguish himself as Commander-in-Chief of the French forces at the Siege of Sebastopol in Crimea in 1855. His reputedly dogged determination led to a successful storming of the Tower of Malakoff, thus concluding that battle and the war itself with a famous victory. For his efforts he was promoted to the rank of Marshal of France, and upon his return to Paris became a Senator and was given the title Duke of Malakoff by Napoleon III. After a stint as Ambassador to London between March 1858 and May 1859 — during which time one wanders if he might have chanced upon his great-nephew, Jean Frederic, perhaps with the odd warning 'writ on bluish paper' — he became Governor-General of Algeria in 1860, where he died shortly afterwards. Exactly what genes may have given rise to any resemblance between the glorious Duke, the diamond merchant and his comedian–impresario son, we can only speculate. However, we can perhaps detect a shared determination and a certain ruthless ambition in each of these Pélissier family members.

In fact, Harry Pélissier's exotic ancestry was to have a profound influence on his career and, while he liked to appear as very much the cultivated Englishman and was capable of being extremely patriotic in his utterances (though often laced with an ambivalent irony), one feels he was always conscious of himself as being something of an outsider looking in, and thus perhaps all the more able to pick out the eccentricities of his father's adopted nation. By the same token, he was equally drawn, as we shall see, to his continental roots and cultural influences and one gets a sense that somehow these heterogeneous, 'larger-than-life' figures who inhabited his past contributed to the sharp sense of mimicry and comic characterisation that he was later to develop.

'A Russian émigré and an Indian maharanee'

On 27 April 1874, Harry Gabriel Pélissier was born at Elm House, Church End, Finchley in Middlesex. His father, Jean Frederic, had married an English girl called Jennie Keen. Born in Hitchin, Hertfordshire in 1839, Jennie was the daughter of Stephen Keen, a brewer from Faversham in Kent and was just 19 when they married.[25] Harry was to be the youngest of six siblings. In 1859, his eldest sister Minna had been born, followed a year later by twins, Adele and Mell, who only lived to the ages of three and one year respectively. His elder brother Frederick, with whom he maintained a close personal and working relationship throughout his life, was born in 1862 in Paris,[26] and it is interesting to note that this was not long after the period of time in which his Grand-Uncle Aimable was acting as French Ambassador to London. Another sister, Jenny, was born in 1871. Did being the runt in the pack, the youngest of the yield with age differences ranging over fifteen years, foster and encourage Harry's characteristically playful spirit? Within the sanctum of this large suburban family, he most likely had a ready audience for his fun-filled imagination, one that was to prove distinctly useful to him at the outset of his career, and perhaps he never quite lost that child-like sense of being the youngest sibling, the prankster exhibitionist.

At the time of Harry's birth, Church End in Finchley was indeed suburban. In fact, it was little more than a rural village on the outskirts of London. A garden nursery had been established on Ballard's Lane, but otherwise it was an entirely agricultural area of farm cottages,

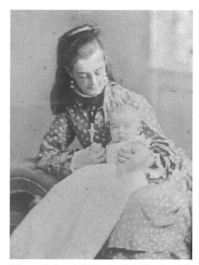

Figure 5. Jennie Pélissier (née Keen), with her baby son Harry, 1874

overseen by a baronial estate at Bibbesworth Manor. There was no rail connection until 1867, when Finchley and Hendon Station was opened by the Edgeware, Highgate and London Railway Company. Today this is Finchley Central Station.[27] As was common in the suburbs of Victorian London, residential development soon followed the rail links and perhaps this is what first drew the Pélissiers to the area – a clean and fresh oasis after the cholera-ridden experience of central London – for Jean Frederic had made enough of a success of his jewellery business to afford a rather grand house with extensive gardens. The playful young Harry would have had acres of wild land in which to run free – although it seems he was forbidden to jump on the flowerbeds, something that inspired him in later life to re-purchase the house and do precisely that![28] Yet, this rustic idyll is not at all how Harry himself viewed his childhood circumstances, leastways not in the riot of his imagination. Among the many fantastical reminisces of 'In the Days of My Youth: An Appreciation of H.G. Pélissier by Himself', an article he put together with the collaboration of Arthur Wimperis and which was published in the *M.A.P.* magazine of June 1909, he wrote:

> Introduced to Life. Mr. Pélissier, despite his foreign-sounding name, is an Englishman by birth, being the only – and we may fairly add – favourite son of a distinguished Russian *émigré* and an Indian maharanee and having been born on the high seas. [*sic*] He is very proud of his country and invariably supports home industries, always buying his soap at the rate of 13 oz. to the pound from Messrs. Smithers of Jonestown, – [ADVT.] Some Early Achievements. At an astonishingly early age he showed unmistakable signs of the humour that was in him, creating shrieks of mirth among his brothers and sisters by tripping up blind old ladies in the street, kicking the crutches from the grasp of a passing cripple, and a thousand other innocent drolleries. These pranks, however, met with no encouragement from the stern old Salvationist, his father, who, while publicly professing an affection for the child, would privately correct him with an ash plant.[29]

Figure 6. Harry, aged 4

Thus, we are introduced to the wild, surreal nonsense, the non-sequiturs and contradictions with which he could describe his childhood experiences. So too, that 'stern old Salvationist', his father, was to go through more than a few satirical representations in the mind of Harry Pélissier during the course of his career. At a later point in the same article, he writes:

> Feelings of Father and Son. It may be said that the father showed a tenderness which he could not have felt, while the son felt a tenderness which he could not have shown.

To add to the absurdist flavour of this autobiographical article, there appears at this point, the illustration of a can of 'Devilled Ham' captioned 'Burial place of the Chicago branch of the Pélissier family'!

The *Appreciation* continues:

> At the age of nine a family council was held to decide whether the lad be educated or sent to Eton, and the former course was adopted with lamentable results as the following anecdote will show: One day while his father was busy lathering a customer, the under gardener rushed in with the news that his favourite cherry tree had been cut down. Hastily laying aside the nets he was mending, the distracted professor hobbled out into the spacious grounds of the old family hovel and found that it was true. The historic oak, one of the only 200 in which the young Pretender ever hid, no longer occupied its position in the centre of the tennis court. Taxed with his guilt the boy denied it. 'Harry!' exclaimed the old soldier sternly, 'that is another story.' 'Oh father!' cried the sensitive lad bursting into tears, 'rebuke me if you will, but not with cant phrases borrowed from Mr. Kipling'. This reply is said to have incensed the quick-tempered baronet so much that Harry had good reason to congratulate himself on the fact that he was wearing the well-known P.D.Q. Double-wool Porous Underclothing at the time. – [ADVT.]

These undeniably dark imaginings that variously characterize his father as a soldier and a professor, a barber and a baronet, are a seemingly spontaneous outpouring worthy of Laurence Sterne. The intermittent references to advertising '[ADVT.]' are a typically sly allusion to what we today would call 'product placement' in the already ubiquitously commercial world of Edwardian England. The final reference to robust underwear is more than likely a dig at the notoriously cruel regime of Highgate School, to which the young Harry would be sent. Though whether he was 'educated' there any more than he might have been at Eton is questionable.

Founded in 1565 by a Royal Charter of Elizabeth I, Highgate School no doubt ranked as an impressive institution in which to have the son of émigré Jean Frederic Antoine Pélissier educated. Having survived a minor scandal in 1827, which involved a High Court action against the Trustees for misappropriation of funds contrary to its founding charitable deed, and the consequent reduction in pupil numbers to just 19, the school had struggled on and rescued its reputation. Under a new headmaster, Dr John Bradley Dyne, free provision for local parish boys had largely disappeared by the 1870s and fee-paying boarding places were introduced, attracting a well-off middle-class clientele. Harry Pélissier found himself among them. His name is to be found in the School Registry, entered in September 1885, when he would have been just eleven years old.[30] He would also, most probably, have found himself on the receiving end of Dr Dyne's merciless birch rod. (Hence the need for that 'P.D.Q Double-wool Porous Underclothing'). The academic regime followed the strict rule book as defined by Dr Arnold at Rugby School, a rigorous house system, the rote learning of the Classics and a strong focus on outdoor athletic activities as the school expanded and took over sports fields in the neighbouring Bishopswood Road.[31] How the indolent, day-dreaming Harry must have responded to this, one can only imagine. In his *Potted Pélissier* of 1913, he has little to say on the subject, preferring to focus in his characteristically whimsical manner, on one of his most prominent attributes, his increasing corpulence:

MY BIRTH AND PARENTAGE/ The smart French Bonne entered my father's sanctum and placed a massy bundle in his arms. 'Bejabers!', said she, 'and it's a proud man ye ought to be this day entoirely.' My father staggered beneath the unexpected weight. 'Himmel!' he exclaimed, 'not twins? Not tri...'[. . .] Mine was a serious-minded family, so my arrival in the world was the occasion of no fireworks or junketings; on the other hand I formed the subject of many domestic conclaves and dissensions. . . . I was accordingly levered into the room by the combined efforts of the domestic staff. At that age (between two and three weeks) it was my habit to call for sustenance at regular intervals of from fifteen to twenty minutes, and this period having elapsed since my last meal I greeted the family at the top of a voice remarkable for its power and resonance.

He goes on to relate how he turned over in bed one night and flattened his

[. . .] old Scotch nurse, one Miriam Solomons [. . .] Poor soul, she was as flat as a pancake [. . .] I was now growing up and attending school regularly, where I was popular with the masters and boys alike; but we have such a surfeit of things said and written on the subject of education nowadays that I feel sure you will feel grateful to me if I leave out all mention of my studies and progress.[32]

In the article entitled 'In The Days Of My Youth', he is more forthright: 'Though I went to several schools – Folkestone, Highgate, and Scarborough – I managed to absorb about as much learning as most boys, possibly less, and was usually at the bottom of my class.' He relates how he won a prize for good handwriting 'by fraud' and goes on to state:

I pocketed the five shillings without a qualm. Like all my money in those days, it was expended on comic songs and theatrical newspapers. The ERA and the STAGE were my favourite reading, and I perused them rigorously, advertisements and all, casually wondering why a 'tall hat' was 'indispensable', and 'drunkards save stamps'. I recall the thrill of excitement on reading that Miss Fitzsomething's 'able rendition of the title role had met with marked approval' and that 'John Smith had proved acceptable'![33]

The non-academic, un-athletic outsider of foreign parentage, with his wildly active imagination, was busily daydreaming of a life in the world of drama and music and play-acting as set out so vividly in the theatrical journals of the day. To pursue such a life would be his determined resolve.

3

The Amateur

Figure 7: H.G. Pélissier, aged 21 1895

Stage or hall?

To the bored and alienated Highgate schoolboy the world depicted in the theatrical journals must have appeared as a vivid wonderland, one of magic and fantasy, replete with possibilities so tantalisingly close at hand, a mere bus ride away into Camden and Soho, and yet presenting the opportunity to tour into the farthest reaches of the Kingdom and the Empire. His fat little knees bent on the bed, elbows folded, palms tucked under his chin, his eyes would have been magnetically drawn to 'Mr. Charles Melville's "Crimes of Paris Company" at the Grand Theatre, Derby',[1] '"The Balloon – The Funniest of all the Farcical Comedies" at the Comedy Theatre, London'[2] or perhaps the '"Compton Comedy Company" under the direction of Mr. Edward Compton at the Gaiety Theatre, Dublin'.[3] He might have drooled with envy as he read of Charles Wyndham at the Criterion who 'was simply delicious, the delighted audience

19

simply laughing themselves out of breath and red in the face over his droll sayings and doings'[4] or marvelled at Mr Dudley Causton at the Gaiety Theatre, London, who 'furnished much diversion by his musical and unmusical imitations, which we have before commended for their mirth-giving qualities.'[5] He even appears at this early age to have produced his own home entertainments. In *M.A.P.* he recalled:

> I built myself a miniature theatre out of wood and cardboard, and produced many favourite pieces, including the Drury Lane pantomimes, to the home audience. These productions ('at enormous cost to the management' in labour, paint and glue) were, I believe, tolerated by the family solely because they kept me quiet for long periods, as the performances themselves must have been exceedingly tiresome, being made up of the minimum of actual show and the maximum of 'stage waits'.[6]

In his relish for *The Era* and *Stage*, Harry was in good company. The second half of the nineteenth century was a golden age for newspaper and periodical publications. Improved print technology and increased literacy were important factors, as was a steadily increasing affluence and urban appetite for news. If we regard print as the cutting edge of the social media of its day, then we can also understand how there would have been a widespread enthusiasm both to create and to consume reading matter. Indeed, there arose a plethora of titles, both national and provincial. *The Times* and *Observer* had both started life in the previous century, but the *The Manchester Guardian, Daily Mail, Western Mail* and *The Illustrated London News* all flourished in this period, to which we can add *The Courier, Chronicle, Sketch* and *Sun* and a whole host more. Major urban centres and provincial towns would have had at least one, perhaps two or three local journals, as well as those produced by clubs and societies, or titles aimed at a particular group like *The Lady* or *Woman*. Each of these would have a theatre page or section dedicated to the latest shows and often their own specialist reviewer. However, it was the *Era* and, later, *The Stage* that stood out for theatre coverage.

The Era was a weekly newspaper, first published in 1838. Though originally it offered general news, being particularly well-regarded for its sports coverage, it became in time the must-read of the theatre world for both professionals and audiences alike. It started life as an outlet mainly for public houses, published on Sundays and with a liberal stance. After only a couple of years, having removed its original editor, Leith Ritchie, it took on a more conservative stance under a new proprietor and editor, Frederick Ledger and from 1881 it appeared on Saturdays. An 1856 advertisement claimed it to be:

> [. . .] the largest Newspaper [*sic*] in the world, containing Sixty-four columns of closely-printed matter in small type. It is the only Weekly Newspaper combining all the advantages of a first-rate sporting journal, with those of a Family Newspaper. Literature and the Metropolitan and Provincial Drama has more space allotted to them in the Era than in any other journal. The Operatic and Musical Intelligence, Home and Continental is always most copious and interesting. [. . .] Invaluable for reviews, news, and general theatrical information and gossip. Also of value are the assorted advertisements by and for actors and companies.[7]

Significantly, *The Era* was the first journal to give any space to the low-brow demi-monde of the music hall, as opposed to the more high-brow world of mainstream theatre. W. McQueen Pope puts it thus:

> Up to 1850, there were many papers which dealt largely or entirely with the Theatre but Music Hall, then still in the 'saloon' stage, hardly got a mention [. . .] the Press as a whole did not regard Music Hall as worthy of space beyond a very occasional and extremely patronising 'mention' if real need arose. The first journal to give it any space was *The Era*; that august journal which became 'The Actor's Bible' [. . .] By degrees and largely because of advertisements, *The Era* began to take more and more of an interest in theatrical affairs and gave weekly reports of theatrical happenings in London and the provincial cities. Now and again a small paragraph about the saloons and music halls got in, often just as a footnote. But as music hall grew so the space devoted to it grew; *The Era* became the great theatrical journal and every member of the profession, stage or hall, had to buy it.[8]

Note the clear distinction that McQueen Pope draws between 'stage' and 'hall'. The world of theatre that so attracted Harry Pélissier and that he dreamed of becoming a part of and devoured so avidly through its journals and reviews and advertisements was in fact two worlds of a very distinct order. Music hall, on the one hand, represented a rough and ready, working-class world as typified by the likes of Little Tich and Dan Leno and Marie Lloyd. On the other side of the tracks, as it were, there existed the mainstream, 'legitimate' theatre of classical and contemporary plays and opera, designed to appeal to a more high-brow, middle-class audience. The former offered a world of comic songs that would often reflect the hard-drinking and hard times of the working people or the champagne lifestyle of decadent upper-class 'Jolly Dogs'[9] as well as more risqué numbers and novelty acts. The latter represented a world of Italian opera or Wagner, of classical plays by the likes of Shakespeare or Congreve, the social comedies of Oscar Wilde, the comic operas of Gilbert and Sullivan, and the 'well-written' drawing-room dramas of Arthur Wing Pinero and John Galsworthy. There was a clear social divide and a sense of 'ne'er the twain shall meet'. A good deal of social snobbery and disapproval was aimed at the music hall by the upper classes and, in return, the working-class would happily mock the grandiose tastes of their 'betters'. According to Laura Ormiston Chant, a vigorous campaigner against what she saw as the moral decadence of popular entertainment:

> The music hall supplies a class of entertainment to suit people who, out of sheer tiredness of brain or want of superior education, could hardly appreciate a play [. . .] The music hall caters for people with a small proportion of brains.[10]

There was also an important legal distinction between music hall and the 'legitimate' licensed theatre. In effect, the Theatres Act of 1843 allowed music halls, which had begun life in the back rooms of alehouses, to be unlicensed provided they only performed musical concerts or any stage work under thirty minutes long and with less than a cast of six. The mainstream, legitimate, licensed theatre was quite another matter. All works performed there were subject to the Lord Chamberlain's scrutiny and required a licence. In the years to come, this anomaly would cause considerable confusion and allow Harry Pélissier his greatest moment of satirical triumph and political impact.[11]

Meanwhile he could only dream of being part of this turbulent world through the pages of theatrical newspapers and magazines. On his sixteenth birthday he might well have given himself a treat with the edition, for example, of *The Era* that was published on 26 April 1890. This is a time when the young Harry Pélissier would almost certainly have been eagerly absorbing and fantasizing over the reports in its columns in order to get a flavour of the theatre worlds as they then were, and this is what his eyes would have chanced upon.

On the front page, five columns of notices announce the appearance of actors and actresses throughout the country. Amongst them, a 'Miss Virginia Bateman appearing as Lady Teazle'[12] and her sister Isabel as Clarissa Harlowe, on tour with the company of Mr Edward Compton, Virginia's husband – a family, unbeknownst to the young Harry, which in time would become his own. After half a dozen such pages, we arrive at advertisements for various dramatic and dancing academies, such as the 'English Dancing School in Covent Garden', and musical and dramatic agencies such as Blackmore's of Garrick Street or MacDermott's of the Strand. Then the reviews of the new shows begin. We can see that a new 'Comic Operatic Romance, *Simon Smith*' has opened at the Victoria Hall in Edgeware; that a 'New and Original Romantic Opera *Thorgrim* by Joseph Bennett' is running at Drury Lane; The Lyric is presenting another opera, *The Red Hussar;* while at Steinway Hall one might have sampled the delights of a vocal recital by Miss Hilda Wilson. There follows a review from Paris of a new play, *Le Roman D'Une Conspiration,* and an exchange of correspondence regarding 'Foreign Music In England', which bemoans the fines and fees currently being enforced on the performance of French music in England following the signing of the Berne Convention. There are extensive articles on 'The Drama in America' and 'Theatrical Gossip' – through which we learn that Mr Henry Irving has retained the services of his cast for the forthcoming dramatized version of *The Bride of Lammermoor.* There follows a review of Frank Benson as Othello at The Globe, more notices and letters, an article on 'The Dramatic Sick Fund' and 'The Thespian Cricket Club', and an extensive article 'About Spanish Theatres', which have 'a certain dingy simplicity'. On page 13 we are presented with five columns of advertisements for such things as 'Hair Destroyer', 'Oriental Tooth-Paste', 'Blair's Gout and Rheumatic Pills' and 'The Great Eastern Railway' with travel times for the Newmarket Races. There is even an advertisement for 'Oxygen! Oxygen! Oxygen! Extracted From the Atmosphere by Bran's Patent Process – 40,000 Cubic Feet always in Stock'.

Only then come the play notices, including the 'Carl Rosa Opera Season' at Drury Lane, '*A Village Priest* by Sydney Grindy at The Haymarket', '*The Gondoliers* at The Savoy', '*The Cabinet Minister* by Arthur Wing Pinero at The Court'; '*As You Like It* at the St. James's Theatre' and so on throughout the West End, Islington and Chelsea and Crystal Palace and the suburbs. A stream of opera and straight plays, either classical or contemporary, dominates the landscape. Even the Theatre Royal Stratford advertises itself as 'A West End Theatre in the East' and presents a season of the Arthur Brundy Opera Company including productions of *The Marriage of Figaro* and *Lucia Di Lammermoor*.

Finally, squeezed into just two narrow columns on the right-hand side of page 14, are the music-hall notices. The Oxford Music Hall on Tottenham Court Road advertises 'All the Stars. The Talk of London' with Dan Leno and Little Tich topping the bill amid a dozen other acts, including Marie Lloyd and Harry Randall. A score of other halls follow including the Metropolitan at Edgeware Road, the Hammersmith Theatre of Varieties and Collins's Music Hall on Islington Green, most of them presenting over a dozen acts at various times of the day. Harry might have spotted the Marylebone Music Hall in the listings, an establishment soon to play a pivotal role in his fortunes. Here 'Pongo the Man Monkey' was heading the bill, to be followed way down the order by the up-and-coming comic singer Gus Elen, who in time would become a huge star of the music halls and the butt of one of Harry's most successful impersonations, a certain 'Gus Squealin''.

It is clear to see in black and white that the theatre is really two very unequal worlds – the mainstream world of straight plays and opera, spread over a dozen and more pages of *The Era*, and another world, the world of music hall and variety, segued into a couple of columns on page 14. However, as the fashion for music hall and its lucrative potential were beginning to gain ground, so the grander halls, such as the Coliseum and the Alhambra began to cater for a more upper-class market. Even within the narrow world of the music hall there began to emerge a hierarchy of the more up-market West End venues at one end, ranging through a spectrum of establishments to the bottom end of local high-street tavern rooms such as the Peckham Varieties. A contemporary writer described it thus:

> London music halls might be roughly grouped into four classes – first the aristocratic variety theatre of the West End, chiefly found in the immediate neighbourhood of Leicester Square; then the smaller less aristocratic West End halls; next the large bourgeois music halls of the less fashionable parts and in the suburbs; last the minor music halls of the poor and squalid districts.[13]

Yet it is this poor and squalid world, the last mentioned, that first caught the young Harry Pélissier's eye. The story of his career would prove to be the gradual drawing together of each of these levels, into one with a less socially divided audience and with more fluid and mixed forms of production flowing between the various stages. Indeed, one of Harry Pélissier's great achievements was to play a pivotal and pioneering role in the breakdown of class barriers in the make-up of the Edwardian theatre audience.[14]

What is also clear from these pages of *The Era* is the sheer enormity of the appetite, not only within London, but around all the provincial cities, for live entertainment. This is a generation that loved to go out and experience shows. Some music halls could house up to five thousand spectators. At a time when the population of London was approximately three million, perhaps on any given night, half the city was engaged in witnessing a theatrical or musical entertainment of some sort. No stay-at-home, take-away, online generation this. There were no such distractions to keep them at home. Originally, it was more of a male preoccupation, of course, the women being left at home to tend to the children and the housework; but, step by step, the women too would be drawn out of doors to escape the humdrum, to gather communally, to witness a spectacle or event and to share the experience. It was in many ways a heroic age of the theatre, deceptively progressive, subversive, experimental and diverse as well as being immensely popular, in one form or another, across all classes.

Upon leaving school, for the next six months, Harry was employed in his father's jewellery business, now based at 63 Berwick Street in Soho.[15] He had moved out of Elm House and taken lodgings at Gloucester House, Harders Road[16] in Peckham, then a semi-rural suburb on the outskirts of south-east London, not unlike Finchley in character, though less well heeled. However, the job in his father's offices proved an unsatisfactory experience and a role to which he was most definitely not suited, as Fitzroy Gardner points out in *Pure Folly*:

> To young Pélissier diamonds, rubies, pearls and sapphires suggested nothing more than a cramped, monotonous life in a dingy room. Probably he would have delighted in casting the pearls before swine had his father not objected to the boy's expressing his love of animals in such an extravagant manner. Although he endeavoured conscientiously to enhance the value of his father's business, as a salesman Harry Pélissier succeeded in completing only one transaction – when he sold himself a diamond ring.[17]

'A ghastly failure'

It is perhaps revealing that at no time does the impeccably middle-class Harry Pélissier express any ambition to be a straight actor or playwright or part of the mainstream, legitimate theatre. His sights are set distinctly low. From the very outset he intended to be a music-hall performer and saw his talents best suited to that endeavour.

> I know that when I suggested adopting the music-hall profession, there was much talk in my family about Marshal Pélissier [. . .] who ended his days in the French equivalent for 'Colney Hatch'.[18]

In other words, the insane asylum![19] Growing up in semi-rural Finchley, Harry would have experienced a dearth of either local theatre or music hall to actually attend. Other than the occasional amateur production at the Kilburn Town Hall, there would have been precious little. However, if he ventured just a few miles into the centre of London, he could sample the delights of scores of music halls, including The Old Mermaid, Hoxton Hall and the Trafalgar in Hackney, Collins and The Wellington in Islington, The Prince Regent and the Windmill in Finsbury or, further east, Lusby's or the Monarch Temperance in Bethnal Green, or to the south, the Windsor Castle and the Olive Branch in Camberwell and dozens more in every borough. Once his father had set up business in Berwick Street, Soho, the delights of the Tivoli on the Strand, the Alhambra, Leicester Square, the Palace on Charing Cross Road and the Oxford on Tottenham Court Road were but a stone's throw away. These represented just the up-market establishments. Furthermore, and of what would prove to be great importance to his West End career, The Royalty (later The New Royalty), a lively experimental theatre presenting early works by Shaw, Synge, Ibsen and Yeats, was on Dean Street in Soho, just a short stroll from his father's jewellery business. Further afield, in Waterloo and Elephant and Castle, Camberwell and Islington, there were literally scores of music halls to choose from. In all, there were thirty music halls in Central London alone and over one hundred and thirty in the wider boroughs.[20] Somewhat frowned upon, lowly and rough they might be, but the temptation seems to have been irresistible. Harry gives his own account:

> All this time I was haunting the stage doors of the music-halls in search of an engagement. I worried the agents for weeks, but, in spite of their numerous promises, my first chance came through a 'bus conductor. I used to ride to the office every morning from Peckham, where I was then living, on his 'bus, and we soon became friendly and confidential. I told him my ambitions and inflicted my songs upon him, which it was a relief to get somebody to hear. He said he could get me an engagement at the 'Peckham Varieties' – Rosemary Branch – having already introduced some beginners there.[21]

Figure 8: Peckham High Street in the 1890s with the Peckham Hippodrome music hall on the left

Note how this anecdote seems to underline the easy-going affability of the young Pélissier, of bourgeois background but able to strike up a cordial relationship with a bus conductor, whom he presumably invited to his rooms to experience a performance of his songs. The ease with which he related to people was a constant feature of his personality, and probably a key element in his success. The bus conductor's assistance proved useful. The Rosemary Branch was one of the earliest and longest-established music halls in south London. Attached to a tavern of the same name, it was situated on the corner of Southampton Way and Commercial Way near the boundary of Camberwell and Peckham and was opened in 1849. It was taken over in 1863 by a certain Thomas Garniss, who renamed it, rather grandiosely, the People's Palace of Varieties. In Frederick Willis's book *Peace and Dripping Toast, Memories of the 1890's*, it is described as:

> [. . .] a long shabby room adjoining the tavern, furnished with chairs and tables, and illuminated with flaming gas brackets. At one end – a stage with footlights screened with blue painted glass. A chairman sat in front of the stage facing the audience. He wore the most deplorable evening dress. Another gent sat at the piano on the stage. Everybody seemed to be drinking and talking while a man in shirt sleeves was dashing about with a tray loaded with glasses of beer. Each turn was announced by the Chair. He rapped with his hammer both to attract attention and to assist applause. A tall gent sang a song about his wife, his trouble and strife. [22]

Some readers might find this description startlingly reminiscent of the 'Up the Creek' alternative comedy club hosted by the late, great Malcolm Hardee in the Deptford of the 1980s. Harry had quite possibly visited the Peckham Varieties prior to his performing there, since it was local to his south London lodgings, but, clearly, he was not put off by the experience. He continues the tale of his journey on the Peckham omnibus and his fortuitous acquaintance, the conductor.

> He was as good as his word, and about the same time, through more 'regular channels' which meant unlimited mulberry and free drinks, I obtained a trial at the Marylebone Music-hall. [23]

The Marylebone Music Hall was a more prestigious and long-established venue. It had been built in 1858 on the site of a pub, The Rose of Normandy at 32–33 High Street, Marylebone, by the pioneering singer and impresario Sam Collins. Collins was of London-Irish descent. His name still lives on in his greatest success, *The Rocky Road to Dublin*, composed especially for him by the established singer-songwriter Harry Clifton. Starting life as a chimney sweep, he made his name at the Canterbury in Southwark, the very first of the custom-built music halls, run by the great impresario Charles Morton. The Marylebone Music Hall cost £8,000 to construct, a considerable fortune in those days, and could accommodate eight hundred people. Already by the 1860s music hall entertainment was becoming a lucrative business. Three years after this purchase Sam Collins went on to buy the Lansdowne Arms in Islington, where he ran an even bigger venue that bore his own name.[24] It opened in 1863, though sadly Collins was hardly able to enjoy the experience, having died within eighteen months. Then the Marylebone Music Hall was taken over by a certain Charles Wilkins, who enjoyed a long career as its manager–chairman. The dapper, cigar-smoking, monocle-bearing Wilkins had an awesome style and reputation all of his own. His obituary in *Entr'acte* on 18 September 1886 describes him thus:

> The late manager-chairman of the Marylebone was quite an autocrat in his way, and his manner of dealing with those delinquents who interfered with their neighbours' enjoyment had more of the *fortiter in re*, perhaps, than the *suaviter in modo* about it. Mr. Wilkins was righteously severe on those young persons who sometimes on Saturday night asserted themselves unnecessarily, and thus produced discomfort and confusion. He would not tolerate deliberate outrages of decorum and was in favour of dealing with such outrages in a summary fashion.[25]

Was Harry Pélissier on the receiving end of this man's righteous severity one wonders? It seems unlikely as Wilkins died in 1886 and by the time of Harry's debut, he had passed on his chairman's gavel. However, one imagines the tradition of his house style may have persisted and, intriguingly, Wilkins was buried in Finchley Cemetery, so one might speculate that some connection with Harry had been made prior to his passing. Among the many stars to appear at the Marylebone Music Hall was Arthur Lloyd, the first of the *Lion Comique*, those dandified versions of the Victorian 'man about town' most famously depicted by George Leybourne as *Champagne Charlie*. An advertisement of 2 February 1884 in the *General Theatre Programme* recounts a typical bill of performers for the Marylebone Music Hall:

> Marylebone Music Hall, High Street, Marylebone. Proprietor Mr. R.F. BOTTING.— Another New Company, including Viscount Walter Munroe (more nobility on the boards); Lily Gray, the Exquisite; Wade and Waller, Burnt Cork Humourists; Charles Carlton and Mami Wentworth, Refined Sketch Artists; Gerrie Russell, Serio-Comic Lady; J.H. Rowen of 'The Medicine Jack' notoriety; the O'Donnell's (James and Kate), with a Variety Show; Will Hartley, a very funny man; J.L. Dixon, Emily Mellon, and Sambo Sutten, with a varied entertainment; George Yates and Harriet Clifford more successful than ever, Charles Wilkins, Manager.[26]

And so it was that the young Harry Pélissier set about his first appearances on the music hall stage, probably at the age of 19 in 1893; first braving the long, shabby room with loud table waiters and dingy gaslight at the Peckham Varieties, to be followed by the boisterous eight hundred strong London Cockney and Irish working-class melée at the Marylebone Music Hall. Were they quite ready for the heavily-built, rather dandified, mop-haired figure of the diamond merchant's son at the piano? He offers his own account:

> I was a ghastly failure at both places, which astonished me much at the time. I do not wonder at it now, for I sang them songs of my own, which, if some of them, notably

'My Fatherland' and 'If It Wasn't For the Likes of Us' have since become popular, were at that time really unsuited to the audiences I inflicted them upon. However, I was paying everybody, and nobody was paying me, so, I didn't actually have bricks thrown at me, I was allowed to continue, always going on first in the bill and being foredoomed to failure.[27]

Let us note that Harry was not deterred by the audience reaction. He 'always' came back for more and even from the outset showed that determination of spirit and ultimate self-confidence to persevere. Let us note also that Harry was apparently 'paying everybody' in order to perform, either directly perhaps or in the purchase of alcohol. He had after all arranged his debut with the said bus conductor by the promise of 'unlimited mulberry and free drinks'. Aspirant pop bands and comedians please note that 'pay to play' is nothing new.

Harry had chosen to make his debut with his own songs – a brave and far-sighted move. The songs he chose were 'Mein Faderland' and 'The Burglar's Song (If It Wasn't For the Likes of Us)' – numbers that were to remain popular in his repertoire throughout his career. 'Mein Faderland' is an outrageous send up of a boisterous German migrant. Little would the audience be aware that the author and performer of the piece was himself the son of a German migrant – unless that is, Harry made a point of telling them, which seems unlikely. Was the ribald caricature represented in this song aimed at his father or perhaps based upon another blood relative? Was Harry trying to reinforce his 'Englishness' by distancing himself from his ancestry and mocking it? At this point in time the relatively strong influx of German and other continental migrants into London was an issue of some contention, as was the build-up of German economic and military might. However, the depiction is not a cruel one, but, in fact, typically of Pélissier, a rather affectionate and joyous one. The worst one can say of this lively Teuton is that he likes to drink and eat and socialize and make merry. Clearly too Harry's natural facility with the language makes for some fun with the accent.

I left my blesset Faterland,
It's choost apout a year,
Und came across to London Town,
To try my fortune here –
Och! England is de place for me,
To you my word I gif! –
I don't go pack to Chermany,
So longer as I lif! –

CHORUS
Och! Faterland, mein Faterland!-
I nefer more shall see,
I don't go pack to Chermany
Tsiss is the place for me!-

I tage a buse in Kampten Town,
At a fery modest rent,
And there I play de fiddle to
A fery great extent.
I play de fiddle all de day —
And sometimes 'das clavier'
And then I in de evening
Go drink the lager beer!

CHORUS

I like your pleasant English ways —
Your sausages on toast,
But the peautiful young English girls —
Is what I like de most!-
I fall in love with ev'ry one,
As down the road they pass —
And as I look I tink dat each
Is petter as de last!

CHORUS

Now I shall tell you what I make,
When summer-time is come,
I take some of those English girls,
To Richmond, for some fun!
A penny steamer first we take,
And den we walk apout, -
And after dat we get to eat-
Bloodwurst mit sauerkraut!

CHORUS

I once with some young English chaps,
A drinking wager won,
But dey underneath de table went,
Before we'd scarce begun!
We drank and drank until dey cry,
'If more we drink we bourst!'
But as for me, - as true I stand!
I'd hardly quenched my thirst!"
Och Faterland, mein Faterland,
I nefer more will see,
I like your good old Bass's beer,
Dat's de beer for me! [28]

Today this may come across as an unacceptable stereotype of a boozing, lecherous German. However, it is equally possible to see in it a rather friendly German expatriate who offers us his music and his food and his company and finally decides he actually prefers our own Bass beer, which one might have thought at least would raise a cheer from the crowd. And given Harry's Franco-German background, it is likely that he could perfectly mimic the accent, in which one hears echoes of Peter Sellers' *Doctor Strangelove*. However, for the audiences at Marylebone and Peckham, it was just too far removed from their own experience to strike a note. There obviously was not enough 'trouble and strife' with the wife in this act. Were they being ironic when they called for a drinking song? Harry continues his tale.

> Finding my own compositions unpopular, I purchased a song from a professional music-hall songwriter, which cost me five shillings, band parts and all, and had a talking chorus, running, as near as I can recollect:

> *'Drink, drink, drink,*
> *Brewers love to brew it;*
> *Drink, drink, drink,*
> *Navvies love to chew it.*
> *Drink, drink, drink,*
> *No matter what you've sunk,*
> *And never give it best until*
> *You're drunk, blind drunk!'*

> Even this, though more adapted to their tastes, can hardly be said to have 'fetched them'. The first time I sang it a beetle-browed ruffian in the gallery inquired: 'When are they going to burn yer?'[29]

The other of his own compositions that Harry chose to perform is a more complex and intriguing one. Eventually published (like 'Mein Faderland' by Reynold's & Co) in 1902, under the title 'If It Wasn't for the Likes O' Huss (A Burglar's Song)', it is oddly prescient of *The Threepenny Opera* by Brecht and Weill. It is deeply satirical and points a direct finger at the hypocrisies and injustices of society as responsible for producing the criminal class and wryly suggests that it is the legal and judicial systems that have most to gain from crime itself.

> *Now I once was an ordinary working man!*
> *Honest? Pooh! As honest as the day!*
> *All my spare time I was teaching in the Sunday School,*
> *but bless your heart, why that game didn't pay*
> *For my family was growin' and my butcher's bill was owin',*
> *I was "spotin'" (1.) every blessed thing I'd got!*
> *When one day I starts a-nickin',*
> *and I took to pocket-pickin'*
> *which regret it from that day to this*
> *I've not! I've not!*

CHORUS

But there's people as'll arguefy and fink
they shows the reason why,
a burglar he's a useless sort of cuss! Ho yuss!
But I asks yer now what would they do,
with all their heaps of men in blue,
if it wasn't for the bloomin' likes of us?
Yuss, us! – if it wasn't for the bloomin' likes of us?

Now one day when I happens to be mouchin' off
with a lady's purse what I 'ad been an' bagged
An interferin' copper come up just behind
and sudden – strike me vulgar – I was lagged! (2.)
Then the old girl starts a-cryin',
"To rob em you was tryin'"
and they hauls me up before the bloomin' beak (3.)
When my little lot was settled,
well I tells ya, I was nettled –
so when the judge says "prisoner you can speak"
I says:

CHORUS

Oh, there's people as'll arguefy and fink
they shows the reason why,
a burglar he's a useless sort of cuss! Ho yuss!
But I asks yer Worship in the Chair,
do you fink as you'd be sittin' there,
if it wasn't for the bloomin' likes of us?
Yuss, us! – if it wasn't for the bloomin' likes of us?!

Now when the judge had heard the words I had to say,
his face it turns into a firey flame!
So, I see by that, that I had touched his stony heart,
but he give me six months hard though just the same
I've pinched an old gent's ticker,
you'd lock up a pocket-picker,
but you can't you see the error as you've made?
Oh go home and ask yer mother,
won't the josser (4.) buy another?
That'll make the whole transaction good for trade.
Can't yer see?

CHORUS

Still, there's people as'll arguefy and fink
they shows the reason why,
a burglar he's a useless sort of cuss! Ho yuss!
But you every one the question shirk,
why you'd all of yer be out of work,
if it wasn't for the bloomin' likes of us?
Yuss, us! - if it wasn't for the bloomin' likes of us?![30]

(1.) pawning; *(2.)* arrested; *(3.)* magistrate; *(4.)* fellow

In *The Threepenny Opera*, near the end of Act 3, MacHeath exclaims:

> Ladies and gentlemen, you see here the vanishing representative of a vanishing class. We bourgeois artisans, who work with honest jemmies on the cash boxes of small shopkeepers, are being swallowed up by the large concerns of the banks. What is a picklock to a bank share? What is the burgling of a bank to the founding of a bank? What is the murder of a man to the employment of a man?[31]

Or take George Bernard Shaw's *Pygmalion*, first produced in New York and London in 1914, some twenty years after Harry had performed his song.

> DOOLITTLE: I'm one of the undeserving poor: that's what I am. Think of what that means to a man. It means he's up agen middle class morality all the time. If there's anything going, and I put in for a bit of it, it's always the same story; 'You're undeserving so you can't have it.' But my needs is as great as the most deserving widow's that ever got money out of six different charities in one week for the death of the same husband [. . .] What is your middle class morality? Just an excuse for never giving me anything [. . .] I'm undeserving and I mean to go on being undeserving.[32]

The comparatively forgotten Harry Pélissier was making a broadly similar satirical point three decades earlier: that morality was relative to social conditions and the joke was that all these splendid occupations, the police and judiciary and merchant trade, all relied for their existence on the humble poor, the pickpocket and burglar! How exactly this young, middle-class ingenue had arrived at such a point of view can only be a matter of speculation. It is doubtful that it was a matter of intellectual conviction, although we know that Charles Dickens was among his favourite authors,[33] and this may have had some influence on his social outlook as well as his vivid style. Rather, it is more likely that Pélissier was already displaying that intuitively anti-authoritarian streak and that innate responsiveness to hypocrisy and the ridiculous that so characterised his personality and career. So too, his social and cultural observations were probably coloured by his alien origins, his disaffection from the strictly disciplined regime of his education and his apparently fractious relationship with his father. Furthermore, his experience of a wide range of social classes and communities through his father's business dealings in Soho – probably much broader than the average Highgate School pupil – must have provided him with a host of characters, dialects and social mores upon which to draw. In time his approach would develop into a veritable scatter gun, whereby all targets were fair game; and ultimately this anti-authoritarian instinct would lead him to an anarchic absurdism that risked losing his audience entirely. However, unlike Brecht or Shaw, in these early forays, Pélissier was performing in a working-class music hall, and to a hostile audience on the receiving end of the very injustice he sought to satirize. The point, you might say, got lost. Harry summed it up thus:

> It was a most disheartening time. My family were naturally horrified at the line I had adopted, and my prospects were of the gloomiest. My experience was that if by Herculean efforts I obtained a trial from a manager, he never paid the slightest attention to my performance. I often used to wonder why on earth they went through the farce of pretending to give me a hearing.[34]

It was time perhaps to try another direction.

4

The Pierrot

*Figure 9. H.G. Pélissier in his trademark
pierrot costume*

Ethiopian Serenaders and Morecambe Minstrels

Christmas came round and we got up an entertainment at my home, purely in an amateur way [. . .] We took the idea from the first troupe of pierrots some of us had seen at Sandown in the Isle of Wight. The members of our company were all amateurs of course; but the idea proved so successful that we became much in request at local charitable institutions.[1]

Fitzroy Gardner picks up the story in *Pure Folly*:

[. . .] to return to his first experience of his father's business – having convinced himself that he was not likely to succeed in that particular line of commerce, he decided to turn his taste for music to pecuniary account, and also devoted himself to stage-managing an amateur pierrot entertainment in his father's back drawing-room. So successful was the first performance that it had to be repeated on several occasions to crowded 'houses' of no more than some thirty persons – the front drawing-room's holding capacity was limited.[2]

Pélissier was understandably keen to get his songs heard and to show off his talents and had therefore decided to engage his family as a ready-made audience, perhaps to try out new ideas. But why the pierrot costumes? From where and when had this fashion for pierrot shows originated? To answer that we have to go outside of London to the booming seaside resorts of the English coastline and to a wholly different tradition of entertainment than either music hall or mainstream theatre. And we have to go back to the mid-nineteenth century and the Emancipation Movement that preceded the American Civil War.

The anti-slavery movement always had a strong following in Great Britain owing to the pioneering work of, amongst others, William Wilberforce. However, it was from the 1830s onwards that black American minstrels, many of them runaway slaves, began to arrive on English shores. It is no coincidence that these first arrivals were at major ports, such as Liverpool and London, Southampton, Dover and Bristol, as many of those who came would have been stowaways or porters aboard ship. Those who could play an instrument, most often a banjo or a fiddle, earned some quick and easy money performing on the quayside or the town parade, the strand or even the beach itself, 'the sands' as it was called. As was to be the case for a later generation, with regard to rhythm and blues and American soul music on Merseyside and on the London dockside of the 1960s, it was these locations of trans-Atlantic commerce and travel that were the first and the foremost to benefit from an easterly cultural migration from America. Gospel songs, work-songs, songs of the chain gang, minstrel dances, the cakewalk and what was eventually to become ragtime and jazz were all beginning to permeate English shores.

In the 1830s, Charles Dibdin wrote his own music and performed the part of a slave called Munro on the West End stage in Isaac Bickerstaffe's *The Padlock*.[3] This part was later taken on by the celebrated black tragedian Ira Aldridge, who arrived in England around 1824 and sang on stage to his own guitar accompaniment – comic songs and proto-minstrel pieces such as 'Possum Up A Gum Tree'.[4] After 18 months touring America, Charles Matthews, a great favourite of Charles Dickens and performer of 'polymonopologues' (self-composed solo works in which he performed all the parts himself), included some 'black fun' by singing that particular number in his own show.[5] 'Black face' minstrelsy, a white impersonation of the black original, was beginning to appear. T. Daddy Rice started a London craze at the Adelphi Theatre in 1836 with his 'Jump Jim Crow'.[6]

In time, and for several decades into the twentieth century, it was the white 'black-face' impersonation that was to dominate. The novel and engaging syncopated rhythm of the music, its immediacy and brightness, the sheer exuberance and fun of it all, and the clear commercial success of the black players both on stage and on the streets, meant perhaps that a white, copy-cat version was inevitable. Money was to be made here and, while on the one hand we may look upon 'black-face' minstrelsy with disdainful hindsight as racist stereotyping (or in today's terms as 'cultural appropriation'), there is also the underlying and undeniable fact that, to coin a phrase, imitation is the sincerest form of flattery. In particular, the minstrel troupes succeeded in the English seaside resorts because, as one comtemporary put it, in comparison to the traditional British music hall:

> [. . .] the minstrel show was by contrast regarded as a form of entertainment where a husband and wife could take their children without fear of being asked embarrassing questions afterwards.[7]

It was the black performers themselves who had blazed the trail (how else would their white impersonators have known what or how to play?) and they maintained their place, although often unrecorded and in the face of the prejudiced favour given to competition from their more privileged white counterparts. Throughout the middle decades of the nineteenth century, anti-slavery choirs known as 'Ethiopian Serenaders' arrived from America, including in their number the celebrated black dancer, William Henry Lane, billed as *Master Juba – The Greatest Dancer in the World*.[8] He stole the show at the Vauxhall Gardens in 1848. Other notable players, of whom we have some record, are Alex Day, who performed with the mixed-race *Morecambe Minstrels* well into the first decade of the twentieth century,[9] Robert Rody, a Jamaican musician who performed in Yarmouth and Henry 'Box' Brown, a popular showman in Liverpool in the 1850s.[10]

In May 1852, the whole phenomenon was to take on extraordinary new proportions, for it was then that Harriet Beecher Stowe's damning, if sentimental, condemnation of American slavery, *Uncle Tom's Cabin*, was published in London. It was an immediate sensation. Within a year there were 23 editions. By the end of 1852, one and a half million copies had been sold in Great Britain and its colonies, while 12 theatrical dramatizations had been produced including four *Uncle Tom* pantos.[11] Add to this the appearance of *Uncle Tom* soap and almanacs, songbooks and even wallpaper and you have some idea of the popular craze that had taken off. Perhaps today we would call it 'hype', but, clearly, even then the marketing men had an eye for a 'spin-off', though all for a good cause you might say. With hindsight, we may look back with an uncomfortable cringe at the patronizing nature of the work (for which the term 'Uncle Tom' has become something of a by-word). However, it certainly had an impact. As a result, those runaway slave minstrels who inhabited the docks and harbours must have appeared even more visible, along with their 'black-face' counterparts.

Importantly this form of musical entertainment could cross the social class divide, unlike the music hall or the classical theatre. Sam Hague, a clog dancer from Sheffield had worked in the United States and formed his own minstrel troupe, consisting of 26 ex-slaves.[12] They first performed in Liverpool on 11 July 1866, under the banner of *The Great American Slave Troupe*. The first time around, it was a commercial failure due to a lack of professional expertise from the players, who mostly returned home to the emancipation that had been won by the Union side in the Civil War. However, a new troupe of players went on to considerable success, including in their line-up 'the black dwarf, Japanese Tommy' (Thomas Dilward), who played fiddle, danced and sang, Neil Solomon and Abe Cox, two comics, and Aaron Banks, a handsome black singer famous for his powerful signature number 'Emancipation Day'.[13] This form of entertainment was slowly beginning to transform British popular culture. A contributor to the *St James' Magazine* of April–September 1868 writes of black entertainers 'continually wandering through the country',[14] while James Greenwood in *The Wilds of London* (1874) remarks how an anti-slavery song, 'Mary Blane', and an old plantation song called 'Poor Jeff' had become popular tavern songs regularly performed in sing-arounds.[15]

Alongside these authentic American imports, the legions of white copy-cat minstrelsy grew into an entire industry that was to reach a peak with the compositions of Stephen Foster and troupes such as *The Mohawk Minstrels* and *The Moore and Burgess Minstrels*. These frequently featured the work of the prolific songwriter Harry Hunter, pieces which sadly often plumbed the depths of patronizing racism in titles such as '"Massa" Sent A Jellygram' and even 'The N***** That Never Knew Nuffin At All'. This, in turn, would lead on to the more sentimental and condescending genre of what was contemporaneously dubbed the 'coon song' with titles like 'De Sun Am A-shining All De Time' and 'My Dear Old Cabin Home'.[16] This was a genre, the vacuous racism of which Pélissier himself satirised and parodied in several songs, such as 'Ypsilanti' and 'Zulu Lulu'. That he was very conscious of the debt that he and other pierrot performers owed to the black American minstrels is made clear in an interview with *The Strand Magazine* in June 1909. Unfortunately, he was constrained to quote the derogatory language of the time to make his point, but the positive and sympathetic thrust of his opinion is clear:

> Years ago, when entertainers in pierrot costume were a novel feature at the seaside, I overheard a mater-familias remark, "What a pity they don't blacken their faces! People always laugh so much at the dear old n*****s'. The dear old n*****s! I too owe them a debt of gratitude. I'm afraid the n*****s have had their day. As one of the best of them remarked to a pierrot reproachfully, 'Taint as if you were content to rub off the bloomin' burnt cork. No. You must go and whitewash yourselves.'[17]

It was as if the anti-slavery intentions of the Emancipation Movement had been turned on their head; such are the machinations of commercialism. However, more importantly, and enduringly, black American music had planted an indelible footprint in British culture. As we shall see, Harry Pélissier was fully aware of all these styles and traditions and was to utilise them in his own way. In particular, the footprint of American minstrelsy had been left on the English coastal ports and towns, for here it was that the original runaway musician slaves had made their escape; and it was here too that a whole transformation was taking place in the English urban and cultural landscape – one that would provide a ready and growing audience for such entertainment. For it was this period of the late nineteenth century that also saw the burgeoning of the English seaside holiday.

In his work *A New England?* G.R. Searle has pointed out that:

> [. . .] by the 1870s the seaside had largely displaced the spa, and the pleasures that it offered were drawing in not only those who could comfortably afford to take a week's holiday on the coast, but also poorer people on day excursions, especially during the August Bank Holiday.[18]

What had made this expansion possible was the rapid development of travel by train. The first intercity passenger steam train between Liverpool and Manchester had opened in 1830 and, during the 1840s, over 10,000 miles of new railway track had been laid, connecting all the major cities. The London and Brighton Railway opened in 1840 with a network of lines that served most of the south London boroughs and extended to the coastal towns of Sussex and Surrey and into parts of Kent and Hampshire.[19] As a result, the coastal towns grew, many becoming fashionable and attractive resorts, and the increasingly prosperous urban working and middle-class now had an affordable means of transport that made these towns accessible.

George IV had made Brighton fashionable for sea bathing, but even his royal horse-drawn carriage would have taken six hours to get there from London. The Brighton Railway reduced that to a mere two hours. On Easter Monday 1862, over 132,000 holidaymakers made the journey.[20] The railways reached Great Yarmouth in 1844, Scarborough in 1845, Blackpool in 1846 and Torquay in 1848. By 1879, between 16,000 and 24,000 day-trippers were arriving in Margate and Ramsgate every Sunday in summer.[21] Booth and Rowntree's contemporary survey states that 75–80% of working-class families could afford an occasional seaside holiday. Two million people visited Blackpool in the 1890s, a number that grew to four million by 1914.[22] By 1900, there were 48 large coastal resorts with a combined population of 900,000, while 200 resorts were named in the fashionable travel guides.[23] Commercial companies and private entrepreneurs were pouring vast sums of capital into piers, theatres and concert halls. In 1879 Blackpool town council astutely secured the power from Parliament to raise its own tax for self-promotion and advertising and, as a result, construction began on its famous Tower in 1891, while its Grand Theatre was built three years later. Brighton Corporation built its three-mile seafront parade and world-famous aquarium in 1901.[24] Consequently, it was boom time for the lodging houses. In the Ilfracombe census of 1889, there were listed 249 such establishments, along with seven boarding houses and 12 hotels.[25] These would have been the natural habitat of the travelling players and minstrels who could afford their prices. At the lowest end of the market, you would share a room, even a bed, with a stranger and buy your own food. You could be charged extra for the use of hot water or the house cruet.

Compton Mackenzie offers a vivid description of such lodgings in his novel *The Adventures of Sylvia Scarlett,* published in 1918. The first part of this work centres around the exploits of a troupe of seaside pierrots, and its informed detail surely owes much to the knowledge and experience he must have gained from working as a sketch writer and lyricist with H.G. Pélissier and *The Follies* during 1910–11:

> The breakfast room was placed below the level of the street: here in an atmosphere of cat-haunted upholstery and broken springs, of over-cooked vegetables and dingy fires, yet withal of a kind of frowsty comfort, Sylvia sometimes met the other lodgers; [. . .] when they got home for dinner at midday, it was impossible to eat, and they used to loll about in the stuffy sitting-room, which the five of them shared in common, while the flies buzzed everywhere. It was never worthwhile to remove the make-up; so, all their faces used to get mottled with pale streaks of perspiration, the rouge on their lips would cake, and their ruffles hung limp and wet, stained round the neck with dirty carmine. Sylvia lost all enjoyment on the tour, and used to lie on the horse-hair sofa that pricked her cheeks, watching distastefully the cold mutton, the dull knives and the spotted cloth, and the stewed fruit over which lay a faint silvery film of staleness: round the room her fellow mountebanks were still seated on the chairs into which they had collapsed when they reached the lodgings, motionless like painted dolls.[26]

The life was hard and competitive, but not without its own rewards as Mackenzie goes on to describe:

> At last, the company, which called itself The Pink Pierrots, was ready to start for the south coast. It took Monkley all his ingenuity to get out of London without paying for the dresses or the properties, but it was managed somehow; and at the beginning of July they pitched a small tent on the beach at Hastings. There were many rival companies, some of which possessed the most elaborate equipment, almost a small theatre with railed-off seats and a large piano; but Sylvia envied none of these its grandeur [. . .] Sylvia enjoyed every moment of the day from the time they left their lodgings, pushing before them the portable piano in the morning sunshine, to the journey home after the last performance, which was given in a circle of rosy lantern light within sound of the sea.[27]

Financially, things could be very tough, as Harry Pelissier pointed out in an interview to *The Daily Telegraph* on the occasion of *The Follies'* 500th appearance at the Apollo theatre:

> There was a lot of money lost over us at the start, but we picked up more than enough to equalise the balance later. There's one point I should like to emphasise. It may be taken in connection with a remark made one night by an occupant of the gallery. 'That fat fellow', he said to his companion, indicating myself, 'started life on the sands. He then built the Apollo, invented the double-barrelled piano, and then eventually got married to the girl with the golden hair.' I am anxious it should be publicly known that we never performed on the sands. We started on Worthing Pier and I am proud to say at no time have we sunk below its level.[28]

Harry is being economical with the truth, claiming that *The Follies* never played on the beaches, when they almost certainly did (see page 46). Even in the world of seaside pierrots there was clearly a sense of hierarchy and status. It is possible that Pélissier received financial backing from his father's diamond business, or had some savings from his short period of work with the company that enabled him to hire concert halls for his troupe; after all he had been able to pay for his initial appearances in the music halls at Peckham and Marylebone. Nevertheless, even *The Follies* employed the services of a 'bottler', a collector with a jug or a hat or a bottle (the latter preventing the removal by the collector himself of any cash given!) to gather donations from the audience. In Harry's obituary in *The Globe*, it was reported that: 'The collector one day brought him only 16s [16 shillings; 20 shillings = one pound]. and, suspecting that the man was pocketing some of the cash he made the next collection himself. It amounted to 1s.1½d [one shlling and four pence half'penny; 12 pence = one shilling].'[29] Such were the humble beginnings of *The Follies*. To put this in perspective, even a bed in a shared room in a low lodging house might cost 1s.4d per night, or a more upmarket bed and breakfast 3s per night.[30] By October 1913, at the height of their fame, just the monthly running cost of *The Follies* was £29.11s.7d, including a rehearsal room at 6s.9d, fares to Bristol at £3.14s.2d and a business lunch at 8s.9d. This was at a time when their monthly income stood at £1,072.1s.2d. to be shared amongst ten players as well as stagehands.[31] Harry Pélissier's plan to aim high – both metaphorically and literally – and to play the piers and concert halls, as opposed to merely the beaches and parades, was clearly driven by a hard reality, and fortunately it seems to have eventually paid off.

By 1896, when *The Follies* made their debut in Worthing, the pier had already become something of an English institution. Originally functional, intended as a wooden landing stage for paddle steamers, the pier gradually transformed into a promenade for holidaymakers. The first pier specifically designed for such a purpose was built at Southport in 1859. From then on, an average of two new piers a year appeared on the coast during the 1860s and 1870s. Many of them provided the concert halls that were to be such a vital arena in which the minstrel troupes could perform. They took on their own theatrical constructions, sometimes exotically fanciful and fantastic, such as the Blackpool North Pier modelled on the Hindu Temple at Binderabund and the Morecambe Central Pier modelled on the Taj Mahal![32] These dream-like surroundings, the hubbub of the unfamiliar crowds, the summer heat, the smell of sea and sand, the odour of tea houses and ice cream, not to mention the shoulder-rubbing proximity of the people themselves and the mixture of accents and faces, combined with what must have been for many a first experience of the sea, all fed into a surreptitiously erotic, essentially un-English, loss of inhibition. Men might bathe naked, as a birth-right of medieval folklore, but women had to undergo the constrictions of the bathing machine. This was a Victorian hut on wheels in which the bather was constrained to change clothes, and thence be transported to the sea's edge in a full body costume. In time, this construction would gradually disappear as women chose to disrobe more conveniently and cost-effectively under cover of a towel, a beach tent or a mackintosh. The costumes too began to shrink (metaphorically if not literally) and become more revealing, inspired in part perhaps by the short skirts and leotards of the music hall. Though many resorts insisted on a regulation 60 feet distance between men and women bathers, competition from the liberal régimes of continental resorts gradually led to mixed bathing, which was first officially introduced by Llandudno in 1895, followed by Paignton in 1896.[33] 'Yes there's lots of girls besides that I'd like to be beside beside the seaside beside the sea!' crooned the popular music-hall artist Mark Sheridan.[34] England did not quite know it yet, (in some ways perhaps it still does not), but in those heady Victorian seaside days it was experiencing the first stirrings of a sexual revolution – and it was fun.

This was the landscape into which the black American minstrel troupes made their first appearance, soon to be followed and superseded by their 'black-face' white impersonators. These were the initial pioneers, the first generation of the busking seaside entertainers, who amused and captivated holidaymakers on sunny seafront parades, in the end-of-pier concert halls, in portable marquees and stages on the beaches and in the municipal parks and gardens. In many cases, these may have been the first black faces – either real or fake – that these visitors had ever encountered. Certainly, much of the banjo and fiddle music, the choral harmonies, the tales of cotton fields and plantation work would have seemed entirely exotic and novel. Likewise, the entertainers' costumes would often have been deliberately colourful and theatrical, utilizing the top hats and tailcoats, the stripy waistcoats and pants of their American counterparts on the Mississippi and Missouri steamboats. It is hard to overestimate how potentially radical and revolutionary this cultural development was. For the first time, middle and working classes, and to a limited extent black and white, were mixing together relatively freely in a leisurely pursuit, by the balmy shores of an English holiday resort.

A whole new industry was taking root. However, it was potentially far too lucrative to allow just a single genre of entertainment, the troupes of busking minstrels, to exploit its distraction-hungry crowds and their many thousands of pounds of disposable income. The millions now thronging to the seaside would seek out a variety of entertainments. It was time for a new generation of entertainers to hit the beaches. Both inspired and, to a large extent influenced, by the minstrel shows, a somewhat unlikely new style of musical entertainment started to appear on the promenades and parades.

In 1891, the popular French actress Jane May appeared in one of the West End hits of that season. It was called *L'Enfant Prodigue* and it ran at the Prince of Wales Theatre;[35] and a reviewer in *The Spectator* described it thus:

> If there be any lovers of the ancient art of dumb-show as applied to dramatic representation, we strongly recommend them to go and see the very curious 'musical play without words' called *L'Enfant Prodigue'*, now being given at the Prince of Wales Theatre. Real pantomime, a story told entirely by gestures, has almost died out in this country, at any rate as regards the legitimate theatres, though we have been told that very clever pantomimic sketches – generally, of course, of the grotesque kind – are to be seen in music-halls [. . .] But a little domestic drama expressed altogether by gestures, accompanied by music, is, we imagine altogether new in England. And that is what *L'Enfant Prodigue* is [. . .] One of the great points in the first act is the writing of a love-letter by young Pierrot. Mademoiselle Mays' acting, while meditating upon the composition, is one of the most perfect things in the play, and it has not even the help of music.[36]

Was it the striking costumes of the *Commedia dell'Arte*? Or perhaps it was the use of gesture to the accompaniment of music, or the presentation of an entertainment without use of spoken dialogue, thus averting the censure of the Lord Chamberlain. Or was it perhaps the sheer and sudden explosion of popular enthusiasm for this pantomimic display from France? Whatever the inspiration, it was only shortly afterwards that the banjoist Clifford Essex put together his own troupe of pierrot-costumed musicians for a show at Henley Regatta in 1891. This too proved to be wildly successful and, as a result, a whole new genre of entertainment was about to hit the holiday resorts of the English coast.

Rather as, some years before, *Uncle Tom's Cabin* and the minstrel shows had been much imitated, so too Clifford Essex's company was widely copied and there appeared a wild frenzy of newly formed professional and amateur pierrot troupes, among the most famous and successful of which were Will Catlin's *Royal Pierrots* and George Royle's *Fol-De-Rols*.[37] Over the next two decades and beyond, it was to become the dominant form of entertainment at the seaside and even in concert halls and clubs in provincial towns and cities around the country. The musical and comic content would borrow heavily from the minstrel repertoire, utilizing banjo songs from the southern United States, but there was also the addition of light classical and parlour pieces, humorous music-hall songs and sentimental ballads. Above all, the dazzling white and black pierrot costumes allowed the performers to stand out from the crowd as they gathered an audience and sold tickets or 'bottled' for their living.

Meanwhile, Harry Pélissier, ensconced in his Peckham lodgings and encouraged by the success of his own home-produced pierrot shows and the response of his family audience, was realising by now that the environment of the working-class music hall was not his natural home. He looked instead for an already up and running troupe that he could join. Some years later, in a magazine article, he jokingly invents the fiction that, as well as having gone to Highgate, he also attended school in Folkestone and Scarborough.[38] Both of these are seaside resorts, and the implication is that this where he received his real, vocational education – from the pierrot and minstrel shows he would have witnessed during those ubiquitous family holidays. This was the genteel genre of entertainment that Harry Pélissier would come to dominate and radically transform into an almost unrecognisably surreal, satirical and subversive stage act.[39]

The Baddeley Troupe

First, however, he had to make his initial tentative steps into touring theatrical work. It was probably in response to an advertisement in *The Era* or *Stage* that Harry was taken on by an amateur company of players based in south London and called *The Baddeley Troupe*.[40] This was a group of six performers that had recently been formed by the famous tennis pairing of the Baddeley brothers, Wilfrid and Herbert. Sports clubs such as Henley and Wimbledon provided something of a cradle for amateur musical and theatrical troupes. The Victorian amateur was wide-ranging in his enthusiasms. Born in Bromley in 1872, Herbert had reached the Wimbledon singles semi-finals three times between 1894 and 1896, and in 1891 and 1894–96, he and his brother Wilfrid had won the male doubles title four times. Wilfrid, the better known player, won the Wimbledon singles title three times between 1891 and 1895.[41] His first win over Joshua Pim in 1891 at the age of 19 years and five months made him, until Boris Becker in 1985, the youngest men's singles champion at Wimbledon. He was also runner-up three times between 1893 and 1896. In 1895 both brothers qualified as solicitors and, from then on, concentrated most of their energies on their legal careers at their father's family firm in Leadenhall Street.[42] However, with their amateur interest (so typical of Victorian times) in music and theatre, even Wimbledon tennis being then entirely non-professional of course, and approaching retirement from the game, they decided to form an amateur concert band of pierrots called *The Baddeley Troupe*. Initially, this would have put on musical events at sporting clubs like Wimbledon itself and Henley. In a short space of time, however, the troupe was taken over by the manager-player, S. Sherrington Chinn,[43] under whose direction it started to become a more professional outfit and to seek engagements further afield, outside of London. Chinn himself had sporting connections, having acted as Secretary for Henley Sports Club, where it is quite possible that he saw, and was inspired by, Clifford Essex performing his original pierrot show.

This was the troupe that, at some point in 1895, Harry Pélissier was to join. From the very start he seems to have made a huge impression. Whereas, in general, pierrot companies tended to borrow the repertoire of the American minstrel shows, with the addition of popular chamber pieces, light parlour songs and comic 'turns' and dance routines, under Pélissier's influence *The Baddeley Troupe* displayed an inclination to create its own material or at least modify standard works with its own arrangements and interpretations. The young Harry arrived with a wealth of talent and ideas to contribute. Not only was he a fine pianist and composer, but he could sing and act, play comic roles, write comic lines and lyrics and, with his larger-than-life physique and personality, provide an all-round hub to the programme. In the summer of 1896 – and by now taken over by Harry and renamed *The Follies* – they set about a tour of coastal resorts and principal towns.[44] And what a gruelling tour it was! In fact, it appears that Harry was on the road and working for the whole first year of his employment. It represented a complete change of lifestyle. First, Worthing in August 1896, then on to Folkestone, Hastings and St Leonard's in September; that same month, a trip to Preston in Lancashire and thence back south again to Barnet, Southampton and Portsmouth in November, staying in whatever hotels or seaside lodging houses they could afford. One wonders whether Harry might have had a hand in organising the concert in his local Barnet. Thence to Croydon and Streatham in December; on to Coventry and Tunbridge Wells, Bournemouth and Brighton in January 1897, Ipswich in February, followed by Redhill in March; that same month a journey north to Newcastle and immediately back south again to Ealing; in April, Southampton, Worthing once again in June and, in July, the Isle of Wight, a return to Hastings, then on to Malvern in Somerset, Llandudno in north Wales and South Shields, Newcastle once more, Southport, Liverpool and Aberystwyth in August; in September, Birkenhead, Lytham, Rhyl and, finally, a week-long engagement in October back in the Isle of Wight. One feels breathless just thinking about it.

Figure 10. The original Follies of 1895, including members of The Baddeley Troupe. Back row: Arthur Wimperis, Florence Minty, Harold Allerton, Emerson Carter, H.G. Pélissier. Front row: Doris Lind, Mabel Engelhardt, Cave Chinn, Ethel Ward, Daisy Engelhardt

Initially the troupe would adopt a quite formal pose, seated on stage in a semi-circle in the style of the traditional minstrel show. In those early days, there were usually ten players in all. Four men, including Harry himself along with Arthur Wynne, 'a born comedian whose able rendering of "The Scientific Man" was one of the best things on the programme',[45] Cave Chinn, an 'admirable elocutionist, his masterly recitations of "Prince" and "Kissing Cup's Race" were listened to with rapt attention',[46] and Harold Allerton, who delivered a comic song entitled 'Big Ben'.[47] The men would usually be dressed in black pierrot costumes, alongside six pierrettes in white. Doris Lind sang and danced, while Norah Jones made a specialty of an Irish ballad called 'Kilarney'; Florence Batty played mandolin and Kate Carew shared the piano playing with Harry. They were joined by Miss Mabel Engelhardt's 'delightful singing' and Miss Emerson Carter's 'sweet voice'.[48]

However, it appears that, as the troupe travelled from town to town, there was a high turnover of cast members. Was this for expediency? Were other local people to join the company as they moved across the country? Or does this shedding of cast members reveal a ruthless streak in the young Harry, who was already clearly playing a leading role? Names of players given in the press accounts in each town change with striking rapidity. In Folkestone we are introduced to Mr Harold McKay and the dancers Daisy Dickinson and Mona Clare,[49] while later in Preston Miss E. Jones appears for the first time. The next month, in Barnet, up pops Miss Nellie Reed (who later forged a considerable music hall career of her own), along with Mr Eric Lodge.[50] Still the crew totals ten, so others have lost their place. Once in Southampton, the troupe is joined by Mr Lindsay Hammond and by Miss Evelyn Hughes, Miss Gwyneth Boleyn, Mr Wallie Montagu and Miss Beatrice Scully.[51] Then, in June 1897, it is joined by the Allandale family, Fred and Hetty and their daughter Ethel.[52] Only then do things start to settle down and Ethel will prove to be one of the long-standing regular colleagues of Harry Pélissier. Indeed, Ethel Allandale became a hugely popular and versatile cast member, playing both mandolin and banjo and able to perform sharp comic impersonations (her parents were both experienced 'black-face' minstrels). At one point in the 1900s, she briefly left *The Follies* to take the lead in a West End Gaiety musical, but soon returned and remained with the troupe even after Harry's death in 1913.

It is important to point out that the employment of female performers in a pierrot troupe would have been extremely unusual at the time. In her essay 'Popular Theatre 1895–1940', Sophie Nield suggests that the first instance may have been in Bridlington in 1899 with Bert Grapho's *Jovial Jollies*.[53] However, it is clear that *The Baddeley Troupe*, and after them *The Follies*, included female performers from as early as 1895 and, as such, must have been among the first, if not the very first, to have done so. Indeed, the practice did not become common until well into the next century. Furthermore, the pierrettes took a prominent role on an equal footing with the men. One should stress that, even as a seaside pierrot show, Pélissier was already offering something quite unconventional, not just through the presence of female performers but also by performing largely original material. In many ways the majority of pierrot troupes of the time offered a re-costumed version of the 'black face' minstrel companies performing renditions of plantation-based American banjo songs such as 'My Dear Old Cabin Home' or 'Carry me Back to dear Old Virginy'.[54] According to Nield:

> Usually audiences could expect to enjoy songs, instrumental turns, comic backchat and sketches, and dancing and displays of particular skills, such as juggling [. . .] Many blackface minstrel troupes actually transmuted into whiteface pierrots".[55]

For example, in Bridlington, *The Waterloo Minstrels* simply changed their title and became the *Waterloo Pierrots*.

As Dave Russell has indicated in his book *Popular Song in England, 1840–1914*, pierrot troupes played a crucial role in introducing a more respectable middle-class audience to popular music-hall-style entertainment:

> The Pierrot troupes which formed a central part of the middle-class seaside holiday entertainment from the 1890s leaned heavily upon music-hall song and thus helped persuade the audience that the music hall was not so vulgar after all, or that the vulgarity could be quite entertaining.[56]

Even at this early stage in his career, Pélissier seems to have been singularly ambitious, with his eye set on the London stage. In 1933, Harold Hartley, a former Managing Director of the Exhibition Centre at Earl's Court in west London, recalled in a letter to *The Times* that Pélissier had approached him in the autumn of 1896 with a view to booking one of the halls at his prestigious venue. On being told that there were none available, a determined Pélissier revealed that he was prepared to go to great lengths to secure an engagement and responded by requesting that: 'I should allow him to perform his show in the open [. . .] as they had been performing on the sands at Margate, trusting to the generosity of the crowd for their reward.'[57] In the event, Harry was denied his opportunity and would have to wait a further five years before *The Follies* could play the more prestigious halls of London.

However, by the time they played Hastings in July 1897, the line-up was at least fairly consistent, featuring the likes of Ethel Allandale and Doris Lind and the former manager Sherrington Chin and a newcomer, Ronald Bagnall.[58] However, Arthur Wynne, Harold Allerton, Emerson Carter, Eric Lodge, Evelyn Hughes, Beatrice Scully, Wallie Montagu and Gwyneth Boleyn are to be heard of no more. From here on, their comic trail is lost to history. In the company of Harry Pélissier it would seem, pierrot fools were not suffered gladly.

It was at West Worthing pier in August 1896, within the august columns of *The Worthing Intelligencer*, that the ingenue, novice pierrot, Harry Pélissier received what seems to have been his first press review:

The performance is distinctly original and clever [. . .] Mister H.G. Pélissier has written much of the music [which is] vastly superior to the ordinary comic song of the day.[59]

In particular, what seems to have stood out for the critics and the audiences as a whole, were Harry's renditions of his own pieces, 'A Dog Song' and 'The Drone and the Bumble Bee'. The reviewer continues:

The humorous songs of Mr. H.G. Pélisissier are deserving of their premier position [. . .] His 'A Dog Song' and 'The Drone of the Bumble Bee' are funny, very funny, while the choruses in both are A1.[60]

Harry had made an instant hit and was beginning to stand out as the central figure of the troupe. This opinion is backed up by a further review in *The Folkestone Herald*: 'The lion of the evening was Mr. H. Pélissier, whose original songs "The Drone of the Bumble Bee" and "A Dog Song" were greeted with storms of applause and encores were necessary.'[61] Clearly, 'A Dog Song' was a great hit with audiences and reviewers alike and it is worth looking at in some detail, representing as it does one of Pélissier's earliest and most enduring comic compositions. It begins conventionally enough as a sentimental narrative in the parlour song or music hall tradition:

There once was a mangy little terrier,
petted by a family of three;
There never was a sharper or a merrier
or a yappier little mongrel than he!
His time he passes barking at the carriages,
little children or at other dogs he'll spy,
No brick at night, his ardour e'er discourages,
and at the cats you'll often hear him cry.

(Then suddenly the chorus breaks into a wild howling and barking for a full sixteen bars. One can imagine Harry writhing and wailing on his piano stool, before he comically recovers to calmly and elegantly continue his tale.)

He had no regard for venerable antiquity,
old ladies lived in perpetual dread!
He possessed a most remarkable ubiquity,
his bark was ever cutting through your head!
One morning with his usual low hilarity,
he 'cheeked' a butcher's dog of massive size,
This dog resenting such familiarity,
then commenced poor 'Towser' to chastise!

(The howls of the chorus are now a mixture of little sharp barks from the terrier and vicious snarling of the larger dog. After another full sixteen bars of sonic violence, Harry returns to his theme.)

Next morning when the family took their breakfastes,
Little Towser's head was missing at the board,
The servant says "Ah! Well, mum,
I hexpects as 'e's been took at last to 'eaven – thank the Lord!
The daughter says "Oh what a dreadful loss he is,
Oh, Towser why did you go and die?
But when they took the cover off the dish of sausages,
they heard once more his plaintive little cry! –

(We hear little Towser's intimate faint bark finally dying away into a deathly whimper. The comic pathos of this play on Victorian sentiment is irresistible.)

Now all Towser's little friends around the neighbourhood,
when they heard the noise set up a dismal cry!
And made up their little doggy minds,
they never could allow their comrade unavenged to die!
So each night they gather round outside that butcher's door,
and squatting down upon their little tails,
From twelve at night until the clock is striking four,
they rend the air with sad, soul-searching wails![62]

Now the entire audience is encouraged to participate and can relish the occasion by howling in communal unison as the auditorium is filled with the wails of dozens of human dogs. What a joyous opportunity for a middle-class concert audience to let its hair down, and how they

Figure 11. The Baddley Troupe, 1898, Brighton. H.G. Pélissier, back right

seem to have taken to it, and to this unusual brand of anarchic comedy. Harry Pélissier had struck upon a wilder, more surreal vein of comedy than was typical of either the traditional pierrot or minstrel shows, and it was a vein that he was to develop to immense effect over the coming years.

5

The Folly

Figure 12. H.G. Pélissier presents The Follies, 1907

A great scheme

One thing that many of the early press reviews point out is the originality and novelty of Harry Pélissier's shows. The fact that he was being experimental, pushing the boundaries and trying out something new was not lost on these experienced theatregoers. 'The performance is distinctly original and clever' was the summing-up of *The Worthing Intelligencer*.[1] 'An innovation certainly! [. . .] an entertainment quite off the beaten track' wrote *The Finchley Times*.[2] 'Novel, unique' was the assessment of *The Coventry Times*.[3]

What Harry and his troupe were offering was a new kind of humour and a new kind of show, a fusion of the energy and physicality of the minstrel show, the visual colour and variety of the pierrot show and a silly, anarchic zaniness all of its own. Like another native of Finchley, half a century later, Spike Milligan, Harry Pélissier was bringing a fresh, unpredictable, liberating quality to the performance. For example, like Milligan, Pélissier had a penchant for silly names. Where Spike gave us Neddie Seagoon, Bluebottle, Eccles, Henry Crun and Minnie

Bannister, Harry created Mona Yelba (the Australian sopralto), Miss May de Colté, Gush Squealin', Miss Pretoria Chunks, Earnest Bathos, Beena Flapper and Stilla Flapper, Margarine – the Dream Dancer, Colonel Swanky D. Codder, Miss A. Lotta Bulls, Dr MacNellie, Snooker of Old Burlington and Pansy of Pennsylvania.

So too, there was a love of silly noises and ridiculous accents. One review points out the use of kazoos during the impersonation of bee sounds during 'The Bumble Bee and The Drone'. As already described, 'A Dog Song' involved choruses of incessant barking. Another early sketch involved the troupe impersonating an entire orchestra with vocal mimicry.[4] Like the post World War Two generation, which was so receptive, almost relieved, to hear the hilarious, carefree, manic nonsense of *The Goon Show*, here was an audience released from the straitjacket of the conventional Victorian mainstream theatre or concert hall, a public conscious of imperial conflict abroad and social conflict at home. In short, like *The Goons*, *The Follies* offered a delirious escape from the cares of the real world, and a hidebound world at that. The truth is too, that it was downright sexy. The reviewer of *The Barnet Press* appears to have been somewhat scandalized:

> The artistes were attired á la Pierrot, and their appearance, so far as this locality is concerned, was certainly unique. Perhaps for the local residents of that precise old dame Mother Grundy, the skirts of the ladies were a trifle short. But although we ourselves are sticklers for the proprieties, we must admit that the ladies, short frocked as they were, looked really charming.[5]

In fact, there are more than a few parallels with the phenomenon that was Spike Milligan and *The Goon Show*. Like Pélissier, Spike was the son of a migrant, an Irish soldier, Leo Milligan from County Sligo. Spike himself was born and raised in India. 'There was always a dislocation, a discomfort, a feeling that wherever he belonged it certainly wasn't *here*. He was a foreigner on British soil', wrote Humphrey Carpenter in his biography of that celebrated comedian.[6] How redolent of Harry that sounds, although in his case this 'dislocation' resulted in a re-doubled effort to be English.

Like Harry Pélissier, surrounded by talk and images of Marshal Pélissier at the Siege of Sebastopol, of exotic connections in the worlds of jewellery and finance and perhaps even espionage, Spike grew up with the wild imaginings of his extrovert father, believing that 'we were descended from the kings of Ireland'.[7] 'My father was like Baron Munchausen', he says at one point. 'He thought he'd ridden with Jesse James and robbed banks when he wasn't shooting tigers in Bengal'.[8]

'Spike [. . .] is still a child. He never grew up',[9] wrote Anthony Clare, the psychiatrist and lifelong friend of Spike Milligan. As we shall see, this was also remarked of Harry Pélissier by several who knew him. And, like Spike, Harry loved to mix music with his comedy. Both were self-taught musicians – Spike on the trumpet and Harry on the piano. And while Harry passed away too early to share in the full blossoming of the jazz music that so attracted Spike Milligan, he was certainly drawn to its antecedents in ragtime, two-step and the minstrel songs. Humphrey Carpenter put it thus: 'For some reason, jazz musicians have an especially developed sense of humour. Puns and wisecracks seem to go hand-in-hand with ad-lib musical solos, and there is a deep cynicism that never descends into sneering'.[10]

In fact, Harry Pélissier liked nothing better than to improvise and ad-lib on stage, both at the piano and with his infamously under-rehearsed and cavalier use of his own scripts.

In little more than a year, Pélissier had bought out the company from Sherrington Chinn (who gave up participating altogether after being partially disabled in a train accident in March 1898).[11] According to his own account, Harry then adopted *The Follies* as their company title at the outset of their 1896–97 tour.[12] This was the first use of that name in the English-speaking world, borrowed by Harry from the French *Folies Bergère*. At the age of just 22, the untrained novice in his first professional engagement was now at the head of his own company, writing his own material and composing his own songs for the entire cast. Already he was paving the way for what in time would be called musical revue, diligently honing the personnel of the company, gathering together a fixed troupe of permanent players. Such revues had their theatrical roots in France as Pélissier, with his continental background, would well have appreciated. James Ross Moore has outlined this development:

> It is enough to say that in one form or another revue had been part of the French theatrical world since the late 18th century [. . .] attaining major importance in the 1840s when theatres such as the Folies Trevises opened in Paris. But something about the word folies: [. . .] the word is a variation of feuilles (leaves). Among its variations, feuilles had over time acquired the meaning of a 'house' hidden beneath leaves, a 'field' where clandestine lovers spent romantic evenings. Folies soon branched further to mean the public places where the 18th century French danced, drank and watched small scale entertainments in the open air. Thus the first Folies housed a kind of variety, and Pélissier knew as much in naming his troupe *Follies*. The French Folies moved indoors to such interesting, informal (as contrasted to concert halls) locales as the large Folies Bergère, built in 1869 (its architecture along the lines of the Alhambra in Leicester Square) and devoted to all sorts of pleasure, including romantic assignations.[13]

Is it possible that Pélissier with his intense and extensive reading of the dramatic journals such as *The Era* and *The Stage*, his partial schooling in Switzerland, and his continental parentage had envisaged all along the formation of an English revue-style group on the French model? Certainly, his friend and biographer Fitzroy Gardner seems to think he had just such an ambition in mind from the very outset:

He saw his troupe of pierrots then in the light of the embryo of a great scheme which, under his guidance and inspiration, has become an institution. The entertainment improved in quality, and at the same time the manager's ideas developed on a far larger scale than that of a mere pierrot show.[14]

The troupe enjoyed regular work over the course of the next year, establishing its reputation as it toured around the country from Worthing to Eastbourne, from Ipswich to Croydon and all the way to Newcastle and South Shields and Wales, taking in a host of thriving, bustling seaside towns on the way. However, back in Croydon on 5 December 1896, something close to disaster seems to have struck. They found themselves playing to 'almost an empty hall at the Literary Institution'[15] and likewise the following evening at The Croydon Public Hall.[16] As a result, *The Follies* must have come under some considerable financial strain and could ill afford to receive bad notices. Unfortunately, that is exactly what they did receive from *The Brighton Herald* on 30 January 1897 for their performance at The West Pier in which the talents on offer were described as 'unequal' and half the performers as looking overly serious.[17] Perhaps this had caused some friction in the dressing room. Likewise in *The Brighton Guardian* on 27 January, one artist in particular was singled out for particular criticism. 'Mr. Lindsay Hammond [. . .] sang through his nose' the critic complained derisively.[18]

It was perhaps as a result of this damning criticism that Mr Lindsay Hammond is heard of no more in further press reviews. He and *The Follies* immediately parted company, and this surely demonstrates an early example of Pélissier's willingness to be tough when necessary. The new name that begins to feature regularly, and with grand plaudits, is that of a certain Ronald Bagnall, first mentioned in a review from *The Newcastle Daily Leader* on 9 March 1897. 'Mr. Ronald Bagnall is the gentleman comic and his songs "The Girl In The Big Black Hat" and "The Piccadilly Baronet" are very amusing'.[19] And from *The Newcastle Chronicle* of 8 March 1897, '[. . .] it says much for the musical ability of the company that a large portion of the songs given are the compositions of two members of the company, Mr. H.G. Pélissier and Mr. Ronald Bagnall'.[20]

What had been a show dominated by the singular personality of Harry Pélissier as singer-songwriter, now had two such personalities in a similar role and for a while this seems to have been a highly successful combination.

A review in the *Isle of Wight Observer* of 2 October 1899 reads as follows:

Amongst the men, Mr. H.G. Pélissier was warmly received as an old favourite, and won encores with all his songs, particularly one which was his own composition entitled 'Jane'. Another new and valuable member in the company is Mr. Ronald Bagnall, who made himself popular from the very first. His style is utterly unlike anyone else's, and as regards his songs, he can claim originality. 'The Girl in The Big Black Hat' is remarkably clever and well thought out, so should soon become a success. He also sang two others, accompanying himself at the piano, both of which are quite up-to-date, and at the same time free from coarseness and vulgarity – which cannot be said of most of the comic songs of the present day.[21]

It seems, however, that Harry may not have entirely welcomed the copious praise handed out to his junior colleague. Perhaps there was ultimately room for only one such talent in the company; perhaps the clash of egos was too great. Whatever the reason, Ronald Bagnall is never heard of again in the context of *The Follies*. He left the company and went on to forge a reasonably successful solo career until the end of The Great War, publishing over 20 songs and performing regularly in concert halls, before sadly dying in unrecorded obscurity.[22]

Perhaps significantly, and rather pointedly, there is no mention made of Ronald Bagnall in the short memoir and history of the company by H.G. Pélissier and Fitzroy Gardner, entitled *Pure Folly*, that was published in 1910, despite the fact that his joining *The Follies* in 1896 may well have saved them from oblivion. So, it seems that the parting of these two young singer-songwriter comedians was probably not on the best of terms. This episode serves to underline the ruthless business streak in a man who was already shaping a company after his own image with his sights clearly set on broader horizons. It may also be that the brusque departure of Ronald Bagnall was the decisive spur for Pélissier to move the company on to greater invention and risk-taking. Fitzroy Gardner puts it thus:

> In his earliest days of proprietorship of The Follies, Pélissier conceived the idea of reviving the art of burlesque. His first venture was, strange to say, at Aberystwyth. There he, Lewis Sydney, and Norman Blumé one evening gave a more or less unrehearsed skit on Grand Opera with Sydney, as the orchestra, imitating various musical instruments with his mouth. The three performers enjoyed themselves immensely, while the audience played the part of a refrigerator. But Pélissier was not discouraged. He gradually improved on the original crude effort at rehearsals until at Folkestone the Follies made a feature in their programme of a burlesque of National Music, including Italian Opera. Their next successful attempt in burlesque was a skit on Wordless Plays – *mime-drame*. Then modern musical comedy provided them with a useful theme; Wagnerian Opera followed, and the Follies Cantata (at the Palace Theatre) proved the climax as regards that particular style of skit. Despite the absence of scenery and costume, the Cantata was, in its own way, as clever a bit of genuine burlesque as anything that the Follies have done since.[23]

This revival of burlesque, the addition of dramatic and musical satire to the slapstick clowning and concert pieces of the traditional pierrot show, was to become Pélissier's main focus for the next seven years, as *The Follies* embarked on what was to be a constant tour of provincial towns. Harry's tour diary of 1904[24] records Colchester and Harrogate in July of that year, to be followed relentlessly by Southampton, the Isle of Wight, Felixstowe, Weston-super-Mare, Bexhill, Worthing, St Leonard's, Blackpool, Kingston, Battersea, Birmingham, Norwood, Guildford and Clerkenwell, all in the span of three months.

'Impossible to describe'

Some three years prior to that, however, in 1901 *The Follies* had received their first big break in the business, an invitation to make their introductory appearance in a major London venue, at the Queen's Hall, Langham Place. The troupe was now usually six in number. Pélissier had distilled his company down to his favourite performers, several of whom would stay with him for his remaining years. Dan Everard, who was to be Harry's 'second-in-command' and deputy manager, had joined the troupe, along with Lewis Sydney. Both would be constant stalwarts throughout the rest of his career. The three pierrettes were the ever-present Ethel Allandale, who had now been joined by another regular, Marjorie Napier and by a newcomer, Lucy Webling. As the *Morning Post* reports:

> It is impossible to describe the programme in detail. A large portion of it is parody. We have a Japanese tragedy, a French mimodrama, an absurd edition of 'English Nell', mock dances of all nations and 'The Buttercup Cable' an obvious and very entertaining skit on 'The Daisy Chain'. A mad, merry entertainment it is.[25]

From now on *The Follies'* name would feature more and more in the provincial press, as their fame spread, and their popularity grew, and their unique style of showmanship beguiled both critics and audiences alike. These appearances at Queen's Hall came in a sequence of sell-out shows organised by the great music hall artist, Albert Chevalier. They represented a major breakthrough for Pélissier and his troupe – something he had been striving after ever since his approach to the manager of Earl's Court Exhibition Centre in 1896. It was a clear step up from the grinding provincial touring and seaside resorts and the opportunity had been granted them by one of the greatest names in music hall history. Albert Chevalier was indeed a key figure in the progress of *The Follies*.

Born in Notting Hill in 1861, the son of a French language master at Kensington School and a Welsh mother, Chevalier began his stage career as a straight actor but had his greatest success appearing in burlesques. In 1889 he became the principal comedian at the Avenue theatre and began to write comic songs. It was on 5 February 1891 that Chevalier appeared for the first time on the music-hall stage at the New London Pavilion, Piccadilly Circus. His principal act consisted of the portrayal of a cockney coster with his characteristic peaked cap and checked jacket. He performed relatively sophisticated character songs such as 'Wot'cher! We Knocked 'Em Down the Old Kent Road!' about a Bermondsey couple who inherit a donkey, [upwardly mobile in Victorian terms!] and 'My Old Dutch', a sentimental reminiscence full of acute observation. It was noted at the time how unusual and possibly risk-taking it was for a straight actor to move across from the legitimate theatre to the music halls. However, Chevalier claimed that audiences were ready for something new and more challenging, although the reverse process from music hall to theatre for which he coined the phrase 'the music-hallisation of theatre'[26] was, he thought, the more prevalent direction of travel, and was the development in which Pélissier would prove an active player.

According to his autobiography, *A Record by Himself*, Chevalier received the support of George Bernard Shaw and Arthur Symons, and even the grudging praise of Lewis Carroll, no fan of the music hall. However, he insisted on only playing the major London venues, private performances and selected concert halls in the provinces.[27] That Chevalier should have acted as something of a mentor to *The Follies* is highly significant. Discussing the broadening of the audience for popular entertainment, Dave Russell has pointed out the importance of Chevalier's recitals and concerts in presenting music hall styles to middle-class audiences. He indicates how Chevalier performed at private engagements for fashionable society figures such as Mrs Asquith, Dean Gregory of St Paul's and Lord Rothschild, which according to Russell helped to make music hall more respectable.[28] In time these were footsteps in which Pélissier was to follow, perhaps at Chevalier's instigation, with private engagements for King Edward VII and Winston Churchill among others.[29]

It is likely to have been in one of these provincial halls that Chevalier first came across H.G. Pélissier and *The Follies*. Did he feel a common bond in their risk-taking repertoire? Did he admire Pélissier's comic compositions? Did they strike up a relationship on the basis of their mutual Anglo-Continental origins and similarity of name, which could almost have featured as a rhyme in one of their own songs? Whatever the reason, Chevalier invited *The Follies* to appear as guest artistes on the programme at his hugely successful annual engagement at the Queen's Hall, Langham Place. These twice-daily shows began in 1899 and ran for over one thousand performances. It was the perfect entrée onto the London stage for the budding young troupe and they did not waste their opportunity.

From the Queen's Hall they moved on to the Tivoli on the Strand for a string of performances and, as a consequence of that, they were booked to appear at the Alhambra, Leicester Square. This prestigious emporium was then under the management of Charles Morton, known as 'the father of the halls' for having opened the very first custom-built music hall, the Canterbury on Westminster Bridge Road, way back in 1852. Fitzroy Gardner outlines the story:

> It was during their second engagement at the Alhambra that they gave a trial performance at the Palace. The late Charles Morton [Gardner is writing in 1910] on that occasion committed one of his very few errors of judgement. He decided that the Follies would not suit his house. But the directors persuaded him to give them an engagement, with the result that they appeared six times at the same house in the course of five years.[30]

For once, the author of this passage, Fitzroy Gardner, is being unduly modest, for he himself was one of those directors at the Palace and was himself instrumental in furthering the career of *The Follies*. Their first appearance at the Palace was in 1901. And what an extraordinary leap it must have seemed for a provincial touring company of pierrots and pierettes. The Palace was a vast edifice accommodating an audience of fourteen hundred. Quite a contrast to Worthing Pier! It had been opened in 1891 by Richard D'Oyly Carte as 'The Royal English Opera House' with a premiere of Arthur Sullivan's *Ivanhoe*. This ran for 160 performances, but with no production to follow, it was found necessary to hire the theatre out to Sarah Bernhardt for a season. Following this, it was sold for a loss to the impresario Walter Emden, who in turn converted it into a grand music hall, renaming it the Palace Theatre of Varieties in 1893. What a fitting irony that Harry should make what was in effect his West End debut at a theatre that echoed the name of his very first music hall audition back in 1895 – at the Peckham Rosemary Branch, that other People's Palace of Varieties!

As an interesting aside, the Palace Theatre was at the time of Harry's arrival embroiled in a dispute with the local authorities. Notoriously, it had been refused the construction of a 'promenade', a circuit for the parade of courtesans and prostitutes, at the time extremely popular with a certain strand of clientele. The ban was instituted by the rather stiff-laced London County Council – later itself to be a target of Harry's satire.[31] Interesting, also, to note that as early as March 1897, the Palace Theatre was being used for the screening of early silent films from the American Biograph Company, including pioneering newsreels of events around the world, such as of the Anglo-Boer War, as shot by William Kennedy Laurie Dickson. Even in its heyday, the writing was on the wall for the music hall and live entertainment. What a sense of fast-changing times the late Victorians and Edwardians must have felt. They too had their own global social media to contend with, with all its novelty and unsettling effects.

A royal command performance

The Follies scored such a hit with the audience at the Palace that they were called upon to present a 'command' performance for the King and Queen at a real palace, at Sandringham in Norfolk.[32] The occasion was Queen Alexandra's sixty-first birthday in December 1905. In

Figure 18. Pélissier 'knighted'. Arthur Wimperis cartoon of 1907

particular, their Majesties had been struck by Harry's parody of Wagnerian Opera. This was duly performed at the event, along with Harry and Lewis Sydney singing a love duet to one another entitled *O! Pierreta*, while Marjorie Napier and Dan Everard gave their version of *In Our Canadian Canoe*. The troupe was still six in number, Ethel Allandale and Marjorie Napier having been joined by another pierrette, Gwennie Mars. In the coming years, they would grow to nine as Marjorie Napier retired and the company was joined by Douglas Maclaren, Morris Harvey and Effie Cook while, after several years absence, a former Folly, Muriel George returned. Also appearing on the bill at Sandringham for that occasion was a short drama entitled *Pantaloon* by an up-and-coming young playwright called J.M. Barrie. Over the coming years, Pélissier and Barrie would enjoy something of a fertile, if strained, relationship; and one that would have consequences even beyond the former's early demise.

It would be hard to over-estimate the unprecedented novelty and significance of the rise of this precocious young seaside troupe from provincial piers and concert halls to the very heart of the West End in the span of just a few short years. In 1895, Harry Pélissier had nervously signed up for an amateur company in South London. Within a year, he had audaciously taken it over and put it on a more original and professional footing, daring to perform his own compositions and sketches. By the end of the decade, they had made their introduction into London at the Queen's Hall alongside Albert Chevalier, and from there directly to the Alhambra and the Palace Theatre at the very heart of the West End, and even a Royal command performance at Sandringham. *The Follies* had definitely arrived.

6

The Satirist

Figure 14. H.G. Pélissier as a satirical pantomime
Dame in Bill Bailey

Creation of the modern comedy sketch

In January 1904 at the Palace Theatre, *The Follies* performed their first extended satirical parody: a burlesque of popular pantomime entitled *Bill Bailey*.[1] The Palace, despite its name, was actually a music hall and, as such, treated with a light hand by the Lord Chamberlain. However, the running time for *The Follies* sketch, featuring songs and spoken dialogue, would have been something between 30 and 40 minutes and therefore risked falling foul of the Lord Chamberlain's censorship. Thus far, Harry had offered his audiences comic and sentimental songs and repartee in the standard structure of a series of 'turns' such as one might experience in a conventional music hall programme or concert party. The material could be unusual and wild, but the format was recognisably made up of a quick turnaround of songs and routines. However, all this was about to change now that the troupe was securely established as a favourite act at the Palace Theatre, as Fitzroy Gardner points out:

Pélissier first demonstrated fully the possibilities of himself and his company on more ambitious lines, when he produced at the Palace Theatre his brilliant skit on the conventional Christmas pantomime, entitled 'Bill Bailey'.[2]

There had always been an element of mimicry and pastiche and downright silliness in the songs and comic turns, but now Harry sought to present a longer, more highly developed and sophisticated sketch. This would entail an extended narrative in which the songs and characters were linked and in which there was a specific target to the jokes. *Bill Bailey*, a mock Christmas pantomime, is essentially a show 'gone wrong' and it was to remain a regular feature of *The Follies* repertoire for the next seven years.

With the success of the shows at the Queen's Hall and the Palace came greater revenue and the first real opportunity for Harry Pélissier to realise his comic vision. From now on there would be both scope and resources for the design and construction of an elaborate set and props. During the course of the *Bill Bailey* sketch, incompetent stagehands shamelessly transport scenery in front of the performers on stage, shuffling awkwardly back and forth. Back-drops collapse. *The Follies* dish up a series of outlandish characters, Harry himself presenting the first of his many cross-dressing roles, lampooning Dan Leno's 'Dame' (see Figure 14), while also appearing as the demon-author and the fairy godmother. Typically, each player would now have upwards of a dozen costume changes in the same show thus beginning to distance the company from the purely pierrot image of the seaside troupe and deliberately positioning themselves within a more mainstream milieu. Gwennie Mars plays Cinderella and Norman Blumé a Scotch cat; Lewis Sydney takes on the role of the nasty baron while Dan Everard plays Idle Jack.

What Pélissier is sending up is the lazy ubiquity of a tired Victorian entertainment that had dominated the popular stage for the past 30 years. It was a timely parody of the traditional Christmas show – a seasonal event that, as well as appealing to children, drew in massive adult audiences, arguably representing a kind of 'infantilization' of the general public. Indeed, it was adult entertainers such as Marie Lloyd and Dan Leno and Little Tich who usually headlined these lucrative shows, which could often be hurriedly and cheaply thrown together, particularly in the provincial towns. Today we may think nothing of a sketch that lampoons a popular entertainer. Many of us have grown up with the likes of *Dead Ringers* on Radio 4 and Rory Bremner and *Spitting Image* on television, as well as the take-off sketches of *French and Saunders* and *The Two Ronnies* among others. However, to lampoon living figures in Edwardian England was a radical step that could invite the wrath of the Lord Chamberlain. Fitzroy Gardner was present for the opening night of *Bill Bailey* and the audience's delight and surprise at the novelty of *The Follies'* invention is clear from his account:

Anything more depressing than the circumstances of the first performance can hardly be imagined. I was then associated with the management of the Palace. One of the thickest black fogs I can recall pervaded the auditorium. The house was not half full. Across the lights the company could see great gaps in the stalls. Those who had managed to get to the theatre were by no means in the best of spirits, but before the Follies had been on stage five minutes the attenuated audience from stalls to gallery, was roaring with laughter, which never ceased until after the curtain had fallen on the last scene. Probably no one there that night had realised the scope for burlesque provided by the slavishly conventional characteristics of the ordinary Christmas pantomime. The delightfully subtle treatment of the subject in speech, song, dance and 'business', the quick changes of costume, the grotesque scenery, and not least, the spirit of burlesque conveyed by the music, appealed to the audience to a remarkable degree. Although it was a bold, and intensely subtle satire of an entirely new order – a very daring venture for a music-hall – its success was assured on the first night, and the success not only of that particular production but also of Pélissier's pet scheme of elaborate burlesque, of which *Bill Bailey* was intended, and has proved to be, a mere foretaste.[3]

As usual, the music hall billing retained its novelty and variety. Alongside *The Follies*, at the Palace Theatre that winter of 1904–05, there appeared the singer, Arthur Roberts, a troupe of performing elephants under Madame de Gracia and two Japanese acrobats.[4] However, by putting on a more sophisticated work in a music hall, *The Follies* were beginning to straddle the divide between mainstream middle-class entertainment and the working-class popular routines, the customary short 'turns' of the music hall programme. An antiquated form of comic sketch and melodramas of a similar length had been performed before on the music hall circuit since the 1870s.[5] However, these pieces had their antecedents in clowning and *commedia dell'arte* and even medieval carnival and tended to exclude such 'sophisticated issues as irony, satire, wit, parody and burlesque'.[6] In her seminal article on comic sketches in music hall, Lois Rutherford further points out that they were essentially composed of vulgar comedy predominantly featuring physical and verbal slapstick. In form they tended to ape mainstream theatrical farce, focusing on stereotypical characters and such issues as domestic strife, heavy drinking or unrequited love. By bringing wit and parody and satire to the extended sketch form, Pélissier was offering something quite different. With reference to the

Figure 15. The Follies in Bill Bailey c. 1904

61

older, antiquated style, Rutherford goes on to state: 'In terms of their construction and spirit, comedy sketches closely resembled the vulgar comedy of the pantomime harlequinade, echoing back to primitive carnival scenarios'.[7] Nevertheless, she does recognize the existence of 'the relationship between the rise of music-hall sketches and the shift upmarket which broadened the social base of the public for variety entertainment'.[8] In Pélissier's development of the comic sketch, this already broadening audience base was something he was aware he could artfully exploit and build upon.

For example, in deciding to satirize the pantomime genre in *Bill Bailey*, Pélissier was not only demonstrating a sharp satirical sense, but also his shrewd business acumen, for in so doing he was targeting one of the most prominent and ubiquitous forms of music-hallization of the theatre. As has already been noted, popular artists such as Marie Lloyd and Dan Leno were regularly employed in this period to appear in legitimate licensed theatres like the Theatre Royal Drury Lane.[9] In his book on popular song in England, Dave Russell has pointed out that in this way pantomime contributed to 'bringing the middle classes into contact [. . .] with the singers, for the stars of the pantomime were often music-hall stars'.[10] At the same time, Pélissier was distancing himself from that milieu of music hall in which he had been performing, by the very act of satirising and mocking it. Furthermore, by use of the seemingly arbitrary title of *Bill Bailey*, he was injecting that element of the randomly absurd that was to be such a characteristic feature of his work. In fact, the title derives merely from the fact that the then widely popular song 'Bill Bailey' is performed for no apparent reason at a midway point in the sketch.

Pélissier's extended routine was bound to risk controversy. A legal distinction had been created between licensed mainstream theatres and places of popular entertainment by the Parliamentary Act of 22 August 1843. This had granted powers to the Lord Chamberlain to license stage plays in legitimate mainstream theatres where no 'distilled or Excisable liquor shall be sold',[11] but had granted discretion for exceptions to be made in any 'lawful Fair, Feast or customary Meeting of the like Kind'.[12] Since the passing of that law, popular stage entertainment had expanded enormously and, indeed at the time the Act was passed, the very term music hall had yet to be coined.[13] This left a conspicuous ambiguity as to what did or did not constitute a stage play, as well as a good deal of friction and jealousy between the two sectors. The matter was partially resolved in 1896 by an informal gathering of theatrical managers, whereby they agreed not to take legal proceedings against one another so long as the burlesque or routine was no more than thirty minutes long and was performed with a cast of no more than six.[14] It was into this controversial fault-line that Pélissier was leading *The Follies* and in the coming years his extended satires would test the law to its limit.

At this stage, the Lord Chamberlain's office seems to have turned a blind eye to Pélissier's activities and was in no mood to monitor the music halls. However, other theatre managers clearly took note of *The Follies'* success and began tentatively to follow their lead. In *The British Musical Theatre*, Kurt Ganzl writes of the year 1906: 'The short musical piece had made something of a comeback with the relaxing of the laws regarding plays in the music halls'.[15] That year, the Oxford, Pavilion and Tivoli music halls all followed Pélissier's innovative lead and put on short musical burlesques. Pélissier, it seems, had forged the way in this introduction of a more sophisticated theatrical form to the predominantly working-class audience of the halls.

Newspaper critics welcomed *The Follies'* performance of *Bill Bailey* with enthusiasm. *The Lady's Pictorial* described them thus: 'This brilliant troupe of clever and refined artistes, known as The Follies, are a host in themselves and their burlesque pantomime remains one of the most delightful and wittiest entertainments seen for years'.[16] The plaudits continued. '[. . .] extremely witty' was the assessment of the *Morning Post.*[17] 'One of the cleverest shows of its kind to be seen in London', proclaimed *The Sun.*[18] Furthermore, the long-standing tension between music hall and mainstream theatre is reflected in some of the reviews, as for example in *Bystanders* of 15 February 1905:

> It is refreshing to see that the theatres don't have things all their own way. Many sarcastic things have been said (some of them no doubt justifiable) about the music-hall entertainment when comparing it with the play, but all old scores are wiped off by The Follies at the Palace Theatre. In a screamingly funny medley, 'Bill Bailey', they go further than mere farce, and produce the best satire on the present-day pantomime one could possibly conceive.[19]

That such attention was being given to Pélissier by national newspapers and periodicals was even in itself something of a radical departure. Historically, popular entertainers and productions had for the most part been either sidelined or totally ignored by that portion of the media. However, from this period on and for the best part of a decade *The Follies* were, quite exceptionally, to appear regularly in the national press.[20]

Victorian burlesques

In December 1907, a whole feature appeared in *The Tatler*[21] extolling *The Follies'* revival of the art of burlesque, for it was widely understood that beneath the frivolous buffoonery this was exactly what Pélissier was doing: bringing back to life a somewhat arcane and forgotten but once highly popular and successful theatrical form, only this time in his own unique and pioneering style. In his *Victorian Theatrical Burlesques*, R.W. Schoch gives a concise summary of the nature of the original Victorian burlesques:

> [. . .] rhymed couplets in a parody of the original text; the transposition of the characters from high to low; [. . .] the contemporization of past events; [. . .] the ludicrous re-enactment of classic scenes; [. . .] a pronounced theatrical bias with an emphasis on

stage business, sight gags and special effects; [. . .] relentless puns; and soliloquies and set pieces re-written as lyrics to contemporary songs whether popular, operatic or even minstrel [. . .] Above all burlesques trafficked in topical allusions.[22]

These Victorian parodies had been aimed at a distinctly middle-class, mainstream theatre audience and often assumed at least a passing knowledge of the Greek classics or contemporary theatre productions. *The Illustrated London News* of 18 April 1868 described them as having:

> [. . .] an ideal audience made up of a lower middle-class male who enjoyed the topical satire in *Punch*, his education in the classics would have been similar to that inflicted on a theatregoer during his childhood in the 1840s, when a governess made him learn 'parrot-like' from the old Eton Latin grammar and from a couple of books on ancient myth and history.[23]

As such, these pieces tended to fail in the music halls or among the more working-class venues. Schoch quotes one contemporary observer:

> Burlesques and extravaganzas have never been extremely popular on the south side of the river. An 1861 performance of Burnaud's *Sappho; or Look Before You Leap* at the Standard Theatre in East London 'fell flat [because it required] a more erudite audience' [. . .] west of Temple Bar.[24]

A sample of burlesque titles gives a flavour of the genre: *Endymion; or the Naughty Boy Who Cried for the Moon* by W. Brough, which played at the St James's theatre in 1860; *Agamemnon and Cassandra; or the Prophet and Loss of Troy* by R. Reece at the Prince of Wales, Liverpool in 1868; and *Cupid; or Two Strings to a Beau* by H. P. Stephens at the Royalty in Soho in 1880. In *Alcestis, the Original Strong-Minded Woman* written by Francis Talford in 1850, a modern-dress policeman appears unashamedly amongst the classical togas. In *Antigone Travestie* presented by Edward L. Blanchard in 1845, Antigone refers to an advertisement in the *Sunday Times*:

> *Antigone*
>
> *Beloved Herman, you had best betimes*
> *Try an advertisement in the Sunday Times*
> *Wanted a wife — An amiable young gent*
> *You know the usual style, ten shillings spent*
> *In this way, will secure another bride.*[25]

In London, the highpoint of burlesque was probably reached between the 1860s and 1870s. The Greek classics were a favourite target, but a variety of topics were fair game – Shakespeare, English history, Arabic tales, *bel canto* opera, Sir Walter Scott, Goethe, Ibsen, Pinero and Oscar Wilde to name but a few. Among contemporary plays, Sheridan Knowles's *William Tell* of 1825 was burlesqued six times; Dion Boucicault's *The Corsican Brothers* of 1852, nine times. W.S. Gilbert produced his own Shakespearean burlesque, *Rosencrantz and Gildenstern*, in 1891; and the prolific F.C. Burnand gave us *The Rise and Fall of Richard III; A New Front to an Old Dickey* at the Royalty in 1868; to be followed by *Faust and Loose; or Broken Vows* at Toole's in

1886 and *The Hunchback Back Again; or Peculiar Julia* at the Olympic in 1878. As a form of entertainment, it was not universally welcomed by the critics. '[. . .] indescribable puerility of wit and vulgarity of tone' is how William Archer described it, along with '[. . .] lame metres, cockney rhymes, (and) inane puns'.[26] And this from 'A Word About Our Theatres' in *Fraser's Magazine 57* of February 1858:

> Let anyone [. . .] who has undergone the penance – and it is no slight one – of going to see the burlesques, which either alone or as introduction to pantomimes, are now filling the West-End theatres, ask himself if they are exhibitions which he can with any propriety take any woman or child to witness. The sickening vulgarity of the jokes, the slang allusions, the use of words and phrases unknown in the vocabulary of ladies and gentlemen, the ridicule of associations which are all but sacred, the outrageous carica-ture of grave passions, the exhibition of crowds of girls in costumes only suitable for *poses plastiques* of Leicester Square, above all, the way in which young actresses are made to say and do things which must destroy every shred of modesty and feminine grace in them, make these burlesques pernicious alike to performers and audience.[27]

These pieces were churned out on an industrial scale for their topicality. Often written over-night, the target of the satire would be a closely guarded commercial secret for fear that a rival author or playhouse might steal the idea. They could be rehearsed in a few days and close within a week resulting in a very high turnover of shows. The painfully weak puns that char-acterised the rhyming couplet were the essential ingredient. The following typical example is from *Miss Eily O'Connor* by H.J. Byron, a burlesque of the play *The Colleen Bawn* by Dion Boucicault.

> *I fell in a ravine, with just one crack*
> *And rose up quite a ra-vine maniac*
> *The ferry – patronised by such a swell*
> *Succeeded and I now row ferry well.*[28]

Some theatres, such as Covent Garden, Sadler's Wells, Her Majesty's and the Lyceum, avoided burlesques all together. They were most frequently and successfully performed at the Adelphi, the Olympic and the Strand, and then later at the Gaiety on Wellington Street, which opened in 1868 just opposite the Lyceum. Frederick Robson's transvestite performance of *Medea* under Madame Vestris at the *Olympia* was attended by no less than Charles Dickens, William Thackeray, William Morris, D.G. Rosetti and even Queen Victoria herself. At the Gaiety, the famed quartet of Nellie Farren, E.H. Royce, Kate Vaughan and Edward Terry established itself in a string of successful burlesques including W.S. Gilbert's *Robert le Diable* in 1868; to be followed by *The Lady of Lyon Settled and Married* in 1878; and *The Forty Thieves* in 1880.

Almost 30 years later, one of the Gaiety quartet, Edward Terry, was to prove a pivotal fig-ure in the progress of Harry Pélissier and *The Follies*. However, at this point in time, the origi-nal form of Victorian burlesque had reached the pinnacle of its success and was about to fall steeply out of favour. One contemporary critic put it thus:

[. . .] burlesque is the one species of dramatic work that seems to have lately fallen off. That its fall has been great we will not pretend, for the reason that its estate was never particularly high [. . .] the whole style of burlesque has completely changed of late years. Either audiences do not want, or else authors cannot provide, witty or pointed dialogue, comic situations or incident. These strong features, as they used to be considered, are now altogether ignored, the one object of authors being to find a character in which a favourite low comedian may display his eccentricities.[29]

'A master of improvisation'

MR. H. G. PELISSIER AS HAMLET.

Figure 16. Cartoon of H.G. Pélissier as Hamlet by Max Beerbohm

Gradually the title burlesque would become associated with American vaudeville and striptease, while the British form of burlesque would increasingly adopt more elaborate sets and dancing girls, a three-act narrative and score and eventually evolve into something we would now recognise as musical comedy. H.G. Pélissier would prove a key Figure in that evolution. However, in so doing, his approach and style would be entirely different to the traditional burlesque, creating sketches that were far less heavily reliant on tightly scripted, weak punning rhymes or classical references for the educated middle class. Instead, they allowed for free flowing, often entirely improvised, dialogue and absurdist humour.[30] Indeed, Compton Mackenzie described Pélissier as 'a master of improvisation'.[31] By its very nature, of course, lacking the necessary technology, improvisation of the time went unrecorded, and is therefore difficult to evaluate or define. However, a rare piece of evidence for *The Follies* impromptu style can be found in the text for *Bill Bailey*. Here the following specific direction for improvisation is included: 'Ad Lib [. . .] as National Anthem is playing [. . .] whilst making Grand Mechanical change from High-gate Hill to Baron's Kitchen'.[32] Likewise, the crudely typed scripts in the Lord Chamberlain's Collection are liberally marked with Pélissier's seemingly *ad hoc* hand-written edits and additions. For example, in his burlesque of *Hamlet* a parade of additional cut-out dummy Hamlets enters in the closing scene, bearing name labels that depict a host of distinguished contemporary actors including Martin Harvey, Henry Irving, Herbert Beerbohm Tree, Frank Benson and Sarah Bernhardt, whereupon Shakespeare rises from the grave and shoots Pélissier, the principal Hamlet of the sketch (see Figure 16). There then follows a hand-written stage direction scrawled on the closing page: 'All dance lying flat on their backs as the Safety Curtain (egg-proof) descends'.[33]

It is also clear from this and other examples that Pélissier did not shy away from targeting and naming specific living public figures for satire, something that in the licensed theatre might itself attract the Lord Chamberlain's disapproval. For example, in a song at the finale of a later, revised version of *Bill Bailey* about the recently signed *Entente Cordiale*, he includes the following verse:

> *Mr. Balfour will be teaching golf to President Loubet*
> *Who'll walk about in scarlet coat and putties, all the day*
> *Instead of keeping his eye on the state, he'll keep it on the ball*
> *And that will be the next Entente Cordiale!*[34]

In *Baffles*, a parody of J.M. Barrie's *Peter Pan*, a cast member representing J.M. Barrie exclaims:

> *Enter J.M.B.*
> *Hoots, man, hoots!*
> *I am the Author Man!*
> *And I wrote 'Peter Pan'!*
> *Gold, gold, gold*
> *I've sacks of it about*
> *I'm bound to say I like the way*
> *That Peter's panning out.*[35]

Another crucial difference from the original Victorian burlesques was that Pélissier was composing his own songs as a feature of these sketches, not recycling the popular works of others. Thus, in *Bill Bailey* in addition to the song 'Entente Cordiale', the character of Dick Whittington delivers a musical satire on the avarice of the City of London, entitled 'Gold'. There then follows a mock sentimental ballad for Cinderella called 'The Banyon Tree'. In the next scene the fairy's entrance is accompanied by a mock musical-comedy dance with the opening lines: 'Dear little children of the slums / wearing a garland gay'.[36] The effect is to create a satirical unity between the various scenes that prefigures the development of musical revue.

Encouraged by the critical and popular success of his pantomime burlesque *Bill Bailey* at the Palace Theatre, Pélissier looked for another subject for parody. As previously referenced, the subject he chose was *Hamlet*[37] or rather those many productions of Shakespeare's play that festooned the West End. *Beyond the Fringe* was to mirror this in its own spoof of Shakespeare a half century later. In his definitive study of the satire boom of the 1960s *That Was Satire That Was*, Humphrey Carpenter writes:

Culture has become absurdly precious and elitist, as evidenced by [Dudley] Moore's Britten and Schubert *Lieder* parodies, the mock-German of the latter emphasising that most concert audiences have no idea what the words mean. British theatre is obsessed with the perpetual staging of Shakespeare plays which have long since become meaningless – this sketch [on Shakespeare] has the deeply ironic title 'So That's The Way You Like It'. Though *Beyond the Fringe* had not set out to be satirical, it had gradually developed into a devastating survey of the state of Britain in 1960.[38]

The very same might have been said of Harry Pélissier's *Follies* with regard to the first decade of the twentieth century and with strikingly similar parallels of subject matter and approach. For example, as we have already seen, like Dudley Moore, Harry Pélissier famously and skilfully parodied what he saw as the overblown pomp and clichéd foibles of classical music, in his case not Schubert or Beethoven, but the Teutonic melodrama of Wagner's operas and the canon-blasting grandeur of Tchaikovsky's 1812 Overture. Indeed, Harry Pélissier was an extremely accomplished composer and improviser at the piano, as evidenced by his appearances at the Henry Wood Proms as well as by his hilarious pastiches of classical music. And, like Harry Pélissier, as has already been noted, the satirists of *Beyond the Fringe* created their own parody of Shakespeare, a nonsense version of *Hamlet*. Pélissier's was to prove the most popular sketch or 'potted play' in his *Follies* programme of 1905. *The Morning Post* provided a glowing review:

> Yesterday afternoon, 'The Follies' produced their version of 'Hamlet'. Their idea is that Hamlet has been 'too much i' the Sun' – Inn. He is not mad but has visions as a result of alcoholism. The supposed ghost has no existence. Hamlet has inherited the craving from his father; his uncle is a staunch teetotaller whom Hamlet suspects of having poisoned his father with a glass of pure water. The players, however, refuse to speak the words set down for them, and substitute a mixture of "Bedelia" and "Sammy", which drives Ophelia mad. In the final scene Hamlet throws Ophelia into the river. She is not drowned and turns up at her own funeral. Laertes and Hamlet have a burlesque wrestling match. Hamlet kills the entire cast, as also several dummies, which, bearing the names of several well-known Hamlets, rise in succession from the grave. Finally, the shade of Shakespeare arises and shoots Hamlet dead.[39]

This is all a very long way from the musical hall routines of Marie Lloyd or Dan Leno and its surreal nonsense more closely prefigures the comedy of Spike Milligan or the Cambridge satirists in *Beyond the Fringe*. Like them, Harry Pélissier's target was not so much the Bard himself, but the 'perpetual staging', in overwrought and arcane productions, of his works. Jonathan Miller and company probably had in mind the performances of Donald Wolfit, Laurence Olivier and John Gielgud when they penned the line, 'O saucy Worcester, dost thou lie so still?'[40] At the time of Pélissier's sketch in 1905, there were no less than seven productions of *Hamlet* running concurrently in the capital, including the performances of 'Sir Henry Irving, Forbes Robertson, H.B. Irving, Frank Benson, Martin Harvey and other exponents of the worthy Dane'.[41] By combining drunkenness and Shakespeare in the setting of a tavern and the Royal Dane's castle in one skit, Pélissier knew exactly what he was doing. He was combining two vastly contrasted and conflicting worlds, that of high culture and that of the music hall, and most importantly and pioneeringly, he was doing it in the West End. This point was not missed by the critics at the time and was snobbishly commented upon in some reviews, including that of *The Circle*:

> All admirers of Shakespeare must deeply regret the presentation of the travesty of his 'Hamlet' in the form in which it appears at the Palace Theatre [. . .] in the first scene we have the castle of Elsinore shown with a low-class public house called 'The Sun' in the corner. We are treated to a quantity of taproom talk before we arrive at Scene 2. We now see Hamlet represented as a drunkard who is constantly imbibing whiskey and the King acting the part of a buffoon whose talk is interspersed with 'advertisement gag'. We have the character of Ophelia travestied as a kind of hysterical schoolgirl who rushed about the stage without rhyme or reason. In the third scene, Hamlet still imbibing, throws Ophelia into a rivulet, after which he seats himself with the two gravediggers on the edge of the grave and indulges again, interspersing his comments with snatches from Shakespeare. Ophelia reappears and enacts a ridiculous part. In the end, after some knockabout business in and about the grave, Hamlet is supposed to slay everybody by knocking them on the head with a stage truncheon. Then an impersonation of Shakespeare appears on a pedestal out of the grave and shoots Hamlet with a toy pistol. This is the scene we consider to be in decidedly bad taste – the grave is too solemn and sacred a thing to be made the subject of a music-hall jest.[42]

Too solemn indeed. You can almost feel the bile rising in the reviewer's throat as he contemptuously inserts the phrase 'music-hall jest'. Yet somehow the sneering puritanical tone of the *Circle* critic makes the piece sound even more hilarious. The *Morning Post* too felt obliged to add a coda of regret to its otherwise favourable review. 'It seems a pity that the authors have not found a pleasanter *motif* than drink. One hears and sees a deal too much of it as it is at the less refined variety houses and the Palace audience is not an audience to which it particularly appeals'.[43] In fact, Pélissier's parody of *Hamlet* proved immensely popular and remained in *The Follies* repertoire for years to come. One particular Hamlet, however, was not impressed. In May 1905, Sir Herbert Beerbohm Tree applied for an injunction against *The Follies* preventing them from performing their parody. In fact, Beerbohm Tree, in all his splendid pomp, was a favourite target of Harry Pélissier's and they had something of a bitter-sweet running battle. It was not unknown for Harry to turn up at one of the actor's performances and heckle for the great man to 'speak up!'.

In October 1905, *The Follies* transferred to the King's Theatre, Hammersmith, which was indeed a mainstream establishment. As such, unlike at the Palace or Alhambra, performances would require permission from the Lord Chamberlain's office. Pélissier's sketch *Bill Bailey* was granted its licence on the 11 September 1905.[44] The resulting copy of the script is the only one known to have survived, along with a handful more of Pélissier's satirical pieces, which he himself referred to as 'potted plays'. It is somewhat ironic that we are indebted to the Lord Chamberlain's collection at the British Library for the survival of these manuscripts dating from this period onwards, given that none of them was ever actually published either in Pélissier's lifetime, or indeed since. What were published, however, were over 60 of Pélissier's musical compositions, ranging from the wildly absurd to the socially and politically satirical, and even the romantic, in a variety of styles from Victorian parlour song to light operatic and even minstrel cakewalk. These we shall examine in greater depth in a later chapter. However, it is worth briefly reflecting at this point on how the songs reveal a flavour of Pélissier's political and social satire as, for example, in 'What A Happy Land Is England', co-written with the lyricist Arthur Wimperis:

> *The Lib'rals say they want to save the country from expense*
> *So, they're cutting down the programme of imperial defence*
> *They've reduced the British Army which already was too small*
> *And everybody's happy – but the Kaiser most of all!*[45]

In subsequent verses, Pélissier turns his wit upon a declining birth-rate, the passion of the suffragettes, the pollution of motor cars, price inflation, retailers cheating on their weights and measures, syndicates and trusts monopolising goods, health scares, even a changeable climate. Similarly, in 'What a Funny World We Live In' he once again satirises a social and political system, which, as he sees it, displays anomalies in the law and in artistic censorship:

> *I've been thinking, I've been thinking that this world's a funny spot,*
> *You're born to strife and trouble if you want to be or not;*
> *And suppose you take to stealing when by poverty you're pressed*
> *What you're charged with at the Station all depends on how you're dressed.*
>
> *I've been thinking, I've been thinking though no moral sense we lack*
> *In some things we're absurdly strict, in some insanely slack,*
> *We're very strict for instance on the censorship of plays,*
> *But let the Modern Novelist transgress in many ways.*[46]

Straying into the sphere of political and social satire was to prove especially problematic for Pélissier when it came to the Lord Chamberlain's office, especially as he extended his reach beyond the music hall into the licensed theatre. However, Pélissier was undeterred. Following the success of *Bill Bailey* and *Hamlet* there came a string of satirical parodies targeting in particular those plays that were most successful in the West End, including J.M. Barrie's *What Every Woman Knows* and *Peter Pan*,[47] Hall Caine's *The Christian*, Oscar Wilde's *Salomé*, Arthur Conan-Doyle's *Fires of Fate*[48] and Christopher Marlowe's *Faust*.[49]

The West End

In April 1907 Pélissier took his most ambitious step thus far as an impresario by hiring at his own expense the New Royalty Theatre at 73 Dean Street, Soho. It was a shrewd choice of location, being so near to the West End, while remaining in close proximity to a traditional music hall audience at, amongst other venues, the Oxford on Tottenham Court Road and the

Palace Theatre on Charing Cross Road. It was also of a modest enough size with a seating capacity of 657[50] not to present too much of a financial risk. It was newly opened and renamed, having previously been simply the Royalty. In fact, under that title, it had been a regular venue for private performances of radical works by Ibsen, Shaw, Synge and Yeats among others, variously staged by J.T. Grien's Independent Theatre Society and The Abbey Theatre, Dublin. Its audacious programming may have been one factor in Pélissier's choice of this theatre. With his father's diamond business located around the corner at 63, Berwick Street, its recent history is something with which he would very likely have been familiar. Its reputation for attracting an adventurous clientele and for adopting a risk-taking attitude, would have appeared an attractive option to this daring young impresario. Under the newly installed management of the American Tom Buffen Davis, the New Royalty was looking for a show with fresh appeal and Davis was later to prove a crucial connection for Pélissier when the former assumed management of the Apollo on Shaftesbury Avenue, a venue that *The Follies* were in time to make their West End home.

Their season at the New Royalty was a commercial and critical success[51] so that in September of that year another theatre manager, Edward Terry, who was a rival, felt confident enough to offer Pélissier a prestigious residency at his own, eponymous theatre on the Strand. This would represent yet a further step into the heart of the West End, into a theatre with a somewhat larger capacity of 888 plus standing in the pit[52] and this time Pélissier would not be required to fund the enterprise himself. Edward Terry would have recognised and been attracted to *The Follies* direction of artistic travel; that is to say, into the realms of satire and the extended sketch. As previously noted, he had himself once been a star of burlesque in the 1860s and 1870s. The illegitimate son of Fergus O'Connor, the Irish chartist, he started his theatrical career as a classical actor alongside Henry Irving. However, comedy was soon to prove his forte and he became a master of burlesque at the Royal Strand Theatre and the Gaiety Theatre, where he formed part of a famous quartet alongside Farren, Royce and Vaughan. As part of this celebrated comedic troupe, Terry had reached the peak of his success as a spoof Mephistopheles in *Little Doctor Faust* in 1878. Intriguingly, this was a theme that H.G. Pélissier was himself later to borrow and exploit with even greater success some 30 years after Terry's own efforts.

In 1907, Edward Terry had founded his own theatre by taking over management of a newly built venue on the site of the old Coal Hole (a famous public house and early music hall) and had unashamedly named it Terry's Theatre. The fashion for the old-style burlesque was already fading, so he had decided to concentrate on modern 'straight' plays such as Arthur Wing Pinero's *Sweet Lavender*. But it seems he never lost his love of satire and musical comedy. When *The Follies* began to grow in reputation, Terry would see an opportunity and so it was that, in the autumn of that year, he offered them a prestigious residency at his venue on the Strand. Pélissier was now the unrivalled master of the new comedy – a modern satirical style of burlesque, a wild combination of impersonation, music, clowning and topical commentary. *The Follies* were becoming the toast of London, playing to twice-daily sell-out houses at which anyone who was anyone would be seen. Even the distinguished Sir Herbert Beerbohm Tree regularly popped in for a glass of brandy, along with authors such as G.K. Chesterton and Hilaire Belloc, while Max Beerbohm was happy to provide caricatures for society magazines such as *The Tatler* (see Figure 16), as was E.T. Reed for *Punch* (see Figure 17). The latter, in fact, struck up a lasting friendship with H.G. Pélissier, and the two would exchange correspondence laced with each other's cartoons.

Following their success at Terry's, in February 1908, *The Follies* were contracted once more by Tom Davis to appear at the Apollo Theatre on Shaftesbury Avenue. It seems as if *The Follies* had immediately become such an overnight 'hot ticket', that a sort of bidding war had opened up between rival managements. In fact, the Apollo offered a significantly larger capacity of 1,200, according to *The Stage*[53] or, alternatively, a rather more modest increase to 893 according to Howard,[54] but it was here that *The Follies* were to remain in almost uninterrupted residence until 1912.

A Peter Pan-tomime

As previously noted, another favourite and repeated target for Harry's satire was the author J.M. Barrie. It was during his season at the Royalty that Pélissier had come up with his next hugely successful mock-pantomime entitled *Baffles: a Peter Pan-tomime*,[55] in which he imagines the raffish society playboy Raffles hilariously embroiled in the world of Barrie's *Peter Pan*. Having been encouraged by the response to his *Bill Bailey* and *Hamlet* sketches, Pélissier had turned his attention to whatever productions happened to be popular at the time in the West End; the more popular and successful, indeed, the more appealing as a satirical target. Throughout the first decades of the twentieth century, J.M. Barrie was a hot ticket with the theatre-going audience. The working proximity with Pélissier dated back to the Sandringham Palace performance of December 1905, at which Barrie had presented his one act play *Pantaloon* alongside Pélissier's Wagner parody. In the succeeding years, as we shall see in the next chapter, Pélissier was to have great fun and would run into considerable trouble with his parody of *An Englishman's Home* by Guy du Maurier, a production with which Barrie was closely associated both as a producer and as an editorial associate. This play was not itself written by Barrie, but he did have a considerable hand in the final draft of the script and, being a close friend of the du Maurier family, assisted greatly in getting it performed. More directly, as well as his spoof of *Peter Pan*, Pélissier produced a fairly savage spoof of another of Barrie's own most popular plays, *What Every Woman Knows*.

In *Baffles, A Peter Pan-tomime*, the audience would have easily recognised Pélissier's fusion of *Peter Pan or The Boy Who Never Grows Up*, which had been running at the Duke of York's with various casts since December 1904, with *Raffles, The Amateur Cracksman* by E.W. Hornung, another West End stage hit of the time, currently enjoying a successful run at the Comedy theatre. In the opening scene of Pélissier's sketch, three adults, dressed as children, are crammed into a tiny four-poster bed. Gwennie Mars (a popular cast member) plays 'Gwendy' alongside John and Michael Darling played by Norman Blumé and Dan Everard respectively. They are singing a chorus based on 'The Bogie Man', a popular song of the 1890s. Mrs Darling is struggling to control the massive St Bernard dog, Nana, whom she joins in a wordless growling duet of a song. Suddenly, the dog sheds its fur to reveal Harry Pélissier dressed as a Pirate King version of Captain Hook (complete with hook), only, as it turns out, to be a Music Pirate King called 'Baffles', who is hiding from the police with ten thousand copies of the hit song 'Down By The Zuyder Zee' buried on Hampstead Heath. At the time, music copyright laws were extremely vague and routinely ignored and, then as now, music piracy was a hot topic of debate. (Harry was also probably having an ironic joke at his own expense, in that he as much as anyone in theatre was often on the receiving end of criticism or even an injunction for his musical parodies and allusions to other composers' copyright material for his sketches.) Enter Lewis Sydney as 'Peter Tanned', or 'The Boy Who Couldn't Sit Down'. (Highgate School remember, which the young Harry had attended, was notorious in its enthusiasm for severe corporal beatings.) He is carrying a dark lantern and recognisably dressed as the burglar from that other popular play of the time, *Raffles*. He attempts to abduct the 'children' but the wires to the flying apparatus have broken – an announcement is brazenly made to that effect by the stage manager – so Peter tries to take them through the window to 'Blather Blather Land', but they get stuck in the frame and are held back by Baffles, the Pirate King. Tinkerbell is a 'prehistoric nymph' who bangs a massive gong every time Peter makes a mistake or does something foolish. Peter grabs a cigar-case, thinking it is a pistol and points it at the head of Baffles, who coolly announces the following:

> Have you ever pictured Peter when the play Peters out. When Peter begins to pall? In place of a house crowded with bejewelled aristocracy, the stalls become a series of empty *Rose du Barrie* dotted here and there with 3s.9d. blouses and borrowed dress suits, the box office receipts diminished day by day till not a single family adorns the family circle; the pit queue dwindled down until it consists solely of the fireman's wife, the stage doorkeeper's uncle, two dogs and a policeman. Then Mr. Charles Showman [a reference to Charles Frohman, the West End impresario] will 'present' another attraction from the States that'll put your nose out of joint and London will know you no more.[56]

Yes, even children will finally get bored with endless versions of Peter Pan. Peter Tanned is resigned to his fate and agrees to share the proceeds of the pirated music. During the whole under-rehearsed proceedings, the cast are forgetting their lines, ad-libbing and corpsing, adding to the general sense of chaotic nonsense and to the merriment of the audience and the dismay of certain critics. At one moment, an actor representing J.M. Barrie appears on stage and proclaims in a high-pitched Scots accent, 'it's all panning out rather well!'[57]

Perhaps Harry Pélissier was merely having a bit of fun with the idea of Peter Pan and the burglar Raffles entering simultaneously through the same bedroom window, but he would also have been conscious of the enormous success of Barrie's play, which, though nominally intended for children, had a massive popular appeal among adults. The only phenomenon that we can compare it to a century later is J.K. Rowling's *Harry Potter* series in all its manifestations. Barrie's piece of fairyland escapism was a perfect target for the down-to-earth satirist. As adults and children alike were drawn into Barrie's reassuring fantasy world, where everything is free of the exigencies of time and change, where children never grow up or grow old or die, it must have appeared as a red rag to a bull for Harry Pélissier to confront the audience with his dysfunctional nonsense, his particular dose of madness. And, much as they loved Barrie's reassuring escapism from the growing insecurities of Edwardian England, so too they relished Harry's chaotic parody.

J.M. Barrie himself was not so impressed. He penned his own review in *Sphere* on 30 March 1907:

> There is great scope for burlesquing *Raffles* but it would not be strictly accurate to say that the opportunity is utilised to the fullest extent by the Follies at the Royalty where we get a compound of *Raffles* and *Peter Pan* under the title *Baffles, a Peter-Pantomime*. The fact that it is a composite effort (by Mr. Pélissier himself and by Arthur Wimperis and Arthur Davenport) may have something to do with its patchwork character, and lack of rehearsal was obvious on the first night. But when all that is admitted, there remains the fact that there is no real idea behind the burlesque. It is funny in little bits, just like the individual songs with which this troupe amuses us. But much of it is amateurish and boyish and its weakness for a pun is quite old-fashioned. Adopting the paranomistic plan of authors I should say that altogether little flashes do not pan out to the length required [perhaps a barbed response to his own appearance as a character in the skit]. The Follies are seen to far greater advantage in their burlesque of a music-hall entertainment, for it gains by jerkiness. Here the authors have really caught the spirit of the thing to be pilloried and present a most scathing criticism of the average programme of the halls. This part of the programme is one of the funniest things now to be seen in London.[58]

It would seem that, in Barrie's eyes, 'scathing criticism' of working-class entertainment was much to be enjoyed, whereas a satire of mainstream West End theatre simply did not 'pan out'. 'Amateur and boyish' were of course terms of praise when they were employed fifty years later by critics to describe *Beyond the Fringe*.[59] Some reviewers and theatregoers simply had yet to catch on to the idea that the unrehearsed wild nonsense of *The Follies* was entirely intentional and exactly what was fresh and new about it. Indeed, that 'there is no real idea behind it' was precisely the idea that *was* behind it: paradoxical and surreal. This low-level war with Barrie was to continue of course, as Pélissier picked on another of his works for satire, *What Every Woman Knows*,[60] Barrie's ambiguous exploration of female emancipation and suffrage. Though perhaps Barrie was to have the last laugh when several years later he would cast Harry's young widow, Fay Compton, as Peter Pan and subsequently wrote a play called *Mary Rose*,[61] inspired in part by her tragic marriage.

'Impudent familiarity'

There followed more 'potted plays', satirical parodies of hit West End productions such as a spoof of *The Christian*,[62] a religious melodrama by Hall Caine, in the parody of which one can hear echoes of Alan Bennett's 'I am an hairy man' from *Beyond the Fringe*.[63] Then there were skits on light comic operas such as *The Merry Widow*[64] and *The Girls From Gottenberg*,[65] for which Harry wrote his own pastiche score; and of *Faust*[66] and *Henry of Navarre*;[67] even of Maud Allan's uninhibited and revolutionary modern dance style in *Salomé*,[68] in which Harry himself performed his most notorious transvestite role.

Another target common to both Pélissier and *Beyond the Fringe* was hypocritical or inappropriate philanthropy and charity. The year that *Beyond the Fringe* appeared at the Edinburgh Festival was also World Refugee Year. Peter Cook and company could not resist sending up the patronising middle-class attitude of fobbing off old clothes onto Oxfam. Cook and Miller play two doctors examining a refugee, played reluctantly by Alan Bennett:

PESKER: Now you may realize, Johann, that a lot of people all over Britain — many of them not very well off, old-age pensioners, vicars, schoolmasters and the like, have sent in some of their dearly valued possessions in order to get you kitted out properly. It's rather like Christmas, isn't it? Or do you have Christmas in — where is it — Bosnia?

BRIGHT: Now this is a vest which has kindly been sent in by the Vicar of Nastbury. It's a beautiful bit of English worsted aertex, you see, Johann.

PESKER: Completely mothproof.[69]

In Pélissier's case, it was the self-serving 'benefit' performance that was his target. In his sketch entitled *Everybody's Benefit* a special fund-raising matinée is arranged for the frail and elderly former star of the musical stage, 'Sarah Judkins'. Great stars are invited to perform. However, it is noted in the programme that these artistes 'reluctantly consented to appear by kind permission of their respective managers'. Furthermore, they insist upon choosing their own time and point out that 'the distinguished actor-manager objected to associating with music-hall folk, and poor little Sarah Judkins, the charitable object, (the forgotten "star" of forty years before) was unrecognised and requested to give up the chair on which she was resting'. In other words, these artistes are not appearing for charitable purposes at all but rather to boost their own image and profile with the public, a phenomenon we might easily recognise in our contemporary media.

As previously noted, it is somewhat ironic that we are fortunate to have surviving copies of a portion, though sadly not all, of the 'potted plays' as a result of the Lord Chamberlain's scrupulous censorship. *Bill Bailey, Hamlet, A Christmas Panto, Fires of Fate* (a spoof on a hit play by Arthur Conan-Doyle), *The Whip, Faust* and *Baffles* were all collected and diligently filed away. In contrast, Harry and his troupe appear to have treated their own copies of the scripts with casual abandon — only one or two fragments have survived in the family collection, or even in the company's scrapbooks and mementos subsequently donated to the Victoria and

Albert Theatre Museum. The scripts, anyway, only give us a partial notion of the actual performances, there being such a rapid turnover of material full of topical, up-to-the-minute jokes, which unlike many of the songs, were never published. Also, as previously stated, a great deal of the performance was actually improvised and ad-libbed on the night – something underlined by impromptu handwritten notes in the margins of the collected scripts. This, one can imagine, was part of the excitement for the audience, happily drawn to a show where they would not quite know what to expect – an approach to theatre-making quite untypical of the Edwardian mainstream, or even of the fixed routines of the music hall. Indeed, Harry's approach – and that of his audience – seem much more redolent of the experimental world of the 1960s and 1970s than of the risk-averse culture that we inhabit at the time of writing. These audiences were stepping out in order to encounter the thrill of something unexpected, something improvised and uncertain. It was very new and different. Like Spike Milligan after him, Harry Pélissier habitually strayed from the written text – sometimes to the discomfort and chagrin of his fellow performers. Fitzroy Gardner describes it thus:

> The spontaneous geniality of his smile is irresistible. Even to the dullest brained among his audience it conveys that which convinces them that there is something funny in what is going on, apart from Pelissier's face and figure, and they laugh with the rest. His attitude of almost impudent familiarity towards his audience fascinates them. When he addresses them before the curtain he does not make a formal announcement, but just chats with them as if he and they were on the most intimate terms. If, during one of these interludes, they receive his remarks with applause that is not quite uproarious, he will sometimes rebuke them with, 'You don't applaud half enough. Go on! Like this.' And then he applauds himself. What other actor would dare stop in the middle of a song or speech and address some late arrival in the stalls with 'You are very late, sir!'? But it never seems to cause offence; the grieved tone of the remonstrance disarms resentment; in fact, I have heard of a party of people who have come very late remark in the vestibule of the Apollo, 'I hope he will spot us and say something funny.[70]

So, it is perhaps to the published song lyrics that we must go for more reliable transcriptions of *The Follies'* performances. For sheer silliness and surreal humour, we have 'A Dog Song', which is also a riff on Victorian sentimentality. Likewise, in 'The Toothbrush and The Sponge'[71] we have a silly fawning love song that might grace the pen of Lewis Carroll. 'Li-Ti-Ti-Ti'[72] is a bit of surreal nonsense in which a farmer turns murderous having eaten too much cheese and an old woman is run over by a tram, all rounded off with the meaningless refrain that is the title of the song.

Once again, it is worth reiterating that it is in the song lyrics that a good deal of the political and social satire comes across most keenly. Pélissier had regular collaborators in the creation of his musical pieces – lyricists such Arthur Wimperis and Arthur Davenport and later on Compton Mackenzie, for example. Here some of the most acerbic satire is to be found. Harry Pélissier's own position, on subjects such as suffragettes and women's rights and immigrant aliens and socialism, can often appear ambiguous, so perhaps some of the more politically reactionary views that are sometimes expressed derive from the pens of his lyricists rather than himself. I rather think that in Pélissier's mind everything was fair game and the range of targets in his songs is extraordinary.

In 'Back To The Land',[73] he sends up the political sloganizing of Lloyd George and his 'back to the land' policies, suggesting that Percival Spencer, the pioneering aeronautist, will crash 'back to the land', that freezing channel swimmers will climb into boats to get 'back to the land', that the North Pole explorer Captain Peary will rush 'back to the land' and that Londoners will all suddenly become knowledgeable farmers as they go '"back to the land'. One hears echoes of the ridicule that fell upon Prime Minister John Major for his 'Back to Basics' campaign of the 1990s.

In 'What A Very Great Improvement It Would Be', Harry sends up fast-food production and touches upon a very modern topic – the provenance of food:

> *If our favourite dishes we were not afraid of*
> *What a very great improvement it would be!*
> *If we only knew what sausages are made of*
> *What a very great improvement it would be!*[74]

Overall, his work presents the image of an Empire and an England in decline, a cosy, complacent Edwardian era that was perhaps more self-evident to the partially 'outsider' son of an immigrant. Again, how very closely this mirrors the satirists of the 1960s, as described by Michael Billington at the time:

> I asked them [the cast of *Beyond the Fringe*],'What are you attacking, what's your gripe?' And they said, 'Complacency'. It was the complacency of Macmillan's England that they really wanted to get at. And I think it's no accident that *Beyond the Fringe* happened when it did. Because the 1950's (which I had been brought up in) had been so complacent, parochial, smug, little England-ish.[75]

One of the stand-out moments of *Beyond the Fringe*, an iconic sketch at its very heart, was Peter Cook's impersonation of the then Prime Minister, Harold Macmillan. Carpenter describes it thus:

> Cook shrewdly chose not so much to caricature MacMillan, as to impersonate him with deadly accuracy [. . .] The Cook mockery was instead directed at Britain's loss of riches and status in the years since the war.[76]

Pélissier's 'Macmillan' was the then Prime Minister, Herbert Asquith, and his Liberal government and, in particular, Winston Churchill. In fact, it was not permissible for Pélissier to impersonate Asquith or Churchill directly because he was still subject to the Lord Chamberlain's strict censure regarding the ban on the representation of living persons, as indeed was Cook 50 years later. In Cook's case – the Lord Chamberlain's Office still being in existence at the time – this was a stricture that he was cleverly able to sidestep at The Establishment through its status as a private members' club, and, as such, not subject to the Lord Chamberlain's licence. In Pélissier's case, his performances at the Apollo were very much dependent on the Lord Chamberlain's public licence – but he simply hoped to be ignored and disregarded as a 'music hall' entertainer, not to be taken seriously. In fact, the targets of Pélissier's sketches and satirical songs were always clear, and much enjoyed by his audience. Perhaps the thrill was enhanced by the sheer sense of taboo, of risk-taking, that was intrinsic to his style.

A good deal of the political and social satire was made even more explicit in the cartoons that appeared in the daily press – political caricatures that borrowed from, and paid homage to, *The Follies* sketches. For example, a bizarre cartoon by Pélissier's friend E.T. Reed appeared in *Punch* magazine depicting the Prime Minister, Herbert Asquith, in a somewhat sorry state, having been to see *The Follies* at the Apollo. In the drawing, the startled and helpless figure of John Bull is depicted tortuously ensnared and strangulated by the coiled figures of Pélissier and Asquith, represented as a pair of giant chicken-crested octopuses (see Figure 17). Despite, or perhaps even because of, Pélissier's satire, Asquith attended *The Follies'* shows, just as Macmillan is reported to have witnessed his impersonation by Peter Cook at The Establishment. The caption to the cartoon suggested that Asquith was more concerned about the satire of his policies than by the actual business of government itself.[77]

Above all, Harry was offering an insight into the real world and real issues, however much they were dressed up in madcap buffoonery, and this represented a step change for the mainstream, popular Edwardian theatre, in particular for the music hall and the concert party repertoire, so dominated by drinking songs, domestic strife and sentimental ballads. Again, there is a strong echo of the 1960s. Thus, Michael Billington commenting on his experience of *Beyond the Fringe*:

> I'd been to those Hermione Gingold revues, *Sweet and Low* and all that, which depended mainly on theatrical gossip, but suddenly this was about the real world, and one was absolutely astonished.[78]

Like the 1960s satirists who were to follow him half a century later, Harry Pélissier had blown the lid off an unspoken reality of political and social insecurity, hypocrisy and decline. And everything in his sights was fair game. Whether it be prominent politicians, celebrated classical composers, the birth rate, price inflation, defence cuts, the provenance of food, the English climate, venerated playwrights and their hit West End shows, music hall performers, *avant-garde* dancers, distinguished actors, the march of technology, suffragettes, the campaign for military recruitment, the place of the migrant in society, free trade or the price of soap, it was all a topic for humour and comic de-bunking. And Harry took it all in his stride with a delicious joy that was infectious to his audience. We cannot know all the ad-libs, the off-the-cuff asides, not much even of the original scripts save what was reported in press reviews and is to be found among the several 'potted play' scripts in the Lord Chamberlain's Collection at the British Library. But we easily discern that Harry Pélissier loved playing the fool and sending up everything in sight, and that his audience loved it too, drawn to the Apollo shows with an infectious delight that resulted in sell-out crowds of every class and background. This was new, fresh and delightful. The 'real world' represented on stage — and with a wicked sense of fun.

7

The Rebel

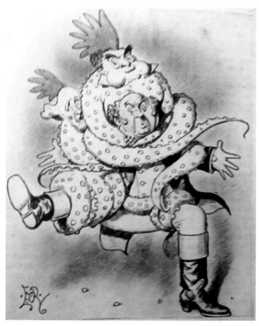

Figure 17. Punch cartoon by E.T. Reed of H.G. Pélissier and Prime Minister Herbert Asquith strangling the figure of John Bull

Cancel culture

It was not long before Pélissier and *The Follies* ran into difficulties with the Lord Chamberlain, whose office was capable of some harsh, not to say baffling, decisions. For example, the Reader of Plays Alexander Redford had banned two works in 1907 – Harley Granville-Barker's *Waste* and Edward Garnett's *The Breaking Point*. No particular reasons had been given, which only helped intensify an even greater sense of injustice. Asked to define his criteria, Redford brazenly stated, 'Simply bringing to bear an official point of view and keeping up a standard. There are no principles that can be defined. I simply follow precedent'.[1] For some this was indeed a breaking point. 'The situation of the Englishman of letters ambitious of writing for the stage', wrote Henry James 'has less dignity – thanks to the censor's arbitrary rights upon his work – than that of any other man of letters of Europe'.[2] In other words, the censorial régime in Britain was perceived to be, and quite possibly was in fact, more arbitrary, authoritarian and restrictive than any other in the Western world. At times, it was downright farcical, as when a production of *The Mikado* was temporarily banned in 1907 on the pretext that it endangered the Anglo-Japanese Alliance!

On 29 October 1907, a letter of protest was published in *The Times*, signed by 71 major dramatists, poets and novelists – many of whom had more radical aesthetic, social or political ideas. These included Henry James himself, W.B. Yeats, George Bernard Shaw, J.M. Barrie, Thomas Hardy, Joseph Conrad, H.G. Wells and John Galsworthy. They demanded to meet with the then Prime Minister, Campbell Bannerman. In the event, rather dismissively, they were finally granted a long-delayed audience, not with the Prime Minister, but with the austerely conservative Home Secretary, Herbert Gladstone, on 22 February 1908. Following this, no further action was taken, which gives some idea of the status attached in the corridors of power to 'men of letters' in the Edwardian world. In December 1908, the issue was raised in Parliament by the Liberal MP Robert Vernon Harcourt, himself an aspiring dramatist, when he introduced a Private Member's Bill seeking to 'abolish the powers of the Lord Chamberlain in respect of stage plays'.[3] This was given equally short shrift by the Government, progressing no further than the first reading.

However, by no means all those engaged in the theatre world were opposed to the Lord Chamberlain's powers. A significant number of theatre managers welcomed the stamp of approval and subsequent barrier to potential legal action that the Lord Chamberlain's licences ensured. Indeed, the vast majority of productions on the English stage fitted perfectly well within the vaguely conservative strictures of the Licensing Act and successfully avoided any cuts. The prevailing attitude of the time among the upper class was summed up by W. Macqueen Pope in his *Carriages at Eleven* of 1948: 'London in the days of Edward VII was a city of smiles, the habitation of wealth, of peace, of security and of power. [The theatre] disregarded the outside march of progress and it had nothing to do with rush or vulgar clamour'.[4] It was a world typified by the drawing-room peccadilloes of that 'respectable darling of late-Victorian middle-class audiences',[5] Arthur Wing Pinero. On the whole, theatre managers also welcomed the stable authority of the censor when putting on their productions, seeing it as a restraining influence against any radical or risky experimentation on the part of the writers themselves. The eminent impresario Charles Hawtrey, the actors Mrs Patrick Campbell, Sir Herbert Beerbohm Tree and Gerald du Maurier all spoke up in defence of the Lord Chamberlain's office. W.S. Gilbert was particularly forthright, stating that: 'I think the stage is not a proper pulpit from which to disseminate doctrines possibly of Anarchism, Socialism and Agnosticism'.[6]

This then was the context in which H.G. Pélissier was about to openly invite controversy. By choosing to satirize a patriotic and, at the time, highly successful and popular new play, he was certain to fall foul of the Lord Chamberlain. The opening night of Pélissier's chosen target, *An Englishman's Home*, in early February 1909, was keenly awaited by an expectant public. There had been much advance publicity, fuelled not least by the mystery of the authorship – which was itself perhaps an early example of deliberate press manipulation and 'hype'. In fact, the author was Guy du Maurier, brother of the actor Gerald, a close friend and associate of J.M. Barrie, who would play no small part in its production. As ever, Harry Pélissier was hot off the starting block, wasting no time in his quest for fresh prey. *The Observer* noted on 14 February:

> As Mr. Pélissier and several of 'The Follies' were to be seen in a box at Wyndham's on Wednesday afternoon, it may be presumed that 'An Englishman's Home' will shortly be potted at the Apollo.[7]

This mention gives witness to the ubiquitous presence of Pélissier, both in the national press and on the West End circuit, and of the scrupulous attention paid to his activities. On 19 February we read in the *Evening Standard*:

> Mr. Pélissier has found it necessary to postpone presenting his new programme at the Apollo Theatre until March 1st, when 'the Follies' will be seen in three 'potted plays' – 'An Englishman's Home', 'The King of Cadonia' and 'What Every Woman Knows'.[8]

This gives further testimony to the speed and alertness with which Harry Pélissier produced his sketches and how fresh and topical they were when presented to the public. In many ways, it is a style more akin to the turnover and topicality of modern-day television and social media and is arguably a pioneering form of those very techniques. *The Pelican* reported on 26 February:

> Next Monday, Mr. Pélissier and his Follies will reach their 101st performance at the Apollo, when a new programme will be given including a skit on 'An Englishman's Home'.[9]

Similar notices followed in *Stage*,[10] *Referee*,[11] *Reynolds*[12] and *The Irish Times*,[13] as well as *The Daily Mail*,[14] *Observer*,[15] *Winning Post*[16] and many other publications. It was national news and Pélissier's spoof was obviously as keenly awaited as the original play had been.

Banned!

It seems that the Lord Chamberlain's office had duly taken note of these press reports, for a formal ban was promptly imposed on *The Follies* sketch, without even recourse to reading Pélissier's script. This too was reported with equal prominence in *The Daily Mirror* on 25 February[17] as well as *The Sun, Daily Mail, Standard, Times, Globe* and *Pall Mall Gazette* of the following day. *The Daily News* ran the following piece:

> EMBARGO ON FUN/ A letter to *The Times* by Robert Harcourt MP headed 'The Censor of Plays' quotes a rather brusque telegram delivered to Pélissier five days prior to the

initial staging of the parody: 'Am instructed to inform you that no skit on *An Englishman's Home* will be licensed for representation by Lord Chamberlain – REDFORD'.[18]

In fact, Robert Harcourt had addressed his letter of 26 February 1909 to several English newspapers, including *The Daily Telegraph* and *Standard* as well as *The Times*. It is worth quoting in full:

> Sir, – Ridicule is often a stronger weapon than argument, and one hopes that the refusal of the Censor to allow the 'Follies' to lay their unhallowed hands on a melodrama called 'An Englishman's Home' will be too great a joke even for actor-managers who support the existing state of affairs. Last year I introduced into Parliament a Bill to remedy this intolerable absurdity, and in one way or another this Bill will reappear. It is for the gentlemen who support the censorship to argue the matter. I have merely to state the position. Mr Pélissier it appears received the following telegram:- 'Am instructed to inform you that no skit on "An Englishman's Home" will be licensed for representation by Lord Chamberlain. – Redford'. Note that no charge is brought against the particular burlesque. The play itself is sacrosanct – a side issue which requires some explanation. No skit is permitted. But what is the central position? Mr Pélissier and his colleagues are artists of high ability but they are essentially in technical and professional language 'variety theatre' or 'music hall' artists. Their early career was at concert and music halls. Gradually they grew in popularity and are able to give a variety entertainment that fills an entire evening bill, which (again technically) is a theatre. They exist, therefore, at the pleasure of Mr Redford. But let them decide to shift their camp and return to their former mode of appearance. Let them arrange to appear under the management of Mr Butt at the Palace 'Theatre' (technically a music hall). They may present in another place of entertainment a few yards from their present pitch this very skit or 'sketch' officially banned at the Apollo, and the Lord Chamberlain and Mr Redford have absolutely no power to say them nay. *Ex hypothesi* this sketch is (in the opinion of these gentlemen) detrimental to the public interest. But what the law says is that this dangerous and undesirable performance may take place in the Charing Cross-road [*sic*] but may on no account take place in Shaftesbury avenue [*sic*]. I ask the plain and simple question, is this situation defended? And by whom? I am, Sir, your obedient servant, Feb.26. ROBERT HARCOURT.[19]

Probably in direct response to Harcourt's reference, a caricature that formed part of Pélissier's regular personal correspondence with E.T. Reed, the *Punch* cartoonist, depicts *The Follies'* maestro with bulls' horns delivering a blow to the rear end of Mr Alfred Butt of the Palace Theatre. The caption reads: 'Butt me no Butts!!' (see Figure 18). The implication is that Pélissier had no intention of returning to play the music halls in order to evade the censor's ban. On 25 February 1909, *The Daily Chronicle* ran the following headline: 'VETOED PLAY / Skit on An Englishman's Home Not Allowed / PROHIBITED HUMOUR'.[20]

That week, similar headlines and stories ran throughout the national press in *The Observer, The Times, The Daily Telegraph* and even in many provincial newspapers and magazines.[21] It is

Figure 18. 'Butt me no Butts!!' Cartoon by E.T.Reed. Sent privately to
H.G. Pélissier.

worth emphasising that all this sustained and intensive press coverage focused on a relatively new music hall and concert party company at a time when, as has already been noted, such performers in general received scant attention. A most unusual and very public scandal was under way. Pélissier had achieved national notoriety through the Lord Chamberlain's censorship of one of his 'potted plays'; one of the first examples perhaps of the controversial banning of a work actually increasing its fame and success – something that nowadays one might consider a common phenomenon.

A fractured society

To understand why the Lord Chamberlain may have felt it necessary to take such swift and arbitrary action, it is necessary to take account of the general political and cultural climate of the time. In essence, despite the superficially prosperous and harmonious appearances alluded to earlier by W. Macqueen Pope, this was an era of deep unease and national insecurity. A decade before, during the Boer War of 1899, the British Empire had been presented with a humiliating dilemma. That mighty global Colossus had found it alarmingly difficult to defeat a motley guerrilla army of Southern African farmers and traders whom they had heavily outnumbered. Not only had Britain suffered severe defeats in the early stages of the war, but it had also drawn widespread international disapproval through what were seen as bullying and cruel tactics. Military weaknesses were revealed that became a matter of sharp debate at home and political divisions were drawn between those who had supported and promoted the war, such as Joseph Chamberlain, the Chief Colonial Secretary, on the one hand and Lloyd George, among others, who had opposed it, on the other.

At the same time, the British public was keenly aware of the increasing military and economic might, both in real and in relative terms, of other world powers – in particular, the United States and Germany. By contrast, the British economy was in a state of stagnation. Its open borders had permitted an influx of cheap foreign goods, whereas Germany and the United States had implemented rigorous systems of protection. In particular, the textile, iron and steel industries were hit badly. Agriculture continued to suffer from falling prices and there was a steady migration of desperately poor, unemployed workers into the towns and cities. The number of agricultural labourers and farm servants dropped from 983,919 in 1881 to only 689,292 in 1901.[22] And, once again, from 1904 onwards overall unemployment began to rise. In 1902 the London boroughs were empowered to set up labour bureaux, while the Unemployed Workmen Act of 1905 allowed local committees to keep a register of unemployed and to raise funds for relief. An embryonic and much-needed welfare state was under way.

Throughout the country, economic development was slowing down. During the last two decades of the nineteenth century, Britain's aggregate income had increased more rapidly than the population. In 1900, it was roughly one third greater than it had been 20 years earlier. By contrast, however, during these opening decades of the twentieth century, it was to stagnate at practically the same figure as that of 1900 for the next 14 years. The result was intense industrial and social unrest. What emerges is a picture of a fractured society. Beneath that complacently idyllic image of a sweetly scented Edwardian summer lawn, complete with white flannels and straw boaters, of punts, croquet and cricket, of imperial splendour and confidence, we see glimpses of a seething underbelly of turmoil and discontent, of nervous tension and the darkest fears.

Increasing trade union campaigning resulted in the 1906 Trades Disputes Act, which effectively confirmed the right to peaceful picketing and secured the unions' legal and financial independence. Following this, the Trade Union Act of 1913 restored their political rights, so that henceforth they were free to take political action provided that first they obtained the authority of their members by a vote. This increasing confidence also encouraged the unions into more militant strike action, rising to a crescendo between 1910 and 1912. Mine-workers, ship-workers and dockers all called strikes for higher wages and gained their demands in this period. There followed a general railway strike in the blazing hot summer of 1911 and, in 1912, once again a general strike of the miners. Inevitably, all this industrial discontent fed into the political arena. A radical wing of the Conservative Party saw a potential solution to the economic stagnation in following the example of Bismarck in Germany and McKinley in the United States by the abandonment of free trade and with a proposed policy of the imposition of protection against foreign workers and goods. This Tory faction was led by the old Boer-Warhorse himself, Joseph Chamberlain, and it was to divide the Conservative Party for a generation and thus facilitate the revival of the Liberal Party under Lloyd George.

In fact, the principal issue at stake was not just the free movement of goods, but also of people. Before the Conservatives had departed office, they were able to pass the Aliens Act of

1905, the aim of which was to restrict the immigration of foreign workers – an obvious appeal to the working-class trades-union vote at a time of high unemployment and labour agitation. It should be remembered that at this time and throughout all the preceding centuries of British history, there had been no such thing as an official passport. As a result, the free passage of migrants and refugees from the Mediterranean and Continental Europe, not to mention Ireland, had dramatically boosted the growth of the British economy and British cities throughout the Victorian era. Between 1880 and 1900, the number of aliens domiciled in Britain had more than doubled and was then close to a third of a million. Added to this, there were the hundreds of thousands of Irish migrants who had contributed to the building of the railways, canals and housing stock in the second half of the nineteenth century. Jewish migration, in particular from Eastern Europe, was at the time a sensitive issue within the trade union movement, leading to the resulting claims that it had given rise to 'sweatshop' labour and pressure on wages. Since the early 1890s, the Trades Union Congress had been demanding a limitation on the entry of destitute aliens.[23] This entire state of affairs, and in particular the presence of 'aliens' and an increasing rate of migration, was to be of great relevance to Harry Pélissier's sketch writing and to the manner in which he satirised du Maurier's 'patriotic' play. It was also something he would have felt with an acute sensitivity himself, given his own family origins.

Thus, it was that issues of a stagnating economy, industrial unrest, trade union militancy and immigration control all fed into the turbulent unease of the early 1900s. However, more than any of these, the decade was dominated by the intense imperial rivalry and the fear of the growing power of that close neighbour across the Channel – Germany. It is against this backdrop and with this major concern in mind that Guy du Maurier was about to present his sensationally popular new play, *An Englishman's Home*.

An Englishman's Home

Broadly, the plot of *An Englishman's Home* hinges upon a typical, middle-class, suburban household finding itself suddenly overrun by an invading foreign army. In this context, du Maurier's play can be seen as an example of what was to be called 'invasion literature': a cultural reflection of the general public unease of the period with regard to hostile threats from foreign powers, in particular Germany. Most prominent among these works would have been H.G. Wells' *The War in the Air* and William Le Queux's *Spies of the Kaiser*. Du Maurier's work was unusual in being a stage work, but the common thread was a siren note of warning that tapped into the spirit of national anxiety.[24]

One of the central conflicts of the play involves an effete young teenager called Geoffrey Smith, depicted in the louche manner of a Wildean aesthete, a regular homophobic target of the era, and the antagonism towards him from an upstanding, patriotic army volunteer called Paul Robinson. Rather inconsistently, the witty Smith is often given the best lines. This aspect of the writing confused many in the audience as to the author's intent. Were they meant to laugh *with* this young Wildean aesthete or *at* him? All seems to be made clear as the play develops and the author's voice rings loud through the polemical remonstrance of the Volunteer Paul:

> Are you all mad? Don't any of you understand? How can you stand here and laugh and joke in the same old way? [. . .] Don't you realize it yet – that the whole damned country is coming down like a house of cards, and that you, and thousands like you, are saying it's not your business, and as long as it doesn't interfere with you, let it go on? And others are just the same, shouting and singing rotten music-hall songs, and thinking they're just going to see some fun! Fun! – oh, my God![25]

Note that the music hall is once again singled out as a symbol of all that is decadent, misguided and rotten. This particular breed of theatrical snobbery was deeply entrenched and revealing. In his summation of the play, Nicholas Hiley is in no doubt as to the ultimate value of the piece: 'It was a real "tuppence coloured" thriller, with simple stirring dialogue and a stock of two-dimensional characters which could have come from a Pollock's toy theatre'.[26] Given all this, it is perhaps unsurprising that Pélissier would have seen it as ripe for satire and it is intriguing to note that, at one point in the drama, a principal character suggests that the rather fey young aesthete, Geoffrey Smith, should go and visit *The Follies* for his musical entertainment. 'My brother has seen the Follies twice', says Ada Jones, a sporty young female in the family household.[27] Clearly Pélissier's troupe was already in du Maurier's sights as an exemplar of all that was wrong in the state of England. (Or perhaps we can thank J.M. Barrie and his own on-going friction with Pélissier for the insertion of this line!)

The brazen militaristic propaganda of the piece was only further underlined when Lord Esher, a colleague of the War Secretary Viscount Haldane, arranged for a recruiting booth to be set up in the foyer of Wyndham's theatre on opening night.[28] The play was clearly considered a propaganda coup for those seeking to bolster enlistment into the armed forces. Esher wrote in *The Daily Mail* on 4 February:

> We do not want people to go away from the play and merely talk and discuss it in much the same sort of way as the crowd in the play at Brentwood shout and cheer and end by doing nothing. We want some practical, orderly, business-like result to follow from it [. . .] We ask you to get men for the Territorial Army.[29]

An editorial in the same edition proclaimed the need for an extra 100,000 Volunteers and extolled the virtues of du Maurier's play. There followed a 'Territorial Saturday' on 13 February, in which seventeen corps of the London Territorial Force marched through their respective London districts. As a result, over 30,000 fresh recruits signed up in the first two months of 1909.[30] A kind of militaristic hysteria was sweeping the nation as a prelude to the Great War and *An Englishman's Home* was very much a part of it. 'It is certain', claimed *The Times*, 'that the fortunate increase in number of recruits would not have been recorded had it not been for the production of a play at Wyndham's Theatre'.[31]

Rather ironically, at one point, a short-lived ban had been placed on the actual play itself. This had been imposed for fear of offending Germany and was only lifted because of military influence within the Lord Chamberlain's office from the likes of the Comptroller of Plays, Douglas Dawson, and from Viscount Haldane. Once the anti-German sentiment of the play had been softened by changing a few names from the explicitly Teutonic to the more amorphous 'Nearland' and 'Empire of the North', then it was passed for performance without any further concern that it might 'cause offence to a friendly power'.[32] In fact, such was the offence caused by the performance of *An Englishman's Home* in Berlin in April 1909 that, rather unsurprisingly, it had to close after one night.[33] The main thrust of the play was well understood - a caution against the military un-preparedness of Britain in the face of a ruthless and over-mighty Germany.[34] Significantly, as Steve Nicholson has pointed out in his definitive history, *The Censorship of British Drama (1900–1968)* , Douglas Dawson was himself 'an active member of the National Defence Association and in favour of universal voluntary service; so, he was undoubtedly very sympathetic to the propagandist message of the play'.[35] In this context, *The Follies* parody would have been regarded in the corridors of power as most unpatriotic and unwelcome and its consequent ban probably inevitable.

The Pélissier sketch might equally have drawn the Lord Chamberlain's attention because it touched upon that other sensitive political issue, immigration. The essential device of his satire was to conflate the two issues of a potential German military invasion and of the actual presence of thousands of German migrants already living and working in Britain. Thus, Pélissier sought to ridicule what he saw as the fear-laden implications of the play with the notion that a friendly invasion of sorts had already occurred, and furthermore that these diverse communities were living in peaceful co-existence. With the announcement of the ban, a division of opinion immediately opened up between the various national and provincial newspapers, either in support of du Maurier's play and the right of the censor to ban anything that mocked it or conversely in support of Pélissier's satire. *The Morning Post*, for example, declared that 'It is undesirable that a play of such serious import should be made the subject of a jest'.[36] *The Daily Graphic* took a different view and wrote sarcastically:

> Once again, the censor of plays has asserted himself. Having safeguarded the Anglo-Japanese alliance by forbidding for a time the performance of 'The Mikado' he is now strengthening the national defences by taking the Territorials under his motherly wing. It is not easy to see how a five-minute burlesque of 'An Englishman's Home' could have endangered our foreign relations.[37]

The Daily Mail on 25 February sounded a more neutral tone: 'The reason for refusing a licence is not quite clear [. . .] The reader of plays, however, is understood to have said that any stage performance likely to cause offence to a foreign power had best be left unperformed and that therefore the skit on 'An Englishman's Home' had best be left unperformed'.[38]

'Let us play it!'

Pélissier was undeterred. In a deliberate and provocative defiance of the ban, *The Follies* raised the curtain at the Apollo Theatre and, on 1 March 1909, presented a bowdlerized version of their sketch. Unfortunately, since the original script was never actually requested or read by the Examiner of Plays it is not among those manuscripts that can be found in the Lord Chamberlain's collection at the British Library, nor have any other transcriptions survived. However, we can piece together an impression from the several press reports of the time. This too presents some difficulty as none of the original written dialogue was actually delivered, which was almost certainly a deliberate ploy on Pélissier's part in order to avoid prosecution both for himself and the management of the Apollo.[39] Extraordinarily, of those reports

Figure 19. Cartoon representation of the set from The Follies' parody of An Englishman's Home

that survive, the fullest account of the sketch's opening scene was provided by an American newspaper, *The New York Sun,* for H.G. Pélissier was by now even making front-page news in the United States. The old transatlantic rivalry seems to have fueled the relish with which the Americans viewed the discomfiture of a British imperial state that they clearly regarded as both less than democratic in nature and diminishing in power:

LONDON MOCKS AT CENSOR/ A BEHIND THE CURTAIN SKIT ON "AN ENGLISHMAN'S HOME"/ The English censor of stage plays has come in for such an amount of unmerciful public chaffing that if his office depended upon the suffrage of the people it would cease to-morrow. SUN readers have already been told how he placed a ban on a skit on the patriotic play "An Englishman's Home". Not only did the Examiner of plays proscribe the particular skit for which a license was sought but he expressly intimated to the author and chief actor that no burlesque of any sort of "An Englishman's Home" would be tolerated. The result has been an entertainment at the Apollo Theatre that has set all London rocking with laughter. Mr. Pélissier, the chieftain of 'The Follies', whose mission is to amuse London by presenting 'potted plays' – skits on current stage pieces – has scored off the censor with excellent effect. His latest exploit took the form of a travesty on the censor's ban. Stepping before the curtain the other evening he began: Though I am a patriot/ There's a play I must not pot/ And went on humorously explaining to the audience how deeply his company regretted to be barred from performing it. "Even now," he said, "they urge me to produce it and . . ." Then the unexpected happened. From behind the curtain a great cry arose from the massed voices of "The Follies." "Let us play it!" they cried. "Let us play it!"/ Mr. Pélissier, in an agony of alarm, cast his eye around the house as if seeking an ambushed censor, and then turned his attention to his mutinous company. He thrust his head through the opening in the curtains, but withdrew it speedily, for the boom of a canon rang out, followed by a crash of shell and the rattle of musketry. In vain he appealed for silence, the bombardment and the shouting behind the curtain continued. Through an opening in the draperies the screaming audience caught sight of an agitated crowd wearing weird foreign military uniforms and of a burning villa. At last, the shouts and shots ceased. Mr. Pélissier fell wounded in the arms of a gold laced invader as the curtain parted, disclosing all that was left of Britannia Villa. There were great yawning gaps in the walls, the garden paths were strewn with furniture. Only a flowerpot remained standing straight with traditional British stolidity in the foreground. A notice board proclaimed that the villa was to let, "Apply to 'The Follies'." During the entire episode, perhaps more amusing than the banned parody itself, the audience never ceased roaring with laughter. It is the biggest joke in town.[40]

This review surely underlines just how daring, playful and improvisatory Pélissier could be. It subverts the notion of a supposedly strait-laced, 'respectable' Edwardian public. This is an audience that exhibits howls of laughter when unexpectedly greeted not only with canon fire, musket shot and an invading army, but a stage set that is apparently on fire! The lead article in *The Daily Telegraph* of 2 March 1909 reported that 'A more hilarious evening was never, perhaps, spent in a London theatre!'. It too gave a lengthy description of the performance, for which it states incidentally that there was no prior billing in the theatre programme – probably a discreet precaution taken in order to avoid forewarning the censor and thus risking closure.[41]

The Daily News of 2 March 1909 reported the occasion thus, offering some more details and insights on the performance:

> Britannia Villa is a jerry-built house at Hampstead. It is full of aliens who are supposed to be making merry on lager, beer, sausages, and other delicacies. Suddenly, the invasion 'arrives'. Parts of the house fall, and on the backs are written legends such as 'Made in Germany' [. . .] Rushing inside, the attacking party recognize the occupants as their long-lost relatives. 'We have come to take England' they cry. But the besieged party reply 'You are too late; we have taken England years ago' [. . .] Eventually everybody is quite happy, the invaders decide to settle down in England because it would be cheaper than fighting.[42]

Nicholas Hiley sums up the overall effect and apparent intention of the spoof:

> The England which the 'Follies' presented was far removed from that of Guy du Maurier's dark vision. Where 'An Englishman's Home' showed a nation under siege, the Follies' burlesque portrayed a cosmopolitan country already rich in cultural difference [. . .] where the original play saw only racial decay and national decline in foreign contacts, the parody offered a happy co-existence.[43]

As Pélissier said himself in dismissive contempt, and clearly mystified by the ban of his potted play:

> I did not doubt for a moment that this little skit on the subject of foreign inhabitants of London would amuse rather than offend foreign countries [. . .] And as regards our attitude towards Germany (if that is the Lord Chamberlain's objection) I may mention that I could not possibly tend myself to any hostile attitude towards that country. My father is German born.[44]

We would have to fast-forward half a century to the appearance of Lenny Bruce at Peter Cook's night-club, The Establishment, for an equally impacting satirical event,[45] and one that would so undermine the credibility and authority of the Lord Chamberlain's office. The press had a field day. *The Star* ran the following headline: 'FOLLIES OUT-FOLLIED/ RIDICULOUS POSITION OF THE CENSOR'S DEPARTMENT'[46] and, on 2 March 1909, it described the performance thus:

> [. . .] the firing continued, otherwise nothing happened – save the audience overwhelmed the Censor's grotesque pronouncement with mighty guffaws of laughter.[47]

Pélissier had performed his 'potted play' by *not* performing it. It was an audacious and inspired act of genius on his part. Pure Dada. More akin to a *Goon Show* or *Monty Python* sketch than anything by his contemporaries. He had made the government look ridiculous with banner headlines of hostile derision and 'with mighty guffaws of laughter'. This was something a politician must surely dread more than anything else – and Pélissier knew it.

'Castigator ridendo'

On 6 March 1909, *The Illustrated London News* published an extensive polemic by G.K. Chesterton that lambasted the government on Pélissier's behalf:

> The Censor of Plays has solemnly written to the manager of that excellent entertainment 'The Follies' in the following immortal and marmoreal words, that no skit upon 'An Englishman's Home' will be passed by the Lord Chamberlain. When I read this of course, my first impression was that the Censor had suddenly perceived with a roar of laughter, how silly his position had always been, and had resolved to end it with one quick pantomime outrage which nobody would be likely to stand. He feels that the best way of abolishing his own grotesque and painful position is to use his own authority against itself. Thus, one fancies, a good Republican might deliberately be a bad king. And so Mr Redford has resolved to do something more wild and witty than anything that has come from Mr. Bernard Shaw. Dramatists can only satirise the thing in theory: Mr. Redford may parody it in practice [. . .] They may very well exchange names, Mr. Pélissier is a real and valuable public critic, a healthy castigator ridendo, a vigilant intelligence which pounces on preposterous attitudes and poisonous affectations. Mr. Pélissier is the Censor, a real censor morum, a guardian of good sense and decency.[48]

Almost immediately, the new Prime Minister, Herbert Asquith, set up a Joint Select Committee to review the law on censorship and the role of the Lord Chamberlain's office. Clearly, this was not simply a belated response to the letter of protest to *The Times* of October 1907, signed by so many distinguished mainstream authors; nor to the further deputation of February 1908 to the Home Office, including a petition against censorship signed by Winston Churchill, Sydney and Beatrice Webb and Max Beerbohm, among others.[49] It seems clear that the public scandal that followed in the wake of *The Follies* performance on 1 March 1909 was the catalyst for this turn of events. In the House of Commons, Robert Harcourt MP, an outspoken supporter of *The Follies,* had made a great deal of the censor's ban on their parody of *An Englishman's Home* in his previously quoted letter *to The Times.* He was, indeed, the most vociferous proponent of reform, and it was perhaps largely through his endeavors that official action was finally taken. George Bernard Shaw certainly thought him the principal protagonist, and thus by implication he acknowledged the importance of H.G. Pélissier. Shaw makes particular mention of the ban on Pélissier's parody in his *Preface* to *The Shewing-up of Blanco Posnet*[50] and in a section sub-headed *Why the Government Intervened,* he makes the following observation:

> The censorship scandal had existed for years without any parliamentary action being taken in the matter and might have existed for many more had it not happened in 1906

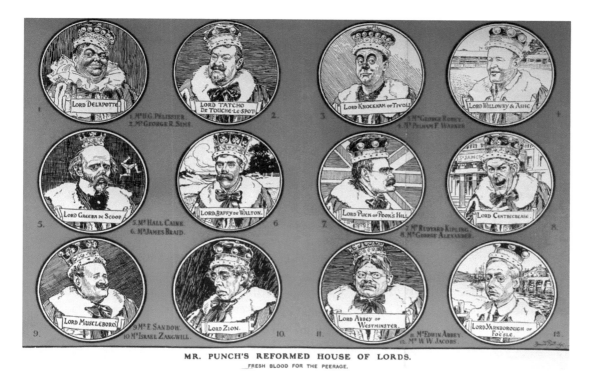

Figure 20: Punch cartoon, 1911. H.G. Pélissier as 'Lord Delapotte' (top left) alongside such notable dignitaries as Rudyard Kipling and Hall Caine in a satirical, alternative House of Lords

that Mr Robert Harcourt entered parliament as a member of the Liberal Party. [. . .] Mr Harcourt informed his leaders he was going to take up the subject of the censorship.[51]

The Committee first convened on 29 July 1909, consisting of five members each of the House of Commons and the House of Lords. It was to meet 12 times in all and to summon forth 49 witnesses, almost exclusively from the mainstream, legitimate theatre. Significantly perhaps, and true to form, hardly a single voice from the world of music hall or variety was interviewed for their opinion (with the exception of the 'respectable' Oswald Stoll) and certainly not from its lower echelons. Steve Nicholson sums up their conclusion as follows:

> Surprisingly, the Committee ultimately produced a series of recommendations which might have gone a considerable way towards ushering in a new era [. . .] It was rather the fact that no legislation was subsequently enacted to turn these recommendations into practice which meant that the system remained essentially the same.[52]

Clearly, Harry Pélissier had come incredibly close – closer than anyone before him – to bringing down the entire house of cards. For what emerges as the main bone of contention in this parliamentary report is the role of the music halls. They, after all, had a free hand to perform what they liked, independent of the regulations that bound the mainstream theatres. It was their position that had made the law seem so asinine. A *Daily Mail* article[53] went to the very heart of the matter. It quoted the current law which allowed any stage work under forty minutes long and with less than a cast of six to be performed without a licence in what were termed 'music halls', while the mainstream, legitimate, licensed theatre was quite another matter. All works performed there – including at Wyndham's or the Apollo – were subject to the censor's scrutiny and required a licence. In other words, Harry Pélissier was perfectly free to take his sketch on to Oxford Street or Tottenham Court Road, into the Alhambra or Collins Music Hall – but it was illegal to perform it on the West End stage. This contradiction lay at the heart of the consequent public furore, at the tabling of questions in Parliament and in the calling of the Joint Select Committee on censorship that met in July 1909. This 'untenable' distinction, as Robert Harcourt dubbed it, between a Theatre and a Music Hall, was 'sheer chaos'.[54]

The Lord Chamberlain's office called it 'the vexed question of Dramatic sketches in Music-Hall'.[55] The Chair of the Committee, Herbert Samuel MP, then also Chancellor of the Duchy of Lancaster, expressed the view that 'These dramatic sketches are themselves objectionable as being representations of either unlicensed stage plays or of condensed and mutilated versions [. . .] and they tend to create a degraded taste for hurried frivolity and brainless Drama'.[56] Plainly, he is referring directly to *The Follies* and what Pélissier called his 'potted plays', or 'condensed and mutilated versions' as Samuel puts it. However, as a leading witness to the Committee, the renowned impresario Oswald Stoll is quoted as saying in the Report: 'The Lord Chamberlain does not want, and does not intend, to be drawn into a policy of prosecuting them [the music halls]'.[57] Or, as the Comptroller in the Lord Chamberlain's office, Sir Douglas Dawson, put it: 'The public interest is to divide the theatre from the music-hall [. . .] people who go to a theatre are loyally composed of a different class to those who go to a music-hall [. . .] and I think it is well to retain that distinction'.[58]

This 'distinction' was the very one that Pélissier had disregarded and worked against throughout his entire working life. Furthermore, it is a 'distinction' that his very success had proved to be illusory. In the song 'What A Very Great Improvement It Would Be' he includes the following verse, which is quite specific in its intent:

> *If this sketch dispute was settled up and ended*
> *What a very great improvement it would be!*
> *If the Theatres and Music Halls were blended*
> *What a very great improvement it would be!*
> *If we put an end to all this petty malice*
> *And George Robey would combine with Mr. Tree*
> *And do a Triple Bar Act at the Palace*
> *What a very great improvement that would be!*[59]

That *The Follies* were quite brazen in their contempt for 'respectability' and for the censor's office is also made clear by this mock disclaimer that was included as part of their Apollo programme:

Extract from Rules of the Lord Chamberlain. The Management earnestly solicit the co-operation of the audience in bringing to their notice any item they may consider inside the bounds of propriety or otherwise objectionable.[60]

His entire output, his burlesques and 'potted plays', his end-of-pier shows and West End revues were all overtly disreputable and entirely aimed at drawing in a mixture of backgrounds and classes and as diverse an audience as possible. *The Follies* played in music halls just as comfortably as they performed on Shaftesbury Avenue or before royalty. But in the very act of dismantling these cultural and social barriers, so came the inevitable consequence that they threw the law into disrepute and the Government and its Select Committee and the Lord Chamberlain's office into confusion.

Virginia Woolf memorably wrote with regard to the London exhibition of paintings by Manet and the Post-Impressionists that had been organized by her friends and associates Clive Bell and Roger Fry, that: 'On or about December 1910, human character changed'.[61] In fact, it had been changing for some while, and Harry Pélissier and his *Follies* had been playing their own significant part in that change. It would be called 'Modernity'. Sadly, the advent of the Great War was to hold a great many of these advances in check for a half century. For the ensuing decade it was du Maurier's militaristic jingoism that was to hold sway. On 7 August 1914, two days after the declaration of war, members of the Cinematograph Exhibitors' Association wrote to the Home Secretary that they would act 'to prevent the exhibition of any films calculated by their character to create a ferment of alarm in the public mind'.[62] The following month, a film version of *An Englishman's Home* by the British and Colonial Film Company went into production at London Studios. It was explicitly anti-German this time and passed for public release by the censor in October 1914. The Lord Chamberlain had won this particular battle and, in fact, with enhanced wartime restrictions the hand of the censor became even heavier; yet another reason perhaps why the name of Harry Pélissier slipped into virtual obscurity. Nicholas Hiley draws a fair conclusion:

The new wave of belligerent patriotism cried out for parody, just as that of 1909 had done, but now there was no reply, for sadly Pélissier had died in September 1913 and in the heat of wartime there was no one to take his place.[63]

In 1912, the Lord Chamberlain conceded that licences would be granted to music halls under his jurisdiction within the general spirit of the 1896 theatre managers' agreement.[64] This represented, in effect, an extension to the existing law of censorship. This was hardly a reform in the direction that Pélissier would have endorsed. However, that it should have come about so relatively quickly after the controversy over *The Follies'* sketch at the Apollo it is surely testimony to his status as a satirist.

G.B. Shaw and H.G. Pélissier

Bernard Shaw came to lament the acknowledged failure of his own considerable efforts, not to say dedication, to the cause of achieving reform of theatre censorship in Britain. In later years he was to write: 'Nobody pays any attention to my solution of the censorship question'.[65] In his biography of Shaw, Michael Holroyd goes on to argue that this failure of democratic, parliamentary means influenced the distinguished playwright towards the direction of violent revolution. 'It made an end for me of the claim of the majority to be taken seriously [. . .] the whole ridiculous transaction was a lesson to me on the futility of treating a parliamentary body with scrupulous courtesy and consideration instead of bullying them and giving them as much trouble as possible'.[66]

It may have been with some envy that he looked upon the relatively greater success of Harry Pélissier and his particular brand of discourteous troublemaking in advancing the reformist cause. He certainly knew of *The Follies*, as is clear from his reference in the preface to *The Shewing Up of Blanco Posnet*. He also attended at least one of their shows, as witnessed by Compton Mackenzie, Pélissier's co-lyricist. In his memoirs he recalls meeting Shaw backstage after a performance of a *Follies'* sketch entitled *Self-Consciousness or the Fourth Wall*, a satire on Shaw's work by Mackenzie himself, in which the great playwright was portrayed on stage. Mackenzie reports that Shaw complained he had been played with a strong Irish accent, whereas he believed himself to possess not a trace.[67] From the surviving programme notes he would appear to have been portrayed by Dan Everard in the role of William Pare, 'President of the Society for the Prevention of Cruelty to Vegetables', a highly Shavian-sounding body (see Figure 21). Pélissier meanwhile had to be content with the role of 'Ibsen's Ghost'. The brazen destruction of 'the fourth wall', both satirically and stylistically and the pursuit of a direct, improvised connection with the audience was a huge part of what *The Follies* sought to offer. Both G.B. Shaw and J.T. Grien, founder of the Independent Theatre Society and a passionate exponent of Ibsen's work, seem to have enjoyed this joke at their own expense.[68]

In March 1909, immediately after the performance of the skit on *An Englishman's Home*, Shaw began his own ventures into writing one-act plays and sketches in a similar vein, of which *The Shewing Up of Blanco Posnet* is the first example. It was quickly followed by *Press Cuttings*, which seems to draw heavily on the Pélissier style. In that particular piece, the Prime Minister (a thinly disguised Herbert Asquith) appears in drag, bearing the comedic name of Balsquith alongside a certain General Mitchener. The influence of music hall and Pélissier's 'potted plays' is evident and, in fact, the work was first publicly performed at a variety theatre in Manchester in August of that year. It is interesting to speculate just how much of an influence H.G. Pélissier may have been on the style of Shaw's later years; intriguing also to note that the actor playing Balsquith was a certain Leon Quartermaine, who would later become the third husband of Harry's widow, Fay Compton. The theatre world of the early twentieth century was a small one indeed.

PÉLISSIER'S POTTED PLAYS.

"BABY MINE"
(COMPTON MACKENZIE).

Zoey ...	...	...	...	... EFFIE COOK
Jim ...	...	...	...	LEWIS SYDNEY
Alfred ...	...	...	...	...DAN EVERARD
Aggie ...	...	...	...	MURIEL GEORGE
Baby Mine	...	...	...	H. G. PÉLISSIER

"No. 37" A Grand Guignol Thrill
(MORRIS HARVEY).

Clifford Borax ...	...	...	MORRIS HARVEY
Milly Stoll-tour (a *Variety Artiste*) (pronounced Stullter)	...		H. G. PÉLISSIER
Nellie Kennington (*Borax's Cousin*)	...		ETHEL ALLANDALE
William Smith (*an Italian Government Clerk*)			...DAN EVERARD
Lieut. Clinton ...	...	...	... BEN
Miss Loofah ...	...	...	... EFFIE COOK
1st Guest ...	...	...	DOUGLAS MACLAREN
2nd Guest ...	...	...	PETER UPCHER
Other Guests ...	MURIEL GEORGE, DOLLIS BROOKE,		
	ETHEL FENTON and FAY COMPTON		

"SELF-CONSCIOUSNESS, or THE FOURTH WALL"
(COMPTON MACKENZIE).

William Pare (*President of the Society for the Prevention of Cruelty to Vegetables*)		...DAN EVERARD
Spitz Bergen (*a Pomeranian Feminist*) ...		MORRIS HARVEY
Jim Nasium (*a Rhodes Scholar and Prussian Blue*) ...	...	DOUGLAS MACLAREN
Colonel Philip Bertram Nutt (*a Militarist*)		LEWIS SYDNEY
Spook (*formerly a fast Bowler, now a Medium*)		PETER UPCHER
Mrs. Peace (*a Member of the Anti-Man Society*)		MURIEL GEORGE
Olla Podrida (*a Portuguese Dancer*)	...	... EFFIE COOK
Charlotte Russe (*a Montenigger Refugee*) ...		...FAY COMPTON
Gladys (*a Victim of Vivisection*)	...	ETHEL ALLANDALE
The Ghost of Ibsen	...	...	H. G. PÉLISSIER

"KISMET"
(MORRIS HARVEY, COMPTON MACKENZIE & H. G. PÉLISSIER).

Cadj (*the Beggar*) ...	...	...	H. G. PÉLISSIER
Wazir Mansur ...	...	...	MORRIS HARVEY
The Caliph (*Son*) } The Shriek (*Father*) }	...	...	LEWIS SYDNEY
Nasir (*the Guide*) ...	...	...	...DAN EVERARD
Kaffir (*Egyptian*) ...	...	...	PETER UPCHER
Marsinah	...	...	...FAY COMPTON
Narjis (*Old Nurse*) ...	...	...	MURIEL GEORGE
Kut-ul-Kulub ...	...	...	... EFFIE COOK
Tailors...	...	...	... BEN AND DICK
Singers	DOUGLAS MACLAREN AND ETHEL ALLANDALE		

Figure 21. An Apollo programme of 1910. The Folies' parody of G.B. Shaw is entitled 'Self-Consciousness or The Fourth Wall'

8

The Impresario

Figure 22. The Follies, 1903 postcard

Exploiting the notoriety

It might be wondered that the impresario and business manager in Pélissier, and indeed Tom Davis the Apollo manager, did not have greater anxiety about the possible financial cost of legal proceedings or closure as a result of this controversy. In fact, the impresario in Pélissier tended to recognize the financial opportunities presented by the publicity. In a string of court injunctions that included actions by the authors of *The Whip*, a melodrama in production at Drury Lane theatre, and most notably by George Edwardes in respect of music copyright regarding both *The Merry Widow* and *The Girls of Gottenberg*, Pélissier had already displayed a phlegmatic sense of business acumen. The latter disputes were settled out of court, but the resulting press publicity meant that *The Follies* played to packed houses for weeks afterwards, Pélissier accounting a net gain of over a thousand pounds.[1] Indeed it was not unknown for Pelissier's 'potted plays' to prove popular with the casts of the very shows he lampooned.[2]

Despite – or indeed perhaps because of – the controversy with the Lord Chamberlain, *The Follies* remained in permanent, uninterrupted residence at the Apollo for almost another three years, until 23 December 1911, and then again after several months of provincial touring, from 28 October to 7 December 1912.[3] Their 500th performance on 13 February 1910 was widely covered in the press, not least because the Prime Minister Herbert Asquith chose to mark the occasion by being in attendance that same week.[4] This was an extraordinary length of run for a West End show, given that, as John Pick has pointed out, during the entire course of the first decade of the twentieth century only 39 shows ran for over 300 performances.[5]

In fact, since taking over the Baddeley Troupe in 1895, Pélissier had led his fellow players on an epic journey out of the sporting clubs of London, on to the piers and promenades of almost every seaside resort in the land and then into the heart of the West End and a command performance at Sandringham Palace. He had shown considerable business acumen in his hiring of the New Royalty theatre and in the company's subsequent progression to Terry's and the Apollo. The budding young composer and sketch-writer was now proving to be quite an exceptional and pioneering theatrical entrepreneur. By this time, after the erratic cast changes of the earlier years, Pélissier had put together a more or less permanent company. The regular male performers were Lewis Sydney and Morris Harvey – who had both begun their careers as straight actors in the legitimate theatre[6] – and Dan Everard, who also acted as something of an accountant-cum-paymaster and would in time take over the management entirely following Pélissier's death. Among the female *Follies*, Ethel Allandale remained a mainstay from the early years, to be joined by Muriel George, Gwennie Mars and Effie Cook.[7] These regular players might be replaced or supplemented from time to time by other performers, but Pélissier had largely succeeded in creating a settled revue-style cast.

What's more, *The Follies* concert and music-hall performances were, broadly speaking, affordable to a wide audience. As a business manager, Pélissier would have been well aware that he had gained his initial followers in the seaside concert venues and music halls and would not wish to lose them. Ticket prices for the music hall could range from six pence for a seat at the Canterbury Hall, to one shilling for the stalls at the South London Palace of Varieties or two shillings and sixpence for a seat and meal at the Oxford Music Hall.[8] This was at a time when ticket prices in a licensed West End theatre could range from five shillings to ten shillings and sixpence, while the average working wage was one pound ten shillings a week.[9] Admittedly, Pélissier was playing the higher class of music halls, away from the cheaper penny gaffs and free-and-easies, which would have provided the staple fare for the poorer lower-paid working-class audiences of the time. For it is clear that, even within the world of the music hall, there was a certain hierarchy of status reflected in the quality of acts and the nature of the clientele, as was noted at the time[10] (see page 23).

Performing as he did at the Alhambra, the Palace, the Tivoli and other music halls in and around the West End, Pélissier may be said to have graduated to the smarter, upper strata of venues. Nevertheless, *The Follies* did venture into the less fashionable suburban and provincial halls. Their seaside appearances on the piers and in the concert halls of holiday resorts would have attracted a wide range of every class of audience, particularly where they had been appearing alfresco on the strands and promenades. Ticket prices for *The Follies'* shows in the provincial concert halls could range from one shilling to three shillings,[11] but otherwise might even rely on the collection of donations, known as 'bottling'.[12] Once *The Follies* had moved on to the more established music halls, their ticket prices mirrored those of the licensed establishments such as the Savoy, which at one time was offering Gilbert and Sullivan's *The Gondoliers* for two shillings and sixpence in the pit,[13] exactly the same as a ticket to see Pélissier in a crowded pit at the Tivoli.[14]

Financial accounts show the steady upward trajectory of *The Follies'* earning capacity. In 1903, for example, a single evening's performance at Queen's Hall in Wood Green on 24 January produced takings of 3s 11d, while in Tunbridge Wells on 28 February just 1s 10d. The yearly total is accounted at £133 13s 0d. In 1904 this rose to a total of £190 3s 6d, the following year to £208 17s 0d. and in 1906 to £274 13s 4d. However, by the time of their run at the Manchester Midland Hotel in January 1907, they were taking considerably more at £6 per night. Their first week in January 1908 at the Apollo theatre produced box office returns of £1,000 rising to £1,500 by the third week of the season.[15] Indeed, such was their success that for a time *The Follies* were able to run a sister company (variously named *The Ragamuffins or Follies Two*), either based at the Manchester Midland Hotel or travelling on tour while the main company continued its run at the London Apollo.[16]

By this time Pélissier was running a flat at 45 Pall Mall as well as the large house in Grove End, Finchley. He was also in possession of two Daimler motor cars, which were often used to transport *The Follies* on their provincial tours, and of a custom-designed Metallurgique car for his own personal use. Sophie Nield suggests that Wilkie Bard, himself a frequent target of *The Follies'* satire, was 'positively the first pierrot to be earning £100' by 1912, but it seems clear that he had a predecessor in Pélissier earning considerably more.[17] His management had placed the company on a completely different financial footing from the days of 'bottling' on the sands of Margate. This in turn meant that they could afford the services of a regular piano accompanist in the form of Louis Laval. In addition to this, a small orchestra was engaged for the Apollo performances, along with the occasional services of conductor–arranger Herman Finck[18] plus a permanent stage manager, Bobby Innes, and a team of three general handy-men-cum-set-builders, and Pélissier's own personal dresser. From 1906 they were also able to employ the services of a dedicated business manager called William Albert with an assistant Frank Huntley, who were responsible for advertising and promotion.[19] The

Figure 23. H.G. Pélissier in his customised Metallurgique

widespread use of posters, often of an absurdist and intriguing nature – such as that by Geoffrey Holme (see Figure 2) featuring a mythical tengee monster dressed in pyjamas[20] – were an essential part of Pélissier's business strategy along with the use of the comical programmes full of visual jokes and spoof advertising that formed an integral part of the evening's entertainment.[21]

As Pélissier had played relatively sophisticated material in music halls, the question remained as to whether the same material could transfer to the legitimate, licensed theatres, and whether a section of the music-hall audience would follow him into those establishments. By the time Pélissier took out his first lease on a West End theatre (at the New Royalty) the reviewer for the *Clarion* rather thought, and perhaps hoped, that they might: 'There's no reason why music hall patrons should not visit the New Royalty – a first step towards reform'.[22] Pélissier's friend and biographer Fitzroy Gardner bears witness that they succeeded in doing precisely that when he states: '*The Follies* have been drawing crowded audiences, representing all classes, to one of the principal West End theatres of London'.[23] The greater mixing of social classes was, of course, not due to the efforts of just one single producer or company. It was rather a process in which Pélissier and *The Follies* had a significant part to play by further developing, as they did, the music-hallisation of theatre. Dave Russell has pointed out with regard to Victorian popular entertainment that 'from about the 1840's, can be identified [. . .] a much larger audience and a widening of its social base'. He goes on:

> [. . .] the music hall audience can be characterized as largely young, [. . .] predominantly male, [. . .] and working class. [. . .] Other social groups were certainly represented, from 'bohemian' army officers, medical students and city gentlemen to shopkeepers,

tradesmen and their wives [. . .] However, the key to maximization lay in attracting that large body of 'respectable' society spanning the upper working class to the middle reaches of the middle class, which had previously largely eschewed the halls.[24]

By taking his music hall act into the West End, Pélissier was arguably making a mainstream licensed venue more openly inviting to the lower classes, while at the same time appealing to a higher-class audience that might be reluctant to attend a music hall. As Russell has pointed out, for this period: 'National attendance statistics do not exist'.[25] Hence the precise make-up of *The Follies'* audience is difficult to ascertain. However, as he had played *al fresco* and on piers and in concert halls on the provincial seaside coast, had played in established music halls and variety theatres, as well as to royalty and political and social dignitaries, and then had established himself in a mainstream theatre in the West End, it would seem that Pélissier as much as anyone had contributed both to the broadening base and to the increased sophistication of popular entertainment. To this we can add the witness of one of his most enthusiastic admirers, the dramaturg and critic J.T. Grein. He it was who had first introduced Henrik Ibsen to a London audience by way of his Independent Theatre Society in 1891, and of Pélissier he had this to say: 'The more I see The Follies, the fonder I grow of their gentle arts, their unflagging inspiration, their wonderful vitality [. . .] the man at the helm, Pélissier, is not merely a *metteur-en-scene* but a clever dramatist, composer and actor'.[26] Grien's returning presence in the audience seems to suggest that Pélissier may also have tapped into that element of the more serious-minded theatre-going audience that favoured the new drama of Ibsen, Shaw and Har-

Figure 24. The Follies at the Apollo Theatre

ley Granville Barker.[27] Furthermore, they seem to have been able to enjoy a joke at their own expense (see Chapter 7, note 68). *The Follies* clearly had a wide appeal.

An unusual photograph, taken during this period from the stage of the Apollo Theatre from a viewpoint behind the cast, that includes a standing Pélissier and four seated *Follies*, reveals a packed house with as many women in attendance as men.[28] Some male figures in the stalls are in evening dress, but many appear in daywear with jackets and straight ties (see Figure 24). As we examine the dress code in the upper circles the attire seems to become more casual. This in itself cannot verify the broad range of *The Follies'* audience but, taken into consideration with the other factors, it lends further credibility to the claim. To this we can add the contemporary testimony of Gardner: 'To my own knowledge every member of the present cabinet has visited the theatre [*i.e.* the Apollo], with two exceptions – some more than once'.[29] Similarly, as has been previously noted, in both costume and design, Pélissier had begun to move the company away from the strict confines of the pierrot concert party. Photographs of the time depict *The Follies* adopting specific character costumes,[30] while their sketches began to involve more elaborate set designs, thus signalling their intention to be regarded as more of a mainstream theatrical company. At the same time, they retained a certain informality in dropping the 'Mister' and 'Miss' in the cast titles of their programme notes, then still the convention in mainstream theatre.

9

The Composer

Figure 25. H.G. Pélissier at the piano by Norman Morrow

'Harry lived and breathed music'

The artistic rebel, the satirist, the pierrot clown, the impresario – these were among the many roles that Harry Pélissier adopted during the course of his short life. However, the one true constant was his love of music and his vocation as a composer.

> After the supper, at which the host himself carved with a tremendous gusto [. . .] we adjourned to a room that seemed full of grand pianos [. . .] We wrestled with rhythms until five or six o'clock of a Sunday morning, when I was allowed to go to bed. At half past eight Pélissier's face rose like a sun above the foot of my bed; he was wrapped in a brilliantly coloured dressing gown. 'Aren't you up *yet?*' he exclaimed, 'Look here, come into my room, I've got a new tune.' I followed him and found another piano at the foot of his bed.[1]

In this extract from his autobiography, Compton Mackenzie is describing his first visit to Elm House, Pélissier's home in Finchley. In fact, Harry Pélissier had at least one piano in every room, in order that he might be able to instantly transcribe any tune that came into his head. On stage, he famously played an especially constructed grand piano with a keyboard on both sides, which was playfully regarded as *The Follies'* mascot[2] (see Figure 26). Harry was as passionate about music and about playing the piano as he was about his comic writing; if not more so. It was at the piano that he made his first ventures into music hall at Peckham and Marylebone with compositions like 'A Dog Song' and 'Mein Faderland', early pieces that remained part of *The Follies'* repertoire throughout his career. It was at the piano that he scored his biggest comedic hits with sharp parodies of Wagner and 'Take-offski'.[3] In all, he had published well over 60 songs and quite probably devised dozens more unpublished and impromptu numbers that have unfortunately not survived. It was at the piano that he proposed to Fay Compton, improvising a comic duet that expressed his marital intentions. And he applied himself diligently to the task of composition. In her memoir *Rosemary*, Fay Compton goes on to point out that it was his habit to work late into the night, only to re-surface feverishly at dawn to work on a new tune or lyric:

> [. . .] at any time of the day or night one was likely to be wakened by the sound of a piano, an organ, a spinet, or some unknown instrument, for Harry slept so badly he often spent more than half the night playing and improvising. [. . .] Harry lived and breathed music; when not rehearsing, writing, designing, acting, or at work on business management, he was composing. It was a dreadful pity that so much of a really high order that he created was lost for lack of time to write it down; the constant demand of the ever-changing Folly bills made it practically impossible for him to do more than provide for these a never-failing supply of ballads, concerted numbers, accompaniments for the quartettes and incidental music for the potted plays and burlesques. Life was a melody with an ever-changing accompaniment, and one motif followed another with a bewildering rapidity; the time was crowded with work and play so intermingled as to become almost indistinguishable, for work was play and play was work in those days.[4]

The variety of his output was equally extraordinary, ranging from savage pastiche to witty satire, anarchic whimsy to dance numbers and poignantly moving love ballads. N.T.P. Murphy in *The New Dictionary of National Biography*, while rightly acknowledging him as the leading satirist of the day, rather misleadingly does him a disservice when he claims he merely composed 'pastiches of [. . .] ballads [. . .] so accurate that it is difficult for modern readers to distinguish them from the originals'.[5] Yes, Harry composed pastiche; but he also wrote serious love songs in deadly earnest, some of which bear comparison with leading composers of the time, such

Figure 26. Harry's trademark piano with two keyboards

as Arthur Sullivan or Jerome Kern and figures soon to emerge like Ivor Novello and Noel Coward.

Broadly speaking there were five principal influences on his musical work. In the first place there was the steady stream of comic and sentimental songs from the music halls. Second, there were the seaside pierrot shows to which Pélissier became professionally attached. These brought to bear the influence of American cakewalk and ragtime and minstrel songs. Then there was the continental strand of cabaret, to which he would have been exposed during his period of schooling in Switzerland and on his frequent trips to Paris, not to mention through his continental family background. Then, there was the world of classical opera, so ubiquitous in London and provincial theatres throughout the second half of the nineteenth century. In addition to all of these, there were the satirical musical interludes of burlesque that gradually transformed into the fashion for whimsical and sentimental musical comedies, which became particularly popular at the Gaiety and the Lyric theatres around the turn of the century. Pélissier dipped his amateur, untrained hand into all these styles, but, above all, they influenced his passion, his imagination and his dedication, and in so doing they led him to come up with something quite advanced and distinct and original.

The typical music hall composition at the time would often have been a drinking song with a lively chorus that invited audience participation, such as 'Champagne Charlie'; or perhaps a sentimental love ballad like 'The Girl in the Gallery'; or a patriotic marching song such as 'Goodbye Dolly Gray'. As we have seen, when Pélissier first hit the Peckham and Marylebone music halls around 1893 with his anarchic 'A Dog Song', complete with a chorus of canine barking, it was most unexpected and resulted in catcalls and heckling and demands for a drinking song. However, the basic structure employed in that particular piece, of a comic narrative in 16-bar verses with a repeated chorus, was borrowed straight from the music-hall tradition. It was only when Pélissier fell under the wing and the influence of his later mentor, Albert Chevalier, that another influence started to come through in his song writing. As we have seen, with compositions like 'My Old Dutch' and 'Knocked 'Em Down the Old Kent Road', Chevalier had taken the standard music-hall song into a more subtle and character-driven direction. Pélissier would take this a significant stage further with intimately personal songs such as 'I Want Somebody to Love Me'[6] and 'My Boy from Barbary'[7] amongst others.

Though influenced by the music hall, Pélissier's songs were far from typical of that genre, and were at times intended as parodies. Significantly, the leading music-hall acts and panto-mime stars of the day were among the favourite targets of *The Follies*. Gwennie Mars turned her impersonations of Harry Lauder and Wilkie Bard into something of a trademark, while Pélissier himself presented a parody of Gus Elen under the soubriquet 'Gus Squealin'. Similarly, while the current of the times following the Boer War and leading up to the First World War was typified in the music hall by a militarist jingoism, Pélissier had the courage and audacity to present a parody of a sentimental soldier's song entitled 'Give My Love to Mother', a cutting satire on the style made popular by G.H. (The Great) MacDermott[8]:

A regiment ordered to the front
A troop-ship on the tide
A little lad in khaki clad
With a bugle by his side
And as the vessel leaves the shore
Amidst the people's cheers
Across the swell, her boy's farewell
His poor old mother hears
Give my love to Mother, and my regards to Leicester Square
Entreat the folk in Regent Street to spread the glad news there!
And tell my dear old Mother, that she may dry her tears
For I'll never have another Mother if I live ten thousand years!
No!!!!!!
I'll never have another Mother if I live ten thousand years![9]

A further example of Pélissier's use of a character-driven song for satirical effect was 'A Burglar's View of Life'. As previously noted (see Chapter 3), he seems to anticipate the moral relativism of George Bernard Shaw in *Pygmalion* or even Bertold Brecht in *Die Dreigroschenoper* in recognizing the role of poverty as a cause of crime, and sardonically suggests that the judiciary is dependent for a living on the activity of criminals. This in itself was a radical stance. Overtly political material or social criticism was, in general, not a typical strand of music-hall performance.[10] As commercial interests developed and the audience base widened, the accepted view is that variety and music-hall programming tended to become even safer and less daring.[11]

Sophie Nield has described popular entertainment of the period as an 'increasingly *respectable* industry'[12] and she goes on to quote Dave Russell in pointing out that 'the assumption of respectability marked the way ahead'.[13] By contrast, in the context of the time, far from seeking respectability, Pélissier and *The Follies* seem to have sailed deliberately close to the wind and even courted controversy and scandal, perhaps with a view to the very idea of attracting a clientele that was otherwise not catered for, or perhaps for the sheer devilry of it. Pélissier offered up the following anecdote in an interview with *The Strand Magazine* of June 1909:

> I was told once of a man who came to see 'The Follies' regularly every evening for a week. He sat in a front stall, and always wore the same sad smile, no matter how funny we were – or tried to be. At last a friend of mine spoke to him and asked him what he thought of the performance. 'It fascinates me', he said; 'I have never seen anything so sad. Grown men and women, and with absolutely no consciousness of sin.'[14]

What the pierrot and minstrel shows brought to Pélissier's compositional style was the American influence, not merely in the dance rhythms and inflections – most evidently seen in 'The Dandy One-Step',[15] for example, which is a straight 2/2 cakewalk, but also in the subtle use of a more relaxed, idiomatic expression in the lyrics – such as:

> *Pansy of Pennsylvania,*
> *She sailed on the Lusitania,*
> *For she had got a mania*
> *To marry an English Marquis*[16]

Or even in a whimsical, surreal number like 'The Toothbrush and the Sponge':

> *Sponge, sponge, dainty little sponge,*
> *Water juggins you must be!*
> *Don't go too far with that lazy loofah,*
> *can't you be content with me?*[17]

It is important to point out that London in the 1890s and early 1900s was the very hub of the musical comedy industry. It was to London that the Americans looked for hit shows to pack the theatres of Broadway and beyond. It was to London that the young Jerome Kern came in 1903, the better and more creatively to pursue his career. In a curious precedent of Beatlemania of the 1960s, by which the British managed to re-package and modulate American rhythm n' blues in such a way that the Americans hungrily bought it back, and as a kind of premonition of Andrew Lloyd-Weber's musical blockbusters of the succeeding decades (loudly proclaimed as 'The Brits Are Coming'), so Edwardian British musical comedy swept the boards of America.

When the young Jerome Kern stopped off in London between his musical studies in Heidelberg, Germany and New York, he was just 18 years old. Within a year, he had signed up with the American impresario Charles Frohman (the producer of J.M. Barrie's plays), to provide additional songs for the transfer of hit London musical shows to Broadway.[18] Among them were *An English Daisy* by Seymour Hicks (one of H.G. Pélissier's regular targets) and *The Earl and the Girl* by Ivan Caryll, for which he composed his first big hit number 'How D'You Like to Spoon With Me?'[19], a song that is still regularly performed on the variety circuit to this day. From 1905 onwards, he was more or less permanently resident in London, where he contributed songs to *The Beauty of Bath* with lyrics by P.G. Wodehouse. This piece was famously and successfully parodied by H.G. Pélissier,[20] much to the author's discomfort, and there can be little doubt that Kern was aware of Pélissier's work and might well have attended his shows (as did many artists who were the subject of his parodies) if only to discover what the popular satirist had come up with! For all its quaint charm, 'How D'You Like to Spoon With Me?' is a pale shadow of Kern's later works for musical theatre, which culminated in the groundbreaking *Showboat* of 1927. What he would have witnessed at the Apollo Theatre was a step towards just such a more intimate and serious and confessional style of song writing and there is every possibility the experience fed into his work. Kern's acquaintanceship with the Pélissier and Compton families clearly deepened over the subsequent years for, in 1914 he accompanied Fay and her new husband, Lauri de Frece, on their honeymoon trip to Coney Island, New York.[21]

'Bien parisienne'

In addition to the pierrot and minstrel shows, and probably reinforced by his continental family background and schooling, Pélissier was able to draw on the tradition of Parisian cabaret and chansons. He made no bones about this, blatantly stealing the name for his pierrot troupe from the *Folies Bergère*. As Fitzroy Gardner makes plain in his memoir *Pure Folly*, as a company *The Follies* was always intended to create something new and original in the English context, and the introduction of a continental influence was very much a part of that.[22] With his intense interest in all things musical and theatrical, it is entirely likely that Pélissier would have come across the great chanteur Aristide Bruant, regularly performing at *Le Chat Noir* night club in the 1880s and 1890s or later at *Le Lapin Agile*, both located in the bohemian district of Montmartre. With his mix of popular song and satire, Bruant developed his own musical genre of *chanson réaliste*, including such favourites as '*La Chanson des Michetons*', '*Meunier tu es cocu*' and '*Nini Peau d'Chien*',[23] which may well have directly inspired Pelissier's own 'A Dog Song'.

That Pélissier was familiar with the music clubs and theatres of Montmartre is further underscored by a cartoon that features in one of *The Follies* programmes for a show at the Palladium. It invites us to enter 'Pallodiseum' through a grotesque portal that represents the gaping mouth of H.G. Pélissier himself and is a clear parody of the gothic and surreal façade of one of the most outrageously decadent music halls in Paris – *Le Cabaret de L'Enfer*.[24]

In an English context, blended with the aforementioned influences, Pélissier was to create his own unique style of 'realistic song'. We have already looked closely in a previous chapter at the forthright and subversive satire contained in 'A Burglar's View of Life', but there would be many further examples such as 'What a Happy Land Is England!', an ironic and comprehensive de-bunking of the state of the nation that strikingly foreshadows Noel Coward's 'There Are Bad Times Just Around the Corner'.[25] There followed 'Back to the Land',[26] a witty send-up of the Asquith government. This bonding of political and social satire to a traditional and popular musical format owed a great deal to the continental influence, a point not lost on the French press itself:

> *L'idée du programme des 'Follies' est bien parisienne. Ce programme est un mélange de revues et de chansons, et une soirée passé á L'Apollo Theatre rappelle bien un peu la gaieté des cabarets de La Butte, sans grivoiserie gauloise.*[27]

[The idea of the 'Follies' programme is very Parisienne. This programme is a mixture of revue and songs, and an evening spent at the Apollo Theatre recalls to a certain extent the gaiety of the cabarets of *La Butte*, without French sauciness.]

Another aspect of Pélissier's compositional style that underscores its Francophile nature is the close resemblance of some of his pieces to the recently burgeoning classical form of *mélodies françaises*. This very particular genre of French song emerged from the mid-nineteenth century operatic composers like Berlioz and Gounod and found its ultimate flowering in the *Belle Epoque* of the *fin de siècle* and early 1900s. For example, Pélissier's songs 'Alone' and 'Awake' share something of the haunting, idealized intimacy that pervades the concert and chamber works of such composers as Reynaldo Hahn, Jules Massenet and Camille Saint-Saens among others. The distinguished French dramaturg Christophe Ghristi has written:

> [. . .] the French *mélodie* finds [inspiration] in the warmth of the conservatory and in the silken and velvet draperies of the salon. It begins life as a precious artefact, the ideal accoutrement for the character of Eisseintes in Huysman's novel *À rebours*.[28]

This particular novel was of course one of the key risqué works of the aesthetic 'Decadent' movement and, as we shall see, a book that was illicitly passed on to Compton Mackenzie by his Wildean associates Lord Alfred Douglas and Robbie Ross. The musical style of *mélodies françaises* was intimately bound up with this movement and it was these particular pieces from his own canon – 'Alone' and 'Awake!' – that Pélissier chose to perform for his Henry Wood promenade concert appearances at Queen's Hall. In keeping with the French style, both were settings of classic poetic verses – respectively by Heinrich Heine and Sir William Davenant – that speak of love's longing and deathly fears. Reynaldo Hahn was himself a successful singer-songwriter and, like his close friend Marcel Proust, 'a virtuoso creator of pastiche'.[29] It is intriguing to speculate as to whether Harry Pélissier might have come across these fellow spirits on one of his frequent trips to Paris.

The mixing of music and comedy in the mainstream theatre was in itself, of course, nothing new. It had been a staple of mainstream Victorian and Edwardian theatre since the D'Oyly Carte productions of W.S. Gilbert and Arthur Sullivan. Indeed, *The Mikado* had been the first show that Pélissier had seen as a child.[30] However, Sullivan's music was in a light operatic style, whereas Pélissier composed mainly in the vernacular; and Gilbert's satire was aimed very much at a 'knowing' middle class with, in Hesketh Pearson's phrase, its 'cutting ridicule of the political game' and of English institutions such as 'parliament, the army, the navy, commerce, the Court'.[31] On the whole, Pélissier's satire was far more wide ranging and broadly based. That is not to say that the influence of classical music had no bearing on his work. As we have seen, his innate skill at the piano enabled him to devise hilarious pastiches of Wagner and Tchaikovsky. He also rose to the challenge of serious classical composition. 'Alone'[32] is a beautifully lyrical setting of Heine's gentle meditation on love and death; while 'Awake!',[33] a rich and extended serenade, shifts artfully from common time to waltz time in a setting of the romantic poem by Sir William Davenant, the 17th-century English Renaissance poet.

It is worth pointing out that Pélissier's music publishers were among the most prominent in the field, including Francis, Day & Hunter, Joseph Williams, and Reynolds & Company. As well as being published in London, his works routinely appeared simultaneously in America, often in the lists of the American publishers E. Schubert & Company of New York. Copies were usually sold at a price of two shillings and such was their popularity that in time they may well have come to represent the larger share of Pélissier's substantial income. In addition to his work with *The Follies,* he pursued a parallel, purely musical career presenting occasional concert evenings under the title of *Pélissiana* (with orchestral arrangements by Herman Finck) conducted by Louis Laval. In fact, by 1901 Pélissier was already a sufficiently respected composer to have been invited to perform his song 'Awake!' on 11 September at Sir Henry Wood's Queen's Hall Prom, alongside works by Tchaikovsky, Gounod and Wagner.[34] This was an engagement that he was invited to repeat in 1903 and again, it seems, in 1912, although sadly on that occasion his worsening health precluded an appearance. This is made known to us in a letter written while he was on tour in Dorset to his young wife, Fay Compton, in the autumn of that year, while she was at home recuperating from the birth of their son, Anthony. In this letter he states:

> I am making an early start for Bournemouth as I am conducting Pélissiana in [*sic*] the pier at 12 this morning – we had special bills printed yesterday – I am getting into trim for the Queen's Hall. I will write again as I have been called late and have only just time to see the orchestra before they begin.[35]

The orchestra he is referring to is the prestigious Bournemouth Symphony Orchestra under Dan, later Sir Dan, Godfrey. In an earlier letter to Fay, he had written:

> Dan Godfrey is letting me have a rehearsal with his orchestra (42) for £7.10.0 so I can get into the way of constructing the 'peace conference' – I think it is very nice of him as I think the orchestra will hate it! - & [*sic*] he is going to give me tips about conducting it properly.[36]

For a concert party artiste, Harry Pélissier was moving in high musical circles. The 'peace conference' composition he refers to was part of a satire on the ultimately ineffectual London Peace Conference convened for the December of that year, at which the major European powers sought to resolve their differences in the Balkans. That Pélissier could contemplate satirising such an event before a crowd of holidaymakers on Bournemouth Pier is surely testimony to both his courage and his topicality as an entertainer. Furthermore, the organist appearing in this routine was, it seems, the highly distinguished Charles John Vincent, then examiner for Trinity College, London. His son Charlie, a professional singer, was at that time appearing with *The Follies*. In a further letter to Fay, Harry wrote:

> Charlie Vincent is a very nice person & [*sic*] extremely intelligent. [. . .] His father will I think play the organ for us at the scenes in the Peace Conference! This is rather a score as he is quite a big shot in the music world and a Mus.B.A. etc – [37]

In the event, it all seems to have been quite a success as Harry rounds off his next letter by stating: 'got another huge reception before and after!'[38] If the Lord Chamberlain was offended by Pélissier's satire, it would appear that the public were not.

Yet another influence on Pélissier's output were the musical comedies of the 1890s that featured at the Gaiety Theatre under George Edwardes. For these, W.S. Gilbert had only contempt, but at the time they were perhaps even more popular than his own Savoy operas. Typically, in these productions, a flimsy romantic plot line would draw together a sequence of light-weight parlour songs and light operatic pieces. The trend was set by *A Gaiety Girl* in 1892, whereupon there followed *The Shop Girl* of 1894 and, over the next two years, *My Girl*, *The Circus Girl* and *A Runaway Girl*.[39] To some extent, the genre was an exploitation of the newly found and increasingly vocal demands of that generation of young women for greater equality and liberation as epitomised by the emergence of the smart and sporty *Gibson Girl*.[40] It was also the brain-child of a shrewd management that had a chorus of beautiful and elegant dancers – The Gaiety Girls – who would feature prominently in every production to the delight of aristocratic 'Stage Door Johnnies', who waited expectantly outside the theatres to escort them to the Mayfair restaurant or club of their choice. The shows often consisted of what Peter Bailey has referred to as a kind of sexualised consumerism, 'a brokered sexuality' and typically featured sentimental romantic story lines with 'an intense glamorization of women' and a mechanical and repetitious chorus line.[41] The music was usually in a light operatic style, which ironically owed a lot to Sullivan. Pélissier offered none of these things. His music tended on the whole towards the vernacular. So too, his scripts tended towards the improvised rather than the strictly disciplined and he could be acerbic and earthy in his wit rather than sentimental. Again, in stark contrast to the Gaiety 'Girl'-themed productions, the female *Follies* had equal prominence and status with the male performers and indeed wore broadly similar costumes, often cross-dressing and taking on male parts. There was little sign of glamorisation here.

Muriel George, for instance, made Pélissier's best-selling ballad 'My Moon' entirely her own, while Effie Cook and Ethel Allandale created their own double act of party girls in 'Beena Flapper' and 'Stilla Flapper', a parody of the Gaiety Girl style. In complete disregard of respectability, these performances were laced with unconventional sexual licence. In her brief hand-written memoir, *A Sketch*, Ethel states quite brazenly: 'I am very fond of smut and never miss an opportunity of talking of drawers and their contents'.[42] In 'My Boy from Barbary', the female protagonist boasts of her love conquests as she courts a North African lover, a song that was daringly transgressive in both respects for its time:

> *A hairdresser well known to fame,*
> *from Barbary to England came*
> *He thought that he would be more free,*
> *until he met with me you see*
> *He was the slowest and the worst I've ever had to woo,*
> *but though he said 'poo-poo' at first,*
> *it was a sham poo-poo*[43]

Sophie Nield has pointed out that: 'the "Girl" narratives almost always closed on a conservative note, of romance or marriage'.[44] In the context of the time, Pélissier's blend of music and comedy and liberal attitudes was clearly offering something rather different, something that today we might call edgy. Indeed, the light operatic and sentimentalised romance of the Gaiety shows was among the targets that he was particularly fond of sending up. Take for example the song 'It Isn't Love – It's Bacchus':

> *For many a deed is Cupid praised that Bacchus has effected*
> *It's high time that the point was raised, the error was corrected*
> *Love may be sweet with distress and jealousy twill rack us*
> *And when man's found true happiness, it isn't love, it's Bacchus.*
>
> *Love makes the world go round they say, how can they be so stupid?*
> *As though this massive lump of clay could get pushed by Cupid*
> *But crawling homewards on the ground lest lamp-posts should attack us*
> *We know what makes the world go round, it isn't love, it's Bacchus*[45]

Amongst Pélissier's satires we can recognise several that were aimed specifically at the Gaiety productions. Examples include his parodies of George Grossmith's *The Girls of Gottenberg* or Franz Léhar's *The Merry Widow* or *The Beauty of Bath* by Seymour Hicks and Cosmo Hamilton. Once again, in aiming his sights on this particular genre he was displaying his characteristic business acumen. As Peter Bailey makes clear: 'With its extensive provincial hinterland and wide media exposure, musical comedy commanded an audience that made it broadly as well as wildly popular'.[46] Characteristically Pélissier recognised that this was an avenue he could exploit to his commercial as well as artistic advantage, drawing on that broadening audience familiar with the genre he was satirising. Indeed, Harry's principal interest in these 'Girl' shows would have been as a satirist. They provided the inspiration for his deliberately over-sentimental parodies such as 'Dreaming'[47] and 'I Want the Moon'.[48] These works are sharply perceptive, on-the-money send-ups of a whole genre of flimsy musical comedy – but they also stand up as viable songs in their own right. So, indeed, when N.T.P. Murphy writes that 'Pelissier's pastiches of [. . .] ballads were so accurate that it is difficult for modern readers to distinguish them from the originals',[49] he rightly draws attention to this particular strand of his work but misses entirely the greater portion of his output, which is written very much in earnest. Harry would also have had an eye to the continuing success and popularity of this particular musical genre and was most likely inspired by it to attempt his own full-length musical comedy. Entitled *All Change Here*[50] and performed at the Alhambra in 1910, it was well-received on opening night, but, for reasons that we shall discuss, became a rare and extremely damaging failure for *The Follies* impresario. It was never to be Pélissier's destiny to create a successful full-length, single-narrative musical comedy, but he did most certainly help pave the way. In the context of Edwardian music hall, and indeed other musical comedy of the time, *The Follies* were as untypical an act as they had been among the pierrot troupes and concert parties of the provincial seaside.

In many ways, several of Pélissier's compositions prefigure those of Ivor Novello and Noel Coward, anticipating their romantic and witty style a decade and more before either of them was actively composing. Novello did not arrive in London until 1913, aged twenty, by which time Pélissier had died and *The Follies* were no longer appearing at the Apollo. The principal influence that fell upon Novello was more likely from light classical parlour songs and the Gaiety shows. His mother, Clara Novello Davies, was established as a highly regarded singing teacher and counted members of the Gaiety cast among her students.[51] However, one can sense a kinship of authentic sentiment and classically influenced structure and melody between Pélissier and the works of the younger composer. The former had published dozens of works that were available to amateur players and burgeoning professionals alike at the time and, in the relatively small world of music theatre, it is interesting to note that Novello was part of the social set that mixed with Fay Compton. The original hand-written score of Novello's 'Thoughts of You'[52] of 1917 is in the Pélissier family possession, bequeathed by Fay to her son Anthony.

Another member of Novello's social set, a budding young actor, songwriter and author who might well have attended *The Follies'* shows at the Apollo Theatre was Noel Coward. He had already begun his career as a child actor in the West End at the Garrick and Savoy theatres and would shortly be cast in *Peter Pan*. What might he have made of Harry's bold and witty musical transgressions? One can easily sense in some of Pélissier's works a hint of what was to come from Coward's imagination. For example, 'My Boy from Barbary', with its catchy and dramatic opening verses that lead us into a haunting refrain with an utterly camp undertone, arguably prefigures Noel Coward's 'Mad About the Boy'.[53] Just as in that particular song, we are surreptitiously aware that in the composer's mind it is in fact a man writing the love lyric about another man – even though the song is expressed through a female character – so Pélissier offers us a sly pining lament of unrequited transgressive passion.

> *My boy from Barbary, he curls my hair for me,*
> *makes transformations on the strict Q.T.*
> *Pads and peroxides, he uses so skilfully –*
> *a finer barber never came from Barbary!*
> *About his native land he raves*
> *and tells me all about his closest shaves*
> *If there a man should raise a razor to a maid,*
> *his ways amaze her*
> *Sunshine there the baldest braves,*
> *though singeing's bad for some,*
> *they always get their hair in waves*
> *and all their bays are rum.*[54]

Coward later became a close friend and colleague of Fay Compton's. He would have been well aware of her marital history and her deceased husband's work and fame. In the coming years, Fay was cast in the 1941 premier of Noel Coward's *Blithe Spirit*, appearing as Ruth Condomine. He also provided her son, Anthony Pélissier, with his first professional engagement as an actor. Perhaps the Master was tacitly acknowledging a debt to a previous maestro of musical theatre, Anthony's father.

Authentic intimacy

Above all, what Harry Pélissier brought to his musical creations was a kind of intimacy and authenticity. On stage, in performance, he made a point of approaching the audience directly. He would happily banter and improvise with them. In a style that a future ex-pierrot comedian, Max Miller, would later make his own, Harry Pélissier stood close to the footlights, breaking down any sense of a 'fourth wall'. There he would deliver his opening monologues on any theme that came to him, engaging in improvised banter with the audience. The style and delivery of his songs reflected this. Even when they are sardonic or satirical, they are curiously confessional. 'My Boy from Barbary' is simultaneously droll and tragic in a way that draws one into the heart of the character; so too 'I Want Somebody to Love Me', 'My Moon' and a host of others. In many ways, it is this authentic intimacy that I suggest was Pélissier's most original and significant contribution to popular musical theatre. It represents a step change from Jerome Kern's 'Do You Want to Spoon with Me?' or the trite simplicity of the Gaiety shows such as *The Shop Girl*. It takes us into quite a different place from the bold, brash orchestral world of the Savoy Operas and Gilbert's self-consciously clever word plays. It is closer to the cabaret world of Aristide Bruant, but in a distinctly English mode. In this way, Pélissier's songbook and brilliantly short-lived revues represent a slender stepping-stone to the great musical plays of the 1920s and 1930s and beyond.

H.G. Pélissier by no means composed all the lyrics himself. 'Pansy of Pennsylvania', for example, was penned by Morris Harvey – a regular Folly in the later years – whilst 'My Boy from Barbary' was the work of Arthur Davenport, Pélissier's most frequent and long-lasting collaborator. But Harry's personal input would have been crucial. He would often provide the initial idea for a song and adapt the lyric as he devised the setting. And, unlike many of the other music hall and pierrot performers, he was composing material for himself and for his troupe. Indeed, Harry Pélissier was very much a singer-songwriter in the modern sense. His principal collaborators in this endeavour were the lyricists Arthur Wimperis and Arthur Davenport, as well as Compton Mackenzie and occasionally other *Folly* cast members such as Morris Harvey. However, Harry's first known collaborator as a lyricist was his own brother Frederick who provided the verses for 'Mein Faderland', evidently inspired by their own father, or at least by their Germanic family origins. It was probably one of the first songs they performed together in their youthful home-grown entertainments.

His first co-writing partner of real significance was Arthur Wimperis. An almost exact contemporary, also being born in 1874, and a fellow Londoner, the exact circumstances of their meeting are a mystery. However, it is highly possible that they met while attending music halls, perhaps even during auditions. Whatever the circumstances, it seems clear that Harry gave Wimperis his first opening into the musical world. 'My Lodestar',[55] a minstrel-inspired cakewalk for which Wimperis provided the jaunty lyrics, was Pelissier's earliest published work. Issued by Francis, Day & Hunter, it carries the copyright date of 1893, at which time they would both still have been just 19 years of age. This appears to have been a very early one-off for both of them. At the time, Wimperis was working as an illustrator for *Graphic* magazine and from 1899 to 1902 he was enlisted as a cavalryman in the Boer War. It was not until 1904, when *The Follies* had begun to establish themselves more firmly on the London circuit, that Pélissier and Wimperis collaborated once again. This time it was on the bitterly satirical

'What A Happy Land Is England'. A similar line is explored in 'What A Very Great Improvement It Would Be' of 1906,[56] which was followed over the next couple of years by a sequence of light ballads, including 'Under The Weeping Willow'[57] and the pastiche minstrel number 'Zulu Lulu'.[58] Their final collaboration came in 1909 with 'A Garden of Roses',[59] but by this time Wimperis was establishing himself in his own right as a librettist and lyricist with a light comedy called *The Dairymaids* (produced in 1906).[60] Following this, he was invited to contribute to the highly popular and lucrative Gaiety shows, including *The Sunshine Girl* and *The Girl in a Taxi*.

In the 1930s Arthur Wimperis took up a screen-writing career for Alexander Korda and, having transferred to Hollywood, was presented with an Academy Award for Best Screenplay for *Mrs. Miniver* in 1942.[61] However, it seems clear that it was Harry Pélissier who gave him his first real start in show-business. At one point, he even appears as a performing cast member in a *Follies'* photograph (see Figure 10) and, as we shall see, it was Wimperis, of all Pélissier's collaborators, who had the sharpest business brain when it came to opportunities and royalties.

By far the most regular and long-serving of all Harry's writing partners was Arthur Davenport. He either co-wrote with Harry or provided all the lyrics for 28 of his published works, nearly half the output. He seems to have started around the same time as Wimperis returned in 1904, providing another minstrel pastiche in the form of 'Our Canadian Canoe'[62] (a number that was included at the private Sandringham performance for Queen Alexandra) and he continued to come up with a wide variety of numbers right into the heyday of *The Follies'* appearances at the Apollo in 1910. The songs range from the quaintly surreal 'The Toothbrush and the Sponge' to the wittily sophisticated 'Jane from Maiden Lane'[63] to the sharply satirical 'What A Funny World We Live In'.[64] Together, one imagines that Davenport and Pélissier must have spent many hundreds of hours seated together at the piano, occasionally co-creating the verses, as they did on the coyly satirical 'Mother's Maxims',[65] – a song in which a daughter innocently misconstrues her parent's warnings with contradictory results, and 'Contrary Mary',[66] a strange comic number about the use of fertiliser in a Covent Garden vegetable nursery, which is not all that it seems (see note in Appendix C).

Davenport too, for a while, was a performing *Folly*. In fact, he married another cast member, Muriel George, who had joined the company in 1902 when she was aged just 19.[67] None of this, however, prevented what seems to have been a rather abrupt dismissal of his services in 1910. We shall examine the circumstances in due course, but Davenport's disappearance is the reason why Harry was looking for a new lyricist and collaborator when he chanced upon the talents of a budding young writer called Compton Mackenzie. Pélissier's immediate necessity was to find a collaborator for the imminent full-length musical comedy that he had been booked to provide for the Alhambra that forthcoming winter. Up to that point, Harry had neither a theme nor a title nor any of the songs. The whole thing was merely an ambition, an aspiration even – possibly spurred on by the success that Arthur Wimperis was then currently enjoying with his own quite radically innovative musical comedy at the Shaftesbury Theatre. This was entitled *The Arcadians*[68] and it opened in April 1909, transferring to Broadway at the Liberty Theater the following January. Pélissier might well have felt a little peeved and upset that his former long-time collaborator, someone to whom he had given such a prominent entrée into the world of musical theatre, should have joined forces with the rival composers Howard Monckton and Lionel Talbot. And not only that, but that they had seemingly employed Pélissier's very own characteristic style of mixing together various musical idioms; as for example in placing the vernacular music hall song 'All Down Piccadilly' alongside a light operatic piece like 'Arcady'. *The Arcadians* is a rightly famous work, much enjoyed even to this day, but arguably its originality owes a lot to the ground-breaking work of *The Follies* revues, and Pélissier may well have felt that he had had a march stolen upon him.

All Change Here

Having taken on the role of Harry's librettist, Compton Mackenzie or Monty as he was known to friends and family, worked feverishly hard on the forthcoming show. This is vividly portrayed, not only in his memoirs of the period, but also in the novel that it inspired, *Carnival*[69] – a work that itself was to enjoy great success and which was later, somewhat ironically, not to say incestuously, adapted into a musical in the 1930s. However, Monty's stint as Pélissier's lyricist was to be rather short-lived. Only two of their collaborations were to be published, 'The Big Bamboo',[70] a fun melodrama on a theme of oriental passion, and 'Return to The Simple Life',[71] a skit on the urbanite's inability to deal with country ways. This latter piece was part of the score for the sadly doomed experimental revue that was to be *All Change Here*.

Figure 27. Compton Mackenzie, 1911

The fundamental idea behind this show was that the year 1910 had been a thoroughly dreadful one that saw not only a horridly wet summer and the death of King Edward VII, but also economic and social turmoil, industrial strikes and so on. Pélissier proposed that by some magic formula and by use of the familiar railway cry 'All change here!' that all of this could be reversed. Perhaps it was not the funniest premise to start with, although worse ideas have been known to succeed, but from the outset the project was hampered by two giant pitfalls. On the one hand, the Lord Chamberlain, still irked and smarting from his spat with Pélissier over *An Englishman's Home*, had strictly forbidden any actual spoken dialogue to be employed in the piece. The Alhambra was a music hall and as such could not present anything that resembled a straight play, in such a place

119

spoken dialogue would be heavily restricted by law. This, of course, denied Harry one of his most effective and characteristic tools. Second, and for reasons that seemed curious even to Compton Mackenzie, Harry himself refused to take the central role. Instead, he gifted that part to the Irish actor who had introduced him to Monty, a certain Shiel Barry.

Perhaps the very notion of a non-speaking role consisting entirely of song and dance rather daunted the verbally dexterous Pélissier. Furthermore, the nature of the piece meant that it would be more formally constructed and there would be little or no opportunity for improvisation, for ad-libs and spontaneous banter with the audience, surely one of the most appealing aspects of Harry's style. More probably, perhaps, he wished to continue performing with *The Follies* show still running at the Apollo. Whatever the reason, his omission from the cast robbed the whole production of its biggest star and draw. As a result, it relied heavily on the formulaic chorus of beautiful dancing girls (much to Monty's delight and his inspiration for *Carnival*) and audiences were bemused as to whether or not they were watching a satire. It fell ineptly and heavily between stools, closing humiliatingly within a couple of weeks of its opening night in January of 1911. In many ways, this was to mark the beginning of the end for Harry and *The Follies;* certainly, of Harry's dream of creating a serious, extended work of satirical musical theatre.

Both his principal lyricists, Wimperis and Davenport, had also provided spoken dialogue for some of the 'potted plays'; in the case of Wimperis, a large measure of the pantomime sketch *Bill Bailey* as well as parts of *Baffles* and the music hall parodies. He also collaborated on the drawing of 'An Invaluable Map to the Apollo Theatre' and several other cartoons for the programmes and even a spoof biography of Pélissier that was published in *M.A.P.* magazine. Davenport co-wrote the extended musical sketch that was *Love's Garden* as well as contributing to the 'potted plays' of *Faust* and *Hamlet*. Davenport had started out as an actor and, according to Fitzroy Gardner's 1910 memoir, 'at one time he was *The Follies'* stage manager, and understudied his chief – in fact, he actually appeared for him at the Palace Theatre on two occasions with considerable success'.[72]

However, they also shared another less wholesome trait – a taste for alcohol. Arthur Davenport drank every bit as copiously as his boss and, for this reason, gained the nickname of 'Fish'. It was possibly this that prompted his abrupt dismissal from the troupe in the autumn of 1910. It certainly meant that in later years he hit hard times. A letter dated 17 January 1913 finds him writing to Pélissier, pleading for what he regards as an outstanding payment of £24 15s. 6d. He goes on to write: 'It was certainly not my fault that you made no use of me at the Empire pantomime rehearsals'.[73] Indeed, he seems to have been treated in a quite cavalier fashion. In November of that year, after Harry's demise, we find him pleading once more, this time to Dan Everard, who had taken over from Harry as *The Follies'* manager: 'Dear Dan, what about that claim you were going to make for me on poor old H.G.'s estate?' (*The Follies* were still performing at this point). 'Hope the show is going strong – I hear it is. If you could let me have a couple of seats this week, I should love to see it. When you want a new show I'm on.'[74]

It is August 1914 when we find him writing to Dan Everard yet again:

> Dear Dan, you haven't answered my last letter & now I'm really in a rotten hole [. . .] Only one revue of mine is out now owing to the war, & the royalties from the other I've had to draw in advance [. . .] Can't £25 be raised to see me through the worst? Yours Arthur Davenport.[75]

He adds rather tragically that he has to face a summons that Thursday at the Edgware County Sessions. In stark contrast, Arthur Wimperis did not find himself having to make such special pleading. Indeed, he seems to have been far more business-like and hard-headed in his dealings. A document dated 8 June 1904 clearly states that he will receive:

> Two guineas for each individual number and one further guinea if published — Comic songs excepted [. . .] A.H. Wimperis' name to be added in brackets on programme to all items written by him. The appearance of his name on Music Hall programmes not guaranteed but it will be put in when possible.

This is then brusquely signed: 'I agree to the above. H.G. Pélissier'.[76] Nevertheless, disputes seem to have arisen. In a letter dated 20 October 1908, Wimperis claims to be owed £10 for a programme design. Shrewdly, he has stopped the printing. He writes:

> Dear Pélissier [. . .] You should have waited a few days more until the programme was actually in the press. Then when I'd finished you might have diddled me to your heart's content. As it is, all the drawings & some contents of the letter press & ideas are mine and are still my property [. . .] I don't anticipate any great ructions over this because I'm pretty sure you'll see my demand is quite fair & that I mean what I say.[77]

Arthur Wimperis went on to a lucrative and distinguished film career, while poor Davenport went to the County Sessions, alcoholism, divorce and an early death. All artists it would seem are best advised to keep a good business head about them. Pélissier certainly did. The seasons at the Apollo Theatre made him a very wealthy man with a fortune amounting to well over one million pounds; a fortune that he instinctively knew how to enjoy to the full in his wildly hedonistic lifestyle — as a true bohemian.

Clearly, a significant aspect of Harry Pélissier's career was the endeavor to develop a wholly new concept of musical theatre. He was building on the 'Great British Songbook' as represented by the works of the many considerable and prolific music hall artists and light classical, concert and show-song composers of the time. In so doing, he was taking that tradition into a new and radical direction. It was a style that he melded with great subtlety into the tradition of burlesque to develop a more continental style of revue, something more coherent than the light and gaudy song and dance musical comedies as typified by the Gaiety Theatre. Furthermore, in his appeal to popular taste, in his desire to attract a wide and inclusive audience, in his employment of the American minstrel, ragtime and jazz rhythms and lyric styles that he had encountered in the coastal resorts, he was even attempting to develop a popular musical theatre that could reach beyond the more strictly middle-class, light operatic world of Gilbert and Sullivan.

For all the aforementioned reasons, he represents a crucial link between those many late Victorian and Edwardian forms and the genre we now understand as the modern musical. And he did it, not just through his sheer range, not just through his mixture of the serious and the satirical, the anarchic and the sentimental – though all of this was important. He did it most especially by being intimate and confessional and quite brazenly and recognisably direct and authentic in a way that neither Gilbert and Sullivan nor the world of burlesque and revue, nor music hall, nor, even up to this point, the likes of Jerome Kern or Ivor Novello had ever achieved in quite the same way. In short, he had laid the foundations of English musical revue.

10

The Caricaturist

Figure 28. H.G. Pélissier, self-caricature, Granta Magazine, 1912

'A definite art-form'

It may have been noted that I have, in referring to the work of 'The Follies', used the word caricature. I did so out of regard for the feelings of Mr. Pélissier who is not pleased at being described as a burlesquer. He prefers to be known as a caricaturist. He would argue that there is a considerable distinction, and that burlesque, as it is generally understood, is foreign to the work he undertakes.[1]

As if to underline the point, this item in the *Manchester Chronicle* of 19 May 1907, is accompanied by several images of *The Follies* sketched by their regular cartoonist Mab. In fact, what *The Follies* were doing was quite pioneering and distinct from either the traditional burlesque or pierrot shows, or indeed from the minstrel or concert parties or from the work of any other popular performers of the time – although it utilised certain elements from all of them. In a similar way, it also drew heavily from the world of the press cartoonists, comic illustrations being a regular feature of *The Follies'* printed theatre programmes. These included their satirical map of the West End, directing the audience to bogus drinking establishments *en route* to the Apollo, and their lampoons of advertisements. On top of this, there regularly appeared characteristically bizarre and enigmatic posters emblazoned around the streets and railway stations of London, such as the one that featured the gazeeka-like animal in pyjamas (see Figure 2) or that showing a guitar-playing elephant. In this regard Pélissier employed the services of a whole range of professional illustrators, including Geoffrey Holme, Norman Morrow, John Bull and Arthur Wimperis.

The world of commercial advertisements was a perpetual target. Indeed, it is arguable that Pélissier had the intrinsic contradictions and absurdities of consumer society in his sights well ahead of his time. For example, *The Follies'* programmes might feature mock advertisements for the following:

> Bovotine or Beef Glue – it sticks everything – may be used as a beverage – an ox in a tuppenny tube.[2] /The Akou Vibra Massage – electrical treatment for deafness.[3] /Face Glaze – Miss Fay Compton before using Face Glaze [an image of a cat-like face in a hat]; Miss Fay Compton after using Face Glaze [Fay's face covered in spots][4]

In years to come, the device of mock advertisements would of course become a regular form of satire employed by the comic troupe of *Monty Python's Flying Circus,* but at the time it would

PÉLIXIR. *For Infants and Inebriates.*

Absolutely the latest thing in Animal Spirits.

Figure 29. A spoof advertisement from a Follies programme

have appeared quite fresh and novel, especially appearing in a theatre programme. In return, *The Follies* became themselves a favourite subject of the newspaper cartoonists, their comical images featuring in a whole host of national periodicals from *The Tatler* and *The Daily Dispatch* to *The Sketch* and *The Illustrated London News*. The celebrated *Punch* cartoonist E.T. Reed struck up a personal friendship with H.G. Pélissier involving correspondence that would sometimes include hastily drawn comic sketches of the comedian (see Figures 18 and 30). On 23 February 1910, *Punch* published Reed's savage caricature of prime minister Asquith enmeshed in the tentacles of a chicken-crested Harry Pélissier with the caption: 'Don't Worry About This. Go And See The Follies!' (see Figure 17).[5]

Arthur Moreland produced a wonderful set of individual caricatures of the troupe for 'Opera Hat', a regular feature article in *Stage and Stalls*, including the figures of Gwennie Mars, Morris Harvey and Dan Everard.[6] And even Harry liked to join in the fun, adding impromptu cartoons of himself or Fay or sometimes of a dog (their favourite animal) to the pages of his letters. Fay too revealed a considerable talent for drawing when *The Granta*, a Cambridge student magazine, published a portrait sketch of her husband in February 1912 alongside a series of cartoons by Pélissier himself, which included a self-portrait.[7]

Fitzroy Gardner was quick to perceive the connection between Pélissier's entertainment and the world of visual art:

> What Aubrey Beardsley did for Art, Pélissier and the Follies may be said to have done for Humour, with this difference – that whereas Beardsley's influence may have proved somewhat ephemeral owing to his having passed away before his cult became an artistic vogue, the Follies have survived the turning-point in their career and have been able to encourage the evolution of their cult until it has become a popular vogue. A 'school' of humour appeals to a larger public than a school of illustration.[8]

What Fitzroy Gardner could not have known, writing in 1910, was that, just three years later, Harry Pélissier would die of cirrhosis and that the memory of his 'cult' would be all but obliterated by the Great War. The visual aspect of his school of humour, however, (rather like Beardsley's school of art in the retro fashions of 'Swinging London'), successfully re-surfaced with a vengeance in the 1960s and 1970s in *Monty Python's Flying Circus*. And here too, in a similar fashion, the comic animations of Terry Gilliam would be intrinsically interwoven with the sketch performances of the cast. Gardner goes on to say:

> And how the frail-blooded artist would have been delighted with the robust fun-maker, each an artist in his own way! How Beardsley would have enjoyed drawing a poster for the Follies! And how Pélissier would have cheered the, sometimes, morbid young draughtsman!"[9]

In fact, Beardsley delighted in producing the sharply delineated figures of pierrots in many of his most haunting images such as *The Scarlet Pastorale*, in which a pair of mysteriously suspended candelabras hang in the air above a fat Harlequin, while behind him masquerade a group of be-wigged and cloven-footed pierrots.[10] For *The Savoy* magazine, he produced an equally enigmatic illustration, *The Death of Pierrot*, as a retinue of hushed and elaborately costumed figures mourn a tiny pierrot in a massive four-poster bed.[11] Beardsley died in 1898 before *The Follies* had reached the pinnacle of their success, but both he and his friend and mentor, the poet Arthur Symons, were devotees of the music hall and concert entertainment and there is every chance that they may have come across the robust figure of H.G. Pélissier during their nightly revels. Be that as it may, there is certainly no doubting the electric interaction and influence, one upon the other, of the fine art and the theatrical worlds of this period. The novelist and biographer Denis Mackail captured the ingenuity of Pélissier's art-form in a reminiscence for *The Times*, composed 20 years after the comedian's death.

> Do you remember the form of one of his typical programmes? You had the theatre in such a helpless and hysterical condition last time that it was almost like a douche of cold water when the curtain again rose on a conventional troupe of pierrots, when a contralto sang a ballad in a coloured spotlight, or a couple of Follies took part in a sentimental seaside duet. But he was watching you as he sat there at the piano, and it was all part of his plan. You must be lulled and soothed, you must even reach the verge of asking yourself whether you were not being bored. Then a flash of humour, and you sat up, and you wanted more; but still you were not going to get it. Again you must be teased and kept on tenterhooks, but still you were not going to get it. No shortage of jokes in that fat round head, but you must join him in pierrot-land before he would show you what he could do. You must get to know his company before they all began turning into creatures of his fantastic imagination. His entertainment was a definite art-form. He knew precisely what he was doing.[12]

It was an art-form that would find its true heirs half a century later in the counterculture of the 1960s and 1970s that was to finally overturn the Lord Chamberlain's censorship. Matthew Morrison has drawn attention to the 'cartoon style' of theatre in this period, which had

Figure 30. H.G. Pélissier with the Punch cartoonist E.T. Reed

'become so prevalent in the lunchtime movement' as exemplified by productions at the Soho Theatre. He quotes Peter Ansorge in his definition of the style:

> The dialogue, action and conflict work in a very basic Punch and Judy manner. We never learn about the characters in any precise way, there is no intention of expressing any psychological or human depth. Rather the characters engage in a very different kind of struggle, a comic summary.[13]

This could as well characterize the 'potted play' caricatures of *The Follies* and further exemplifies just how forward-thinking and *avant-garde* they were as a theatrical company.

11

The Bohemian

Figure 31. H.G. Pélissier as Bacchus in the musical fantasy Love's Garden, 1911

'A bottle of brandy a day'

For one of their seasons in the West End, the back page of *The Follies* programme was taken up with an 'invaluable map' (see Figure 32).[1] It rather pointlessly informed members of the audience 'HOW TO GET TO THE APOLLO THEATRE'. They would already have arrived, of course, having purchased the map in the foyer, but that was of no importance in the absurdist thinking of *The Follies*. This 'map' consisted of a street plan of the West End with arrows and cartoon fingers pointing in random and opposite directions, instructing one to set off

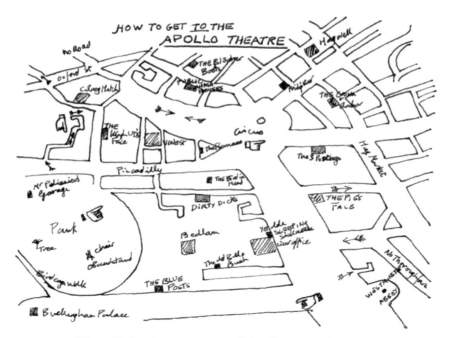

Figure 32. Spoof programme map offering directions to the Apollo

from Piccadilly by way of Dirty Dicks, Bedlam and The Bird in Hand; thence to make one's way through Piccadilly Circus to The Vines and Romano's. From there one might stagger on to Oxford Street and replenish oneself at The Boar and The Blucher Boots, usefully located opposite public wash houses. This may well have been a knowing nod to the well-informed as public wash houses in the West End were a favoured venue for clandestine meetings among the illegal gay community. Then, assuming he or she still had the capacity, the ardent theatre-goer could crawl back towards the Haymarket and imbibe at Ye Olde Sleeping Sicknesse and The Pig's Face before setting off once again for Shaftesbury Avenue, presumably in a suitably inebriated state to fully appreciate *The Follies* satire. Alternative routes might take in a dozen or more other houses of recreation and, given that the Apollo Theatre itself is nowhere to be seen on the map, one might partake of an endless circle of drinking and sight-seeing without ever reaching the intended destination.

In fact, as so often with Pélissier, this street plan was itself a skit – on a map issued a few years earlier by the Scala Theatre and given to potential patrons and London cabbies as a travel guide. In Pélissier's 'invaluable map', however, almost every route culminates in a cul-de-sac or a public house and just about the only recognisably authentic landmark is Buckingham Palace. The map is a practical joke, one of Pélissier's favourite pastimes, but it also points to a more trenchant aspect of the man himself: his hedonistic lifestyle. Pélissier was a notoriously brazen and shameless *bon vivant*. A heavy drinker, his preferred beverage was a bottle of brandy enjoyed with a trademark German cigar.

Figure 33. Norman Morrow's cartoon of The Follies in rehearsal

A cartoon by the caricaturist Norman Morrow depicts 'THE FOLLIES SUNDAY AT HOME'.[2] (see Figure 33). Harry can be seen recumbent on a chaise-longue, complete with Turkish fez and slippers, a smoking jacket and pierrot trousers, composing a musical score as he draws on a hookah pipe sarcastically labelled 'milk' beside a brandy glass and a soda siphon. Many of his songs glory in the delights of alcohol. 'It Isn't Love, It's Bacchus'[3] is a mock-sentimental ballad that provides the central motif for the musical revue *Love's Garden*,[4] while a drunken Hamlet is the core joke of his 'potted' Shakespeare. He loved to drink, and he loved to joke about drinking. Fitzroy Gardner recalls one of his favourite anecdotes:

> A friend who had met with an accident to his arm, from which recovery was very slow, remarked to him, 'I am getting sick of the whole thing. I've half a mind to cut it off and wear a cork arm'. 'What sort of bottle will you have at the end?' inquired Pélissier.[5]

Sadly, however, drink was to prove his undoing. In 1913, his cause of death was diagnosed as cirrhosis of the liver and, as we shall see, his final poignant love letters to his young wife, Fay Compton, are at times painfully expressive of his declining health and abilities, whereby his mind seems to stray erratically, his temper to explode sometimes into physical violence and even his handwriting to become barely legible. However, at the height of his fame in the decade between 1901 and 1911, he appears to have been perfectly fit. Over this period, he drew on an almost super-human energy and dedication at all hours of the day and night to apply himself to his music and comedy, while at the same time managing to revel in a wildly hedonistic lifestyle, in a manner that seems fairly typical of the bohemian social set of the time.

'A long history of bisexuality'

In a word, Harry Pélissier lived for pleasure. In fact, he was one of its most vociferous and vocal exponents, a veritable proselytiser for the libertine and the indulgent. In the scale of things, one might be tempted to think that this counted against him. However, one could equally argue the case that he was shamelessly un-hypocritical about it, as generous in his granting of gifts, hospitality and professional opportunities to others as he was to himself. In many ways, he represented a *tour de force* of brazen candour against reactionary and puritanical cant and humbug, against inhibition and the official moral censure of his time. Picking up on the overtly sensual work of 1890s aesthetes like Oscar Wilde, Arthur Symons and Aubrey Beardsley, he provided a breath of fresh air, a rebel voice and an attitude in direct opposition to the prevalent, rather stuffy and repressive, morality. He drank, he smoked, he earned his living in the shadily disrespectful *demi-monde* of the music hall and concert party and he was sexually promiscuous, certainly with young women and almost certainly with young men as well. According to Compton Mackenzie's biographer, Andro Linklater, Mackenzie informed his mother that Harry was:

> [. . .] an alcoholic drinking a bottle of brandy a day and given to various depravities that her son could only hint at but consisted in fact of a long history of bisexuality.[6]

Jaudy Pélisser, Harry's grandson, has also made reference to this aspect of Harry's nature:

> He was known to be a bit of a scandalous figure, who had died of alcohol, and the rumour was that he was probably bisexual. It was never said in any judgemental way; but in a factual way; there was just an acceptance that he was a very colourful character.[7]

Jaudy Pélissier also alludes to an occasion when his great-uncle Compton Mackenzie reminisced about how Harry Pélissier had in fact made a pass at him, further underlining his sexual ambivalence. No specific reference to Pélissier's sexuality is made in any of his surviving diaries or letters or in Fitzroy Gardner's personal account, but one has to bear in mind that the climate of the times would have necessitated great caution and even clandestine secrecy when it came to homosexual activity. The year that saw the beginning of Harry Pélissier's professional stage career, 1895, was the very same year that witnessed the imprisonment of Oscar Wilde in Reading Gaol. However, notorious as the Wilde case is, immortalised in his own poetry and letters and in a whole series of worthy stage dramatisations and films, it is not necessarily appreciated that his particular case was the tip of a very large iceberg, and that the persecution of male homosexuals in particular became increasingly widespread and intense in the decades preceding the Great War. Indeed, many homosexuals, such as Lord Arthur Somerset and Lord Battersea and, indeed, Wilde himself after his release from prison, were either prosecuted and imprisoned or sent into involuntary exile.

In 1885, what became known as the Labouchére Amendment was enacted, being an adjustment to the Offences Against the Person Act of 1861, by which it became possible to prosecute male citizens for procuring or committing 'an act of gross indecency'. To this was added the 1898 Vagrancy Law Amendment Act, which contained a clause against men 'in any public place [who] solicit or importune for immoral purposes'. In other words, it was no longer necessary that a sexual act be committed in order to occasion arrest. The mere exchange of a look or a gesture, an indication of interest or solicitation could make a citizen vulnerable. And many were. There was a sharp rise in arrests and prosecutions between 1890 and 1894, and then again after the Wilde trial between 1895 and 1900. There followed a continued but slight increase between 1900 and 1909 and, then again, a sharp rise between 1910 and 1914 for prosecutions involving 'gross indecency'. Intriguingly, those for actual sodomy fell while those for 'attempted sodomy' doubled. The average total for all three 'crimes' in London grew from 58 per year between 1905 and 1909 to 76 from 1910 to 1914.[8] Curiously, this intensifying persecution of sexual liberty closely and simultaneously mirrored the escalating regime of theatrical censorship and of the jingoistic march to war. Steve Nicholson has commented: 'Perhaps at no other time in the century were national and international politics bound together quite so publicly and overtly with sexual morality'.[9]

All of these factors contributed to and sustained a fearful atmosphere for the bisexual and homosexual communities of London in particular. There hovered about them the potential to be arrested just for talking in the street. According to the homosexual diarist and activist, George Ives, London was one of the most puritanical and tyrannical cities in Europe. The private rooms, chambers, or 'dens' as they were known of single males could be searched by police, as in the case of those of Alfred Taylor at 13 Little College Street, often referenced in the Wilde trial. These addresses would frequently be abandoned so that the occupant might avoid drawing the attention of the authorities, as in the case of George Ives who, among many changes, moved from flat E4 at The Albany to 56 St. James's Street and then on to Park Road, Regent's Park.[10]

From youthful lodgings in Peckham, Harry had taken up residence at 64 Regents Park Road, becoming a near neighbour of the homosexual rights activist George Ives and then, following that, a further move to Grove End in St John's Wood. All this took place while he was travelling around the country with *The Follies* on tour, moving from various lodging houses and hotels in the provinces and when, in his later years, he also maintained his suburban house in Finchley. His tour diaries for *The Follies* list pages of addresses alongside various names, both male and female, mostly in England, though many of them in Paris.[11] Their identity and purpose are not clear. They were quite possibly convenient boarding-houses, though they might just as easily have been establishments offering more sensual pursuits. None of this is to say that this peripatetic existence in itself represents evidence of clandestine sexual activity. However, it would be entirely consistent with the cautious behaviour exhibited by the gay and bisexual community in the repressive climate of the time.

When E.M. Forster wrote *Maurice* in 1914, he was too fearful to allow its publication in his own lifetime. The work was finally released in 1971, long after his death, in an era when the laws regarding both censorship and homosexuality had finally been repealed. This, perhaps his finest novel, is wracked with the personal guilt, terror and inner conflict of the homosexual's plight in the first decades of the twentieth century. Towards the conclusion, the subject matter and language of the novel become more explicit as the central character develops a more courageous and fulfilled acceptance of his own nature. However, in the earlier chapters, the tone is decidedly euphemistic. 'He hadn't known it could be mentioned',[12] Forster writes of the eponymous Maurice at one point, mirroring Lord Alfred Douglas's 'love that dare not speak its name'. There is talk of 'criminal morbidity' and 'the Hell of disgust'[13] by those of a repressive, puritanical outlook, such as the schoolmaster, Durham. 'Aesthete', 'effete youth' and 'bohemian' are used as by-words and metaphors for a sexual inclination that is feared and distrusted in equal measure. Again, this language and the underlying attitudes very much mirror those that were employed in *An Englishman's Home*. So repressive and conflicted is the lead character's predicament that, midway in the novel, he resorts and surrenders to hypnotic aversion therapy, reflecting the spurious psycho-analytical science predominant at the time. Add to this the fear of criminal prosecution and blackmail, which surfaces towards the conclusion, and it is little wonder that private lives of the period were shrouded in nefarious activity, obfuscation and secrecy and that what written evidence remains is inevitably sparse and elusive.

In many ways, the aesthetic movement provided an impulse and a 'cover' for the nineteenth century gay community, first inspired by Walt Whitman in America and then picked up by both Bram Stoker and Oscar Wilde in Ireland[14] before they both moved to London. It was a social sphere in which people like Stoker and Wilde gravitated naturally to the theatre. The burgeoning West End of the late nineteenth century became a familiar cruising ground for homosexuals. The Alhambra, the Empire and the St James theatre – which housed Oscar Wilde's greatest triumphs – all became favourite meeting-places; likewise, the bars and cafés in the surrounding area such as The Café Royale, Kettner's, the Criterion, the Trocadero on Piccadilly Circus and the Earls Court Exhibition Hall. Ernest Boulton and Frederick Park, the openly transvestite couple known as 'Fanny & Stella', were arrested in women's clothes outside the Strand Theatre in April 1870. They were, in fact, acquitted as there was no evidence of actual sodomy having taken place.[15] However, this was an occurrence that may have provoked Labouchère – himself a writer and friend of the great actor-manager Henry Irving – to introduce his even stricter amendment to the law in 1885.

Pélissier's collaborator, Compton Mackenzie makes much in his youthful memoirs of his liaisons with the bohemian, homosexual community of West London. In particular, he recalls his association with Wilde's entourage, which included Lord Alfred Douglas, Reggie Turner and Robbie Ross.[16] Indeed, Mackenzie's fulsome memoirs, written in the 1960s, display relatively outspoken support of the homosexual community he had befriended, something that was courageously unusual for the time. His early works were released through the novice young publisher Martin Secker, who also took up the cause of D.H. Lawrence, another author who was pioneeringly explicit on sexual matters. Secker also published the young Arthur Ransome, who revelled in his own bohemianism. In 1907 Ransome had brought out *Bohemia in London*, in which he reveals that it was in a typical Soho café that he appears to have lost his virginity:

> Close round the corner opposite the Algerian is a pretty white café [. . .] I came here in the pride of my first twenty-guinea cheque and was introduced with due ceremony to Jeanne downstairs.[17]

In 1913, Secker would publish H.G. Pélissier's own absurdist memoir *Potted Pélissier* (possibly on the recommendation of Compton Mackenzie) and, while this whimsical account lacks any sexual candour, the same cannot be said of his stage productions. *The Follies* shows at the Apollo were, for the time, outrageously 'camp'. It is significant that 'Fanny & Stella' had been arrested *outside* the Strand Theatre while *inside* they had been free to exhibit and entertain, even from the gallery. On stage, drag and transvestism had become ubiquitous in the panto-

Figure 35. Douglas 'Boy' Maclaren (above)

Figure 34. H.G. Pélissier as Maud Allan's Salomé (left)

mime houses and music halls. H.G. Pélissier took full advantage of this freedom, flaunting himself not merely as a satirical 'Dame' in the manner of Dan Leno in his pantomime burlesque, but also as an outrageously erotic and sparsely clad Salomé in his 'potted' version of Maud Allan's notorious dance routine, itself an interpretation of Wilde's scandalous and banned stage play. Other cast members would also regularly cross-dress. Gwennie Mars, for example, made a trademark routine of her Harry Lauder impersonation, while young Douglas 'Boy' Maclaren took the role of Violet Vanbrugh in the 'potted' version of Henri Bernstein's *Samson*. Maclaren liked to sport two rather immense beauty spots (see Figure 35) and, of his performance as Violet Vanbrugh, Fitzroy Gardner commented dryly that it had 'pleased him [Maclaren], and possibly some of the audience, immensely'.[18]

'I am dead'

There is also some evidence to suggest that, not untypically of the period, Harry indulged in smoking hashish, and possibly even opium if *The Follies'* hookah sketch is to be taken literally.[19] By night, he moved in a fashionable set that included his self-styled bohemian biographer Fitzroy Gardner and also the up and coming young novelist, Compton Mackenzie, as well as the critic and caricaturist Max Beerbohm and other glitterati of the Edwardian West End. He dressed with sartorial ostentation, spent money with abandon and held famously lavish parties, both at his house in Finchley and at his Pall Mall apartment. And he loved motoring, as Fitzroy Gardner recalls:

> Motoring is as necessary to him as sleep is to some people. Sometimes he combines the two when he has his chauffeur with him. On Saturday night after the performance, he hustles one or two of the company, or other friends, into his car and drives them to Brighton, Ramsgate or Folkestone, bringing them back on the Monday afternoon. He is a good, and wonderful to relate, very careful driver.[20]

In fact, he was demonstrably reckless behind the wheel, being on at least one occasion prosecuted for speeding, whilst on another he famously crashed his Daimler Silver Knight into a wall at the former village of Withdean outside Brighton. *The Daily Mirror* of 9 September 1909 reported the incident:

> Mr. Pélissier was thrown from the vehicle, but fortunately, escaped with nothing worse than a shaking. The picture, taken after the accident, shows Mr. Pélissier standing in front of the wrecked car.[21]

In the published photograph, the bonnet and wings are a crumpled heap. That night *The Evening News* ran the following article: 'I AM DEAD. Mr. Pélissier On A Fact Which Nobody Seems To Have Noticed'.[22] Having heard of the motor accident and enquired after his health, *The Evening News* had received the following telegram: 'Appearing tonight. Am really dead. But I am such a good actor that nobody has noticed it yet'. [23]

On 24 November 1909, Harry Pélissier was back in court for speeding. He had appealed against a conviction for travelling in excess of 45 mph in South Mimms in April of that year:

> Asked by the presiding magistrate whether it was true that, after a constable had signalled to him to stop, he proceeded on his way, and, turning round, waved his hand to the policeman, he replied: 'No, sir, that is impossible.' 'Why impossible?' asked the magistrate. 'Because, sir,' replied Pélissier, 'I could not possibly wave my hand to a man whom I did not know, and I never met the constable before'.[24]

The conviction was upheld, and Harry was fined £10 and ordered to pay costs of 12 shillings.[25] Motoring was then enjoying its first glorious heyday, not just as an elite pastime for the privileged and wealthy, but also in the public sphere. It was not yet the ubiquitous and classless mode of transport it was later to become, but there were already some 85,000 automobiles on British roads, some 15,000 commercial vehicles and 9,000 motorized omnibuses and taxi cabs.[26] Harry's Daimler Silver Knight was a state-of-the-art vehicle with a slide-valve, single-cylinder engine and was a distinctly prestigious and exclusive luxury, as was his rather eccentric custom-built Daimler Metallurgique. (see Figure 23). This, with its pressed-steel chassis, the option of electric lighting and a distinctive V-front radiator, was one of the finest sporting models of the time. Harry loved his motoring and was relishing his new-found wealth. What would become his customary weekend drives to coastal resorts with members of *The Follies* cast and crew are vividly recalled by Compton Mackenzie, one of his regular companions:

> We used to travel in two Daimlers, and the privileges of the road were taken advantage of with a kind of Dickensian relish. On the way to Ramsgate, we used to reach a public house somewhere before Blackheath called, I believe, the *Marquis of Granby*, unless my Dickensian comparison is misleading me. It would then be about ten minutes to twelve, so that it was a pious duty to alight and take advantage of the fact that there were still

Figure 36. A Follies' outing

ten minutes to closing time in order to fortify ourselves with Dickensian drinks for the drive ahead. This hostelry had a curious museum of oddities collected by the landlord, and we drank amid a compendium of the Late Victorian era. The next stop was about one a.m. at a roadside inn where, duly advised of our arrival, the landlady had prepared her speciality – the dish called toad-in-the-hole. I wish I could remember the name and locality of this inn, for we always ate there very heartily. Pélissier knew better than anybody how to motor. To be sure he drove much too fast for my taste, but he made up for this by enjoying an inn, and what is more by getting the best out of that inn. I motor with other people, and they are fobbed off with a miserable ordinary; but with Pélissier even in strange country we never failed to eat and drink magnificently. I can remember the flavour of the cold lamb at Exeter after driving westward from six o'clock of a blazing July morning, and the richness of the wine in Penzance that same evening. We were only once defeated and that was by the – well, by a hotel in Southampton. There we fared abominably, and though I won a large sum over a race and heard the news after lunch, even that did not destroy the memory of the badness. But the best of all our Saturday emigrations were those to the Albion at Brighton. We never wasted a moment on that road over so much as a gin and bitters. Nothing was allowed to take the edge off Mr. Harry Preston's reception and once more I see Pélissier as Gargantua when I recall him to my mind's eye, striding into the sitting-room and inspecting the cathedral of bottles on the sideboard. 'Coronation cuvee?' he asks, eyeing the champagne, and in response to the waiter's reverent nod of assent he beams like a schoolboy at the Christmas pudding.[27]

Clubland

Most of the names of the public houses on Harry's 'invaluable map' of Piccadilly are a satirist's invention. However, he might as easily have used just as many names of actual locations. The late Victorian era was infamous for its alcoholism and consequent wild street disorder, so much so, in fact, that in 1872 the Licensing Act came into force, by which all houses licensed for the sale of alcohol had to close at midnight – later extended to half past. The first night this Act came into operation, the police were engaged in efforts to close the notorious cafés on the west side of the Haymarket. Prior to that, these establishments, with names such as The Algerian, The Moorish, The Turkish and so on, had stayed open until four in the morning, serving champagne to 'Jolly Dogs', a veritable legion of aristocratic and middle-class military officers, students, young professionals, artists, actors, 'lounge lizards' and wastrels who indulged in what we today would call 'binge' drinking, street fighting, vandalism and minor criminality. These were a regular feature of the West End from Covent Garden to Regent Street, especially on a Saturday night.[28]

All that the Licensing Act achieved was to accelerate the opening of more private drinking establishments and the creation of what was to become known as 'Clubland'. A typical Saturday outing would involve an afternoon performance at the Pavilion Music Hall, followed by a trip to the Alhambra; thence to the Argyle Rooms or the Holborn Casino for late dancing and a hurried supper at Scott's. Leicester Square itself, prior to 1880, was described by one contemporary as: 'a desert waste [. . .] used as a depository for deceased felines and discarded pots and pans'.[29]

The site on which the Empire music hall was soon to be built in that very year, was 'covered by a rough temporary structure to which shooting galleries, fat ladies and human skeletons attracted a public of their own'.[30] Just such a shooting gallery in this exact location played a prominent role in Charles Dickens' *Bleak House,* in which he gives a typically vivid description of this derelict, disease-ridden area before it became 'Theatreland'. Other attractions included The Trocadero Restaurant, The Criterion, Cremorne Gardens, The Surrey Gardens and the Westminster Aquarium where one might enjoy a fashionable promenade to the accompaniment of Arthur Sullivan's organ – a novelty that quickly disappeared after just twelve months – giving way to the attraction of boxing kangaroos, Lady Zazel being fired from a canon thrice daily and Miss Beckwith and her female troupe, swimming amongst the fishes in scanty costumes. Following the French example, there then came the arrival of fine dining restaurants – the Café Royal, Verrey's (much favoured by Pélissier), The Criterion and Épitaux –which offered supper-room accommodation for a 'man about town' entertaining young ladies. The Savoy instituted its Supper Club for the after-the-theatre supper party, while its culinary rivals included The Bachelors', at the corner of Hamilton Place, The Wellington in Grosvenor Place, The Guards in Brook Street, The Athenaeum and Brooks, The Beefsteak and The New Club in Covent Garden (once Evans' Supper Rooms, a cradle of the music hall), as well as 'freak clubs' such as the Amphytrion, where no member paid for any drinks! The 'night club', specializing in nocturnal dancing, came into existence around 1890, the first of its kind being The Carnation in Leicester Square. There followed The Regent in Lower Regents Street and Alsatians and The Palm in Oxford Street. Membership of these was cursory and nominal and, in effect, all classes had begun to mix in a frenzy of drinking, dining and dancing. Pélisser's own club membership included the Savage (famous for its hedonistic philosophy), then located in Adelphi Terrace, and The First-Nighter's, both of which sent tributes to his funeral in 1913.[31]

Certain *habituées* of these clubs were known as 'professional beauties'. Amongst the most celebrated was Catherine (Skittles) Walters, a *'grande horizontale'*, well-known to Harry's friend and biographer, Fitzroy Gardner according to his *Reminiscences of a Bohemian.*[32] When it came to notorious mistresses, actresses such as Lily Langtry, consort of the Prince of Wales, later King Edward VII, were especially prominent. Scandal was never far from a life on the stage. Ellen Terry had two children with her lover, the architect Edwin Godwin, though they were never married, while Mrs Patrick Campbell and the dancers Maud Allan and Isadora Duncan were openly libertarian in their lifestyles. For heterosexuals, at least, in bohemian and artistic circles 'free love' was certainly acknowledged and sometimes adopted, though hardly accepted or approved of in wider society.

Pélissier himself, from the very first days of his taking over the management of *The Follies*, quite conspicuously oversaw a steady turnover in members of the cast. These performers would traditionally start at a young age, often learning their trade while acting with the troupe, and thus perhaps also keeping the payroll as economical as possible. During the first years of *The Follies*, out went the more mature performers such as Mabel Engelhardt, Kate Carew and Nellie Reed. In came the teenage Ethel Allandale (along with her parents, Hetty and Fred) in July 1897. The young Miss Evelyn Hughes, despite her rave reviews in the local press lauding her as 'the chief attraction[33] with her vocal impersonations, seems to have lasted barely a month. They came and went these young pierettes – Gwyneth Boleyn, Beatrice Scully, Mona Clare and many more until Harry finally settled on a youthful line-up that included the regular participants Ethel Allandale, Gwennie Mars, Muriel George and Effie Cook, all of whom were fresh-faced *ingénues* when they began their careers with *The Follies*.

An easy-going, familial and friendly ambience seems to have characterized the relationships within the troupe. A wonderful publicity shot for the *Nicotine Quartet* sketch of 1910[34] depicts them all intimately nestled together on exotic cushions, reclining indolently, male and female alike drawing on cigarettes and seeming almost to kiss as they share the exhalations of smoke (see Figure 37). It is intentionally provocative and extremely modern in its feel; in fact, it could easily pass for the cover of a 1960s rock album. At least three married couples were to form out of the troupe. Dan Everard married the latecomer Dollis Brooke, while lyricist Arthur Davenport married the teenage Muriel George and Lewis Sydney married his fellow longstanding colleague Ethel Allandale. It was for this last wedding that, according to Fitzroy

Figure 37. Publicity shot for The Nicotine Quartets sketch

Gardner, Harry called off a long-planned motoring holiday across Europe and performed a U-turn from Paris in order to attend the ceremony:

> Pélissier's relations to his company are unique. He is more of a father or brother than a manager. He is addressed or spoken of by all of them – not as 'the chief' or 'the governor', but simply as 'Harry', and he takes as much interest in their private affairs as in their performance on the stage. When the marriage of Lewis Sydney and Ethel Allandale was fixed to take place at the conclusion of the short tour of the suburban theatres which followed immediately after their spring season at the Apollo last year [1909], 'Harry' being badly in need of a thorough change, had planned a long motor trip through France and Germany, and was compelled to deny himself the pleasure of being at their wedding. But while in Paris, he was overcome by a sensation of remorse and homesickness when he was reminded of his little company by seeing 'Folies Bergere' written large over the entrance to the theatre of that name. The next day he, and his car, and his chauffeur returned to London, and the following morning he turned up at the wedding.[35]

Harry Pélissier clearly loved Paris. He was a fluent French speaker. According to Gardner, part of his education had taken place in France. He made regular visits. Yet, unfortunately, of these we have no written record save a few teasing addresses noted in his pocket account books and tour-date diaries. He was a scrupulous collector of *The Follies* press reviews and he kept detailed accounts of the company's finances and performance dates, but unfortunately there appears to have survived no personal diary. Somewhat perplexing this, as one feels, for such a busy and diligent man, he may well have kept such a diary, at least of business or social meetings and appointments, auditions and rehearsals and the like. Yet none has thus far surfaced. Just as Harry did not, it seems, retain the correspondence he received from Fay (only his letters to her have survived), so, unfortunately for us, he does not seem to have kept any journal of his personal life. Intriguingly, however, a few notes are to be seen on the pages of his *Advance Date Book*, covering the period July 1908 to July 1910.[36] There we find hastily scribbled 'Elysée Palace Hotel, Champs Elysée', 'Regine Hotel, rue de Rivoli', 'Hotel de Paris' and 'Josephine Hotel'. Were these perhaps among his favourite haunts?

On another page, we find scrawled a few names, 'John F. MacDonald 144 l'is boulevard Montaparnasse', and 'Duncan Moms (Brighton)' with a certain 'Arthur Croxton' at the same location and, at '21 Tivoli Terrace North', 'Miss Jenny O'Reilly'.[37] Candidates to join *The Follies* perhaps? However, there may be other explanations.

Harry Pélissier was an erratic personality, given at one moment to great generosity and at another to callous cruelty; his humour could be dark and savage as well as jovial and fun-loving.

Is it possible that his ambivalent sexuality lay at the heart of his conflicted personality, his wild behaviour? Like many great humourists and comedians, from Spike Milligan and Tony Hancock to Frankie Howerd and Kenneth Williams, Harry Pélissier was given to spells of deep introversion and depression followed by outbursts of manic activity and high spirits. In the introduction to his sister's memoir *Rosemary*, it is once again Compton Mackenzie who seems to find the measure of the man more intimately and truthfully than many others of his acquaintance:

> Pélissier was becoming so much obsessed by the importance of humour that his own humour took on a kind of grim seriousness [. . .] It is the common fate of humourists to feel themselves thwarted by the medium which has made them famous. You may find it in Swift as much as in Dan Leno, and genius burned so hotly in Pélissier that towards the end he fancied that the atmosphere of the Follies was stifling him. His marriage with my sister, which at the time struck so many people as a kind of Folly joke, was to Pélissier himself the outward signal of his resolve to conquer fresh territories of the mind. It would take a book to present his psychology adequately and make his complicated personality credible, and I feel that I may have done him an injustice by saying as much as I have without saying a great deal more.[38]

On this ambiguous note, Compton Mackenzie had his final say on the subject of Harry Pélissier.

Figure 38 Morris Harvey as the Count and H.G. Pélissier as the Lady of Vrillac in a 'potted play' of Count Hannibal by Stanley J. Weyman 1911

12

The Romantic

Figure 39. Fay Compton, aged about 22

'Mr. Pélissier's newest joke'

In the autumn of 1911, news broke of the unannounced and improbable marriage of Harry Pélissier to the 17-year-old Fay Compton. *The Daily Mirror* ran the following headline: 'Mr. Pélissier's Newest Joke. Leading Lady As Bride.'[1] Typical of the time (as now perhaps), the caption was surrounded by a full-page spread of paparazzi-style photographs that depicted the newly wed couple rushing down Great Windmill Street, outside St Peter's Church, Soho as they hurriedly tried to escape the unwelcome melée. What the newspapers appeared to disapprove of most was the age difference, Harry being by then 37. However, there may also have been a hint of professional snobbery, for Harry of music hall and concert party fame was

Figure 40. Harry & Fay leave St Peter's Church, Soho on their wedding day, pursued by journalists.1911

marrying into the Compton family, a long-established dynasty of the legitimate, mainstream theatre.

The Bateman–Compton Dynasty, Henry Irving and Ellen Terry

Fay Compton was the youngest daughter of Virginia (née Bateman) and Edward Compton. Both her elder sisters, Viola and Kay, were successful actresses and members of their parents' theatrical troupe, the Compton Comedy Company. Her eldest brother Compton Mackenzie (known within the family circle as 'Monty') had, since the autumn of 1910, been Harry Pélissier's co-writer and was on the verge of a brilliant career as a novelist. The matriarch of the family, Virginia was herself the daughter of the celebrated Hezekiah Bateman, a fabulously successful American impresario, who had first brought Henry Irving to the attention of London audiences and been largely responsible for the launching of his legendary career. This had led to a close family relationship with both Henry Irving and Ellen Terry. In 1880, Irving had bought an Elizabethan country house in Hammersmith called The Grange from Fay Compton's aunt, Kate Bateman. This was the house he intended for his co-habitation with Ellen Terry once he had divorced his wife, Florence.[2] Indeed, Fay's other aunt, Isabel Bateman, had at one time been Terry's predecessor as Irving's leading lady. In 1885, Ellen Terry's brother Charles had become Edward Compton's business manager.[3] The two families were close indeed and, in some ways, Ellen Terry, whose red-haired, pre-Raphaelite beauty Fay Compton somewhat resembled, was something of a godmother and mentor to the young girl and was among the first to encourage her in a stage career. On one occasion, probably around 1902 when Fay was six years old, she was taken backstage at the Lyceum to meet the great diva following a performance of The Merchant of Venice, whereupon Terry declared: 'She is the one who will succeed!'[4] Fay's grandmother, Sydney Frances Bateman, née Cowell, was the equally impressive product of another Anglo-American theatrical dynasty, sister to the first great music hall star Samuel Cowell and a prolific author in her own right. Together, Hezekiah and his young wife (they married when she was just sixteen) were to forge a theatrical empire that took in not just the struggling Sadler's Wells in north London, but also the Lyceum in Drury Lane, while Sydney, specialising in the adaptation of popular novels, saw her melodrama Leah produced with great success in both New York and London.[5]

Fay's father, Edward, was son to Henry Compton, a well-regarded character actor who had gained some critical fame as the gravedigger alongside Irving's Hamlet at the Lyceum. Edward himself, much to his own and Virginia's disappointment no doubt, never quite reached the heights of success that his father-in-law had achieved. He failed to gain a much sought-after foothold in the West End when his adaptation and acting portrayal in Henry James's novel The American achieved neither commercial nor critical success. However, he did maintain a respected touring company, specialising in Restoration and Regency comedy, and eventually leased a chain of theatres throughout the provinces.[6] The Comptons were very much a part of the respectable, licensed theatre world, whereas Harry Pélissier represented all that was lowbrow and perhaps seen as rather vulgar in popular entertainment. Hence, it was this, as much as the age difference, that may have shocked the national press.

Scandal!

The early twentieth century was replete with scandals in high society. In recent years, the affair of Edward, Prince of Wales and the actress Lily Langtry, the divorce proceedings of Lady Colin Campbell and the illegitimate children and unmarried co-habitation of Ellen Terry had all been in the public eye. Most notorious of all perhaps, there followed the uninhibited dance displays of Maud Allan in her adaptation of Oscar Wilde's Salomé and her inclusion in the subsequent Black Book of Noel Pemberton Billing MP, which contained the names of 47,000 alleged 'sexual perverts' said to be spying on behalf of Germany.[7] Though Harry's marriage was small beer and unspectacular by comparison, it presented useful ammunition to those enemies of the irrepressible satirist who would have liked to see him brought down from his perch. Harry and Fay were married on 16 September 1911. Nine months later, in July 1912, their son Anthony was born, following which, after barely a year, Harry Pélissier was to die on 25 September 1913. So it was that within the span of just two years that the confirmed bachelor and self-proclaimed bohemian became not only a husband and a father, but also the victim of a sudden and fatal illness, leaving behind a widow and single mother of just 19 years of age.

Although a topic of notoriety, Harry's courtship of the young Fay Compton seems to have been condoned, and quite possibly even initiated and encouraged, by her mother Virginia. A substantial part of Harry and Fay's personal correspondence from this period has survived in the private family collection, and clearly reveals that they were known to each other some two or three years prior to their marriage and long before Fay joined *The Follies*. However, this was never openly acknowledged by the family either at the time or in any of their subsequent memoirs. Indeed, the accounts of various family members regarding these events contradict each other on several key points and it seems clear that the relationship, though initially platonic, was also in some measure clandestine and secretive. Moreover, it was Fay's mother Virginia, not his young wife, who was to nurse the dying Pélissier through his final weeks.[8] We also now know, through Harry Pélissier's will,[9] that it may well have been Virginia who indirectly was to become the principal beneficiary of his fortune; a fact of which, until recently, H.G. Pélissier's descendants were seemingly completely unaware. Indeed, when I met Harry's grandson, Jaudy, one of the first things he remarked to me was how strange it was that so successful a man as H.G. Pélissier should seemingly have left no legacy or inheritance, or nothing at least to his own father, Harry's son, Anthony. It has since become evident that there was indeed a legacy, there was a will and there was a substantial inheritance of £13,038 (well over a million and half pounds in today's money).

Prior to the marriage, the Compton family had been in some financial difficulties. This is a fact attested to by Compton Mackenzie in his memoirs,[10] as well as by Andro Linklater in his biography of the same.[11] Edward Compton had over-reached himself financially with an investment in a chain of theatres that had gone broke. Furthermore, he had backed a friend's gambling bill for £2,000 and was suddenly required to produce the money. *The Bishop's Son*, a play by Hall Caine in which he had invested, and which featured among the cast his own son Monty (Compton Mackenizie), had failed after one week.[12] As a consequence, and much to Monty's discomfort, his allowance was discontinued, and he was forced to fend for himself. Furthermore, Monty's elder brother Frank, having been denied the money from his father to purchase a new uniform for his regiment's deployment to the Far East, impulsively resigned his commission in a fit of fury, eventually turning his back on the entire family and emigrating to Canada. Financially, for the Comptons it was clearly a difficult time. Perhaps as a consequence, Virginia suffered something of a nervous breakdown in the winter of 1910 and shortly afterwards made her way to Sicily, with Fay as her companion, in order to recuperate.

Given these circumstances, Harry Pélissier may have seemed a rather promising catch as a prospective son-in-law, despite his notorious reputation and his somewhat lower theatrical status in the demi-monde of satirical burlesque. He was by now, after all, an extremely wealthy man with his own rather grand house in Finchley, a flat in Pall Mall and a highly successful theatre company holding its own in the fiercely competitive world of the West End. As it transpired, following his sudden death in 1913 and the inheritance of his considerable estate, Virginia Compton found herself able to purchase outright a property at 59 Greek Street in

Soho, The Theatre Girls Club,[13] and, the following year, to enter on something of a spending spree in the high-living style she most preferred.[14]

As to the exact circumstances of how it was that Harry met Fay, accounts vary. As far as Compton Mackenzie was concerned, it was he who introduced his sister to Harry in the June of 1911.[15] He had been working with Harry Pélissier as a lyric and sketch writer since the previous October and, according to Mackenzie, their introduction came through the Irish actor Shiel Barry, who was a fellow cast member in *The Bishop's Son* at the Garrick Theatre. His account goes as follows:

> Shiel Barry had been engaged by H.G. Pélissier to play the lead in a revue he had contracted to write for an Alhambra production before Christmas and told me he was going to suggest me for writing some of the lyrics. I did not take this seriously; I had seen too much of the theatre's ways to blow bubbles about possibilities.[16]

This revue was the ill-fated *All Change Here*. At the time, Compton Mackenzie was wretchedly ill with influenza, but nevertheless a meeting with Pélissier was arranged:

> I received a telegram from Shiel Barry to say that Pélissier wanted to see me about the revue. Would I come to the Apollo that night and meet him?[17]

All of this is corroborated by Faith Compton Mackenzie in her own memoirs. Mackenzie goes on to describe an evening of feasting and drinking, of composing and conversing, of exchanging ideas and opinions at Verrey's in Regent Street and at Pélissier's house in Finchley. 'If I call that supper Gargantuan,' he records, 'I am not using a trite epithet; since Gargantua himself there may never have been a man who was so much Gargantua as Pélissier was'.[18] As has been previously noted, Mackenzie and Pélissier went on to collaborate on the failed Alhambra revue *All Change Here* and then, more successfully, on *The Follies* songs and sketches once they were all back in their regular home of the Apollo Theatre in the spring of 1911. In May of that year, along with Mackenzie's wife Faith, all three of them moved in together to share the flat at 45 Pall Mall – though not by all accounts an actual *ménage á trois*, certainly something mildly scandalous in appearance and actively discouraged for that reason by Faith's family members, as in their eyes Harry Pélissier already had a reputation for 'loose living'.

However, it is at this point that the accounts of the various protagonists begin to diverge. According to Mackenzie, it was he who introduced Pélissier to his young sister Fay in 1911 during a trip to the family home at Riviere in Cornwall. 'In that blazing June,' he writes, 'Pélissier agreed to drive down to Cornwall one Saturday. My father's tour was finished; he and my mother were both at Riviere. So was Fay, of whom I had spoken to Pélissier and who was to meet her now for the first time'.[19]

In fact, seemingly unbeknown to her elder brother, Fay and Harry had already known one another for some considerable time. Indeed, they had been engaging in personal correspondence for at least the past two years and had clearly already met in person on several occasions.[20] It is not at all clear why Compton Mackenzie should have been unaware of this. One

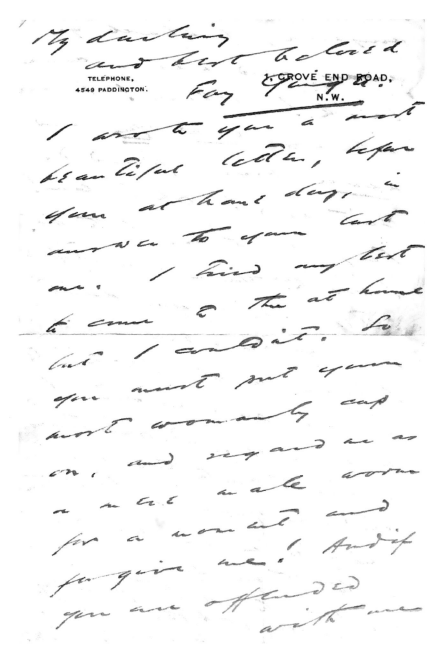

TELEPHONE,
4549 PADDINGTON.

1, GROVE END ROAD,
N.W.

Figure 41. A letter to 'Fay Ginger' from Harry, 9 July 1909

can only surmise that he was being kept in the dark by both parties, if not others as well, because such a familiarity would have been considered in some sense inappropriate. As indeed in due course it was, not least by Mackenzie himself.

So how then *did* Harry meet Fay? The secrecy that seems to have surrounded their relationship, and the differing accounts of family members, make it difficult to ascertain with any certainty. Added to this, of the surviving correspondence in the Pélissier family collection, only Harry's letters to Fay still exist (or a portion of them at least), and this despite his repeated requests to Fay that they be destroyed or at least hidden. Clearly, Fay felt sufficient sentimental attachment to resist these pleas and his letters to her were not only retained but passed on to future generations. For Harry's part, it seems clear that either he had no desire to retain Fay's correspondence, or his life was so peripatetic and unsettled, not to say chaotic, that they were simply mislaid in the general mayhem. That said, it is possible to discern a probable time sequence for the letters that remain, and from that to deduce what Fay herself may have written. The correspondence, and these speculations, have formed the basis of my novel *Pélissier's Folly*. The following, in brief, is an outline of the rationale.

The very first extant letter was written from Harry's address at the time, at 62 Regent's Park Road, Camden. It would appear to date from 1909, when Fay would have been 14 years old and still in attendance at Leatherhead School. It is clear that they had already met and were on fairly affectionate terms as the letter refers to: 'Dearest Fay Ginger, My love' and is signed off 'Harry'.[21]

What seems most likely is that Fay had met Harry backstage at the Apollo after attending a performance of *The Follies*. Being so young, she would have been escorted, most probably by her mother. Virginia Compton was an avid theatre goer and having retired from acting herself, would have been of assistance to her husband Edward in looking out for new authors and works to produce. While Edward's tastes may have leaned towards the more conservative and commercial, Virginia seems to have been quite wide-ranging and daring in her choices. For example, she had taken her son Monty to see Bernard Shaw's *Candida* at the Royal Court in 1905; an author whom, incidentally, Monty referred to as 'the only dramatist with a brain'.[22] Apart from managing and acting on tour with the Compton Comedy Company, Edward had leased a chain of provincial theatres, which would always be in search of current material. He had also enjoyed some financial and critical success through his investment in the musical comedy *The Arcadians* at the Shaftesbury Theatre.

So, it is not at all unlikely that Virginia would have taken her daughter to see *The Follies*. Indeed, in her own memoir, *Rosemary*, published in 1926, some thirteen years after Harry's death, Fay actually recalls having seen them as a child. The context given is that Monty had seen his sister perform in an amateur production at their home in Cornwall. The conversation is related as follows:

'[. . .] you were remarkably good in that ridiculous entertainment of yours in Cornwall this summer.'

'Oh that!'

'Yes, "This, That and The Other" [. . .] An imitation of the Follies of course, but not bad – not at all bad.'

'Well, you see we've been to the Follies tons of times. I'd rather go there than to any other theatre in London.'[23]

Thus, it is made plain that Fay had indeed attended *Follies'* performances at the Apollo. Even so, she goes on to maintain the fiction that her introduction to Harry Pélissier was via her brother Monty. However, in this case she makes no mention of Harry and Monty's visit to Cornwall in the June of 1911. Instead, she claims that their first encounter was during her audition for *The Follies* in London the following month, as arranged by her brother, something that simply cannot be true, given the existence of their prior correspondence. Even after the passage of more than a decade, the true history was not to be revealed.

A theatrical mentor

Figure 42. Fay Compton as a Folly, aged 18

It is interesting therefore to speculate as to how and why the correspondence began. In this regard, it may be of some relevance to note that Fay, rather curiously, was being discouraged by her parents from becoming a professional actress; and this, despite the family's well-connected and distinguished theatrical background and her siblings comparatively easy *entrée* on to the stage. It is clear from her own memoirs and from those of her brother Monty and of his wife, Faith, that Fay had been a rather sickly child, frequently suffering from a recurrent appendicitis. Given the immense physical and mental demands of the profession at that time, her parents seem to have considered her simply not up to the task. Undaunted, Fay would insist on being given her chance. In this context, it seems most probable that she herself, having once met Harry Pélissier backstage at the Apollo, may have instigated the correspondence with him in the hope of gaining some foothold on the stage. In time, of course, that is exactly what was to transpire. Unfortunately, as previously pointed out, none of Fay's letters have survived to confirm this. However, an early letter of Harry's, clearly postmarked 9 July 1909 and addressed from his then accommodation at Grove End in St John's Wood, likens Fay to 'the incomparable Mrs Siddons'[24] and would very much seem to be an encouragement to her to pursue her acting ambitions. Slowly, over the course of the succeeding years, Harry Pélissier appears to have become something of a theatrical mentor to the aspiring, but seemingly thwarted, Fay Compton.

Their correspondence continued throughout the latter part of 1909 and up to the end of 1910, by which time her brother Monty would have been working for *The Follies*. The tone becomes increasingly affectionate, if on the whole paternal and playful, even at times intimate. For example, Harry makes repeated reference to what appears to be his then female companion, who went by the name of Susanne and who had also clearly been introduced to Fay. Again and again, Harry seems to offer Fay professional encouragement to become an actress. 'Are you going on stage when you finish [at school]?' he writes. 'And, when you get your own company will you engage me? I can sing, and dance, and I can juggle with four oranges really rather nicely. My Dear Love. Yours affectionately, Harry'.[25]

It is not possible to know from this distance of time whether or not Virginia was actually aware of her young daughter's regular correspondence. It seems unlikely, given the attitudes of herself and her husband, that they would have welcomed Pélissier's encouragements to Fay to take up the stage. However, once the marriage proposal was made, Virginia at least seems to have proffered no objections, certainly not as regards the discrepancy in their ages or, indeed, Pélissier's reputed lifestyle. This may have been partly a reflection of her socially conservative family origins, which were in the southern states of America. Her own father, Hezekiah Bateman, had married her mother when she was just 16 years old. We should reflect at this point that, in the Victorian and Edwardian eras, marriages in general took place at a much earlier age than they do today. The legal age of consent had been just 12 until 1875, at which time it was raised to 13 by way of the Offences Against the Person Act. It was subsequently raised to 16 in the Criminal Law Amendment Act of 1885, where it remains to this day, provided there is parental consent. Queen Victoria was just 18 when she married Prince Albert, and her daughter, The Princess Royal, barely 17 when she married Prince Frederick, Crown Prince of Germany, whom she had been officially 'courting' since the age of 15. This was the moral and marital context in which Virginia Compton spent the formative period of her life. Furthermore, in 1901, life expectancy for a man was 48 and for a woman it was 52. One in ten women might expect to die in childbirth before the age of 25, so how much more dangerous would childbirth have been for her later in life. By the mid-twentieth century, the average marital age for women had increased to 22 along with a life expectancy of 66 and 71 for men and women respectively. In Edwardian times, the marriage of a 17-year-old would not have seemed so very exceptional.

Hezekiah and Sydney went on to have six children, of which Virginia was the second youngest. By all accounts (and we have only Virginia's own unpublished memoir and anecdotal family recollections to rely on),[26] she had a cruel and stern upbringing. Her two elder sisters, Kate and Ellen, were obliged to perform on stage at a very young age, becoming child stars on tour in the United States and England. This was a period in which, until a daughter was married, she might be expected to contribute to the family income. This too may have had some bearing on the Comptons willingness to see their daughter married, their financial circumstances being somewhat straitened at the time. However, far from being merely pragmatic, the harshness of the Bateman children's upbringing seems at times more like cruelty for cruelty's sake. In one instance, the teenage Virginia was for several years refused treatment for an infected eye until finally an eminent London surgeon insisted upon it and, by then, she was permanently disfigured. 'I'm afraid Mother let this happen on purpose' Virginia recounts in her memoir, 'I can't imagine anything else. I was very pretty and always having nice things said to me and of me, and I suppose she thought to be disfigured would be good for me. I daresay it was, for I never grumbled or reproached her'.[27]

Virginia Compton then goes on to recount a most bizarre and disturbing sequence of events involving her younger sister Isabel and Henry Irving. Sydney Bateman had taken the 33-year-old actor, then a fast-rising star, under her wing with a kind of maternal devotion. He began staying at the Bateman's residence during rehearsals, rather than returning home to his wife, a situation that persisted for the best part of four years. In his biography of Compton Mackenzie, Andro Linklater describes it thus: 'To keep him from drinking she [Virginia's mother] provided cups of beef tea and every night brought him back home from the theatre. To that extent her behaviour was irreproachable, but she also apparently believed that her youngest daughter should become his mistress'. [28] At the time, Isabel was just 15. Virginia vividly recounts how she had to stay up late at night to chaperone her sister and protect her from Irving's advances. It was not until Isabel was 18 years of age that she could summon the courage to tell her mother that she would refuse Irving's company. Nevertheless, she went on to become his leading lady at the Lyceum for several years, until, through the influence of its then manager, Bram Stoker, she was replaced by Ellen Terry. Isabel went on in adult life to form a Celibate Society with a friend and eventually to join an Anglican order of nuns at Wantage in Oxfordshire, where she was to become Mother Superior.[29] Given these childhood experiences, it is perhaps not surprising that Virginia seems to have been profoundly affected and what finally emerges is a truly complex and ultimately rather disturbing figure. Andro Linklater characterises it thus:

> [. . .] in the course of an unhappy and unstable childhood she had learned to exert an ironclad control over her emotions. Dominated by a cruel and ruthless mother, she was on the surface no more than a competent and biddable actress with an excellent memory for lines.[30]

Neglecting to care for her own children in person, Virginia had hired a drunken and bullying nanny by the name of Annie Curry, who was to prove the scourge of Compton Mackenzie's young life. Linklater summarises:

> Her coldness [Virginia's], like her acceptance of Annie Curry's unthinking discipline, arose, he [Monty] decided later from her fear of being accused of spoiling him. 'My mother was always convinced,' he wrote, 'that anything she herself very much wanted

to do was the wrong thing to do.' And so instead of giving way to her real wish to lavish affection on him, she deliberately made herself remote, and refused to replace Annie Curry long after she knew her to be a liar and a drunkard.[31]

A picture emerges of a deeply troubled individual, someone capable of passionate feelings, yet at the same time capable of rigorously repressing those feelings; someone who could be ruthless and cold and at the same time extravagant and ambitious. Over her children she held an iron grip:

> Even when he was in his fifties, Monty still sought her approval and her displeasure still made him as uncomfortable as in childhood [. . .] She was at war with herself, and her children were caught up in the battle.[32]

One thing is certain – Virginia carried within her person that deep conservatism, in all things domestic and religious, of the southern states of America. 'My mother,' Monty explains, 'like her own mother before her, thought that a girl could not be married soon enough.'[33] Furthermore, Virginia may well have carried a huge weight of resentment through her emotional life in having been denied the opportunity, when aged just 24, to marry the dashing and successful young actor-manager Walter Clayton, with whom she had fallen in love. Instead, Virginia was instructed by her mother to stay with the family company and tend to her newly widowed needs. This she dutifully did until 1881, when upon her mother's death she was free at last to marry and her choice fell upon another successful actor-manager, Edward Compton. But by now she was 30 years old, and the marriage contains every sign of mutual convenience rather than heady romance. As Andro Linklater puts it, 'Brought up without affection or attention, her emotions were wild and fanciful, but she imposed upon them a rigid discipline that was constantly at war with her desires'.[34]

Pragmatic and rather stern as Virginia's attitude to Fay may have been, it is also possible that she saw in Harry Pélissier the prospect a good marriage. She certainly would have admired his abundant talent, and the fact that it had led to the type of commercial and critical success in the West End that had so eluded her husband, Edward. In this respect, and in others, Virginia may have seen some resemblance in Harry Pélissier to her own adored much-lamented father, Hezekiah Bateman. The former certainly seems to have shared the latter's temperament and driving ambition. Hezekiah was nicknamed 'Chain-Lightning' for his explosive temper; likewise, Harry Pélissier was renowned for his sudden switches of mood and emotional outbursts. Both came, in their different ways, from unpromising non-theatrical backgrounds to achieve great success in dominating a particular niche of the theatrical world. At the time of her daughter's marriage, H.G. Pélissier may have seemed a very good catch indeed. Furthermore, if Fay was indeed so set on a stage career, where better to begin than in the heart of the West End?

For a while, over the early months of 1911, the correspondence appears to have ceased. During that period, Fay accompanied her mother to Taormina in Sicily for a period of convalescence before taking her place at a finishing school in Paris in May of that year. However, the letters quickly resumed upon her return, and it was soon afterwards that she was offered the opportunity to audition for *The Follies*. This took place in London at the Apollo Theatre in July 1911, with Faith Mackenzie providing the piano accompaniment while Monty sat alongside Harry Pélissier in judgement on his no-doubt nerve-stricken sister. The audition was a success and Fay Compton was offered her first professional stage role at the grand sum of two shillings and six pence per week – subject to her parents' approval. Edward consented on a provisional basis, allowing Fay to rehearse with *The Follies* in order to see how she progressed before he would give his final judgement.

That August, following a rehearsal at Riviere, the Comptons' rural retreat in Cornwall, Harry invited Fay and Faith to accompany him on one of his regular jaunts to Margate. Faith records the episode in some detail in her memoir *As Much As I Dare*. At this time, by Faith's account, Harry was truly infatuated with the young ingenue:

> In the open car we set out. The sky was a copper dome; there was not a breath of air. Harry sat in front with a bottle of eau-de-Cologne which he sprinkled continually on his head, making the coarse pepper and salt hair stand up like burnt grass. Margate was little better. Sea breezes could not cool the red-hot esplanades and hotels after weeks of baking. Fay was pale and tired when we arrived and soon, she was in agonies of pain with one of her chronic tummy-aches (later it turned out that her appendix was responsible). Harry was in a wild state, and suddenly 'took against me' as though I were responsible for her illness. She always had chlorodyne for these attacks, and we sent out for some. While I was pouring it out for her drop by drop, Harry came into the room. 'What are you doing?' he shouted. 'Pouring out Fay's chlorodyne.' 'No, you don't.' He rushed at me and seized the bottle. 'I'll do this thank you very much.' I let him do it and decided to go back to town, writing Monty to meet me. As soon as I knew that Fay was better and that another chaperon [*sic*] was on her way down, I left. London was still under a copper dome. But Monty met me at Victoria, the only man in London who had the sense to be dressed entirely in white.[35]

Unknown to either Faith or Monty, or indeed Fay's parents, some weeks before, in the late July of that year, Harry had already proposed to Fay and she had accepted. It was during one of their rehearsals at Elm House. Fay Compton vividly recalls the episode in her memoir, *Rosemary*:

> Meals at Finchley never seemed to take place under a quota of at least sixteen guests, all talking, laughing, joking and sometimes intentionally, sometimes unintentionally, providing material for the inimitable Folly burlesques. It was a most comfortable house to stay in but disturbing to sleep in, for at any time during the night one was liable to be wakened by the sound of a piano, an organ, a spinet, or some unknown instrument, for Harry slept so badly he often spent half the night playing and improvising. He had a delightful Samoyede dog named Polar, and I recall the sensation of there being something about the way he welcomed me when I first arrived at Elm House, as much as to say: 'You may not know it but I know that you are going to

stay here for a considerable time, permit me to show you over the house, in order that you may become accustomed to your new home as soon as possible,' and he led me to every room and all over the garden. It was only a few days later that Harry proposed to me. He was resting from a vigorous set of tennis, lying flat on his back on a gravel path of all uncomfortable spots to choose, and when he observed, 'Fay, will you marry me?' I thought he was joking, and pelted him with tennis balls, telling him not to be a foolish, fat fellow. Everybody who knew him or saw him on the stage will remember Harry's amazing personality, how attractive he was by reason of his gifts, how lovable by reason of himself, and who was I to be proof against his magnetism? About a week later, during which I learnt he was not in jest, I was kneeling on the chesterfield that stood at the back of his favourite piano, my arms on it, my head on them, watching him play; he looked up and asked me the same question again – and this time I answered 'Yes.' Immediately he burst into a little song, 'Fay, Fay, Fay, will you never run away?' turning it into a triumphal march as the improvisation continued.[36]

Their entire courtship and romance had been conducted in the shadows. However, once Fay declared her intentions, Virginia and Edward gave their consent, perhaps ruefully aware that Fay had been left unchaperoned, and potentially compromised, during their stay in Margate. By contrast, her brother Monty was incandescent with fury. He pleaded with his parents to forbid the marriage. In Octave Four of his memoirs, he writes:

I tackled my mother and told her that she must break off such a lunatic match. Pélissier was thirty-eight [*sic*], Fay was sixteen; Pélissier would be an emotional problem for a worldly-wise widow; he was drinking never less than a bottle of brandy a day and sometimes two. My mother, like her mother before her, thought that a girl could not be married soon enough. The attitude of the old South in her blood. No protest or argument of mine availed; [. . .] I tackled Pélissier, who persisted in saying that Faith's jealousy of Fay was the reason why she had persuaded me to object to the marriage. Then I told all my reasons for objecting to it, apart from the brandy; let those reasons remain in oblivion.[37]

And in oblivion those reasons have indeed remained ever since, Monty seeming to know such insalubrious, possibly scandalous, things about Harry that he could not bring himself to repeat them. He never exchanged another word with his former friend and colleague, choosing to attend neither his wedding nor his funeral. Nor in his later years were those reasons ever expounded upon in his copious written recollections concerning these events, despite his famously forensic and encyclopaedic memory.

The day after their wedding, *The Daily Mirror* printed its cruel headline. The couple had attempted in vain to keep the ceremony a secret from everybody, barring their closest friends and associates, but the news leaked out to the press and what resulted was something of an unruly scrum as they made their 'getaway'. Edward and Virginia Compton and a few chosen friends were present.

The cast and crew of *The Follies*, who in many ways perhaps represented a surrogate family for Harry Pélissier, awaited the happy couple at the Apollo Theatre, where that very afternoon and evening, Fay Compton made her professional acting debut and Harry proudly introduced her on stage as 'Mrs. Pélissier'.[38]

13

The Shadow

Figure 43. H.G. Pélissier by Hana

'The end was already in sight'

Prior to their wedding on 16 September 1911, Fay had been rehearsing with *The Follies* since her audition in July of that year:

> During the afternoon, [of the audition] Harry offered me an engagement as a Folly, at a salary of £3.10s. a week. [. . .] Then began a whirl of a time. Harry was anxious for me to imbue as much of the Folly spirit as possible before rehearsals for the new bill commenced [. . .] My first appearance was the Apollo at the beginning of the autumn of 1911; and there on the evening of September 16th a very large audience of Harry's friends and admirers gave a riotous reception to Mr. and Mrs. H.G.Pélissier. [. . .] A distressing breech of etiquette on my part in these early days that I have often thought of with shame, was when I made the mistake of accepting a dressing-room to myself, and

worse still of Harry's generosity in having it entirely redecorated and refurnished for me throughout. Of course, I should have realized that I was just an inexperienced artist drawing a very small salary and unworthy of either the room or its decorations. I noticed a coldness on the part of the other Folly girls on the subject, and that they did not seem to join in my admiration of the room when it was finished with the enthusiasm I expected. For a very long time now I have understood their resentment and have blushed at how often in my ignorance I must have unwittingly offended that most sensitive of institutions – professional etiquette.[1]

In short, Fay's sudden rise to prominence in the company, her special treatment and starring role caused friction in the previously harmonious 'family' of *The Follies*. She gave an interview to *Era*, published on 4 December 1913, just a few weeks after Harry's death, in order to publicise a role she had just landed as a German schoolgirl in a comedy entitled *La Presidente*. In that interview, Fay outlined her happiest memories of working with *The Follies*:

[. . .] no-one could have finer training anywhere. Every sort of work, from a dainty flapper to a charwoman with three or four minutes to change one's make-up and dress! And, of course, we all had to be able to sing, dance and play the piano. My favourite part when with The Follies was Lady Macbeth when we did a skit on the play. Then I also loved playing the charwoman in The Voice Trial, a part Gwennie Mars created so admirably.[2]

Gwennie Mars, a stalwart of *The Follies* for many years, had left the company and made way for Fay to join. She had, in fact, married an engineer called Burkinshaw and moved to Calcutta.[3] However, these new tensions and divisions within the company were not the only problem. According to Compton Mackenzie and to some press critics of the time, *The Follies* were already in decline when Fay joined them. His collaboration with Harry on *All Change Here*, the large-scale revue at the Alhambra, had turned out to be a massive failure (for reasons already discussed) and the desire to develop the scope of *The Follies* was proving elusive. In his introduction to his sister's memoirs, he writes:

I have heard many people express regret that the Follies ever became more elaborate, and I am perfectly sure that they were at their best in the old days before the Apollo when they did a thirty minutes' turn at the music halls. No doubt if Pélissier, without expansion, could have kept that first fine careless rapture and made all the money his temperament required, it would have been better for him and better for the audience. Unfortunately, no artist can crystallize himself at the moment of his nearest approach to perfection. The real reason why toward the end Pélissier began to lose some of his hold over the public was his own boredom with the development of the Follies. He became exasperated by his own creation. He was like the father of a grown-up family who resents his children's dependence on him, but who at the same time resents equally their daring to suppose themselves capable of the least independence. Without the breath of his life the Follies were dolls [. . .] When my sister joined the Follies the end was already in sight. They were beginning to expire of sophistication in the attempt to keep pace with the public's enjoyment of them to develop as their creator himself was developing.[4]

Both the shows and Harry himself were becoming something of a shadow of their former selves. In *The Times*, 20 years after Harry's death, the novelist Denis Mackail composed a valedictory reminiscence of *The Follies*: 'They bloomed brilliantly, but Pélissier wanted to experiment, and his public it seems were not only conservatives – as all London audiences were assumed to be in those days – in their politics. They did not like his experiments and he fought them, and he lost. Besides he was a sick man now, and clowns must never be sick'.[5]

Harry Pélissier's diary entry for Saturday 16 September 1911 makes no mention of his marriage at St. Peter's Church. It merely states 'Apollo'.[6] Once married, there was no honeymoon for the happy couple; just those two performances on the wedding day itself, followed by an uninterrupted run until Christmas Eve. Only then did they allow themselves a break on Christmas Day until resuming their performances on 26 December at the Empire Leicester Square right through until Sunday 4 February 1912. Harry Pélissier was clearly what in today's terms would be considered a workaholic – of extreme proportions, as in virtually everything he did.

However, it seems clear from the accounts of their schedule contained in the tour date diaries that the West End bookings were growing fewer and shorter in length.[7] In stark contrast to the previous three years, the next two years were to be mostly taken up with provincial touring. This must have represented a rather brusque and wounding about turn for a man whose rise to a long-lasting residency on Shaftesbury Avenue had been little short of meteoric. Perhaps the marriage to the teenage Fay had been a scandal too far, or the theatre managements were becoming less tolerant of Harry's running battle with the Lord Chamberlain and the censor's office, particularly in the increasingly febrile atmosphere of the build-up to war. Then again, in the figures and works he had lampooned, in politicians like Asquith and Churchill, and authors like J.M. Barrie and Arthur Conan-Doyle, he had made too many enemies and his fall from grace with a section of the public after the elaborate disaster of *All Change Here* was beyond repair. Whatever the principal cause, the summer of 1912 saw *The Follies* lose their secure foothold at the Apollo. Once more, they were back on the road on a provincial tour that took in over 16 cities, from Cambridge to Bristol, Birmingham to Aberdeen. It was not until 28 October that they were back once again at the Apollo, and this time for a much shorter season until 7 December.[8] Tom Davis, the Apollo manager, had suffered a sudden cancellation and called on Harry and his troupe to fill in at short notice, which they dutifully did.

'My darling girl'

Fay did not accompany *The Follies* on this latest provincial tour. In the summer of 1912, she was pregnant with their son Harry Anthony, who was born on 27 July. Harry, it seems, was able to take a short weekend break from his touring to visit his bride and their new-born son. Fortuitously, Harry Anthony had been born on a Saturday, and Sundays were the one day of the week that were free of public performances. While he was there, Fay became ill with stomach pains. At first the cause was not understood, and the doctors, having assured Harry that it was merely indigestion, he immediately returned to his touring. However, it soon became apparent that she was suffering once again from acute appendicitis. She remained at the family home at 1 Nevern Square under the convalescent care of her mother and her sister Viola. On receiving the news, Harry wrote from Plymouth, once again, finding himself in regular correspondence with Fay:

> My darling girl,
>
> My goodbye – I am afraid was not all it should have been, but I was afraid I should break down – and so make you worse – Both Doctors assured me that your trouble was simply wind otherwise I should not have gone at all –
>
> Do remember that if you want me to come back a wire will bring me back <u>at once</u> – anyway I shall try to forget my poor pathetic little Fay during the show and drink Mother's advice of Strong Beef tea <u>hard!</u> –
>
> Mother has promised to write to me darling – you add a word if you feel able – I shall telephone and if Viola is out, get one of the nurses to answer it.
>
> (It's very difficult to write in a train!)
>
> I am afraid I am wrong again in asking you to tear up my letters – (I meant to have told you) so if you don't want to <u>don't</u> – but see they are put away in a drawer somewhere.[9]

Once again, this last reference to the letters underlines the probability that their pre-marital friendship and correspondence had indeed been clandestine, and that Harry was anxious it remain a secret. However, the overall tone of his writing reveals a caring and loving husband. Clearly, even under the extraordinary rigours and demands of performing with and managing two fairly large-scale touring companies, and the considerable distances involved, he appears to have made every effort to be with his family. Once recovered, Fay returned to performing with *The Follies*, who were by then back in London appearing at its major music halls. She recounts it thus:

> I was back again at work in the autumn, feeling better than I had done for years, and it was just as well, for we did a season at the Palladium combined with other music halls.[10]

In fact, *The Follies* were booked to perform the pantomime *Aladdin* at the Empire, Leicester Square from Monday 9 December to Saturday 21 December, following which they transferred to the Coliseum until New Year's Eve. From there they moved on to the Palladium until 8 February 1913, all the while fitting in concurrent appearances at other venues throughout

London. Fay recounts the frantic nature of their schedule, quoting from her tour diary at the time:

Appeared in first house at Palladium, accomplished eight changes of costume and make-up, went to and

Appeared at end of first house at Stratford-at-Bow. Another eight changes of costume and make-up.

Appeared at beginning of second house at Stratford. Another eight changes of costume and make-up.

Returned to and

Appeared at end of second house at Palladium. A final eight changes of costume and make-up.[11]

All this, of course, just weeks after giving birth to her son in the most trying of circumstances and having undergone an operation at home for acute appendicitis. However, by this time, it was Harry himself who was beginning to show the first signs of what would prove his fatal illness. Fay goes on to recount an unfortunate incident:

The one and only time the Follies were booed in London was when Harry had undertaken to put on a new show at the Apollo at terribly short notice. [This would have been during their brief impromptu season in December 1912.] We had just over a week to prepare it. He ought to have said 'No', but he loved a task and said 'Yes' instead. The first part – the vaudeville – was good, and all was well; but the second – the potted plays and burlesque – was under-rehearsed and vague, in fact n.g. [*sic*] The gallery booed; the pit joined in. Harry, in a sporting spirit, told us to boo back; but we had allowed the audience to lose their sense of humour. They did not realize it was meant as a joke and became more than unfriendly. That Christmas, the sad time of distress and discouragement began, for Harry was starting his fatal illness.[12]

Saturday 7 December 1912 was to prove Harry Pélissier's last appearance at the Apollo, the theatre he had made so much his home. After their stints at the Empire, the Coliseum and Palladium and various other metropolitan music halls, *The Follies* resumed their provincial tour. This time Fay did not join them. It seems likely that she had only returned to the company while the engagements were in London and that now they both considered it better she stay at Nevern Square with her new-born son. Another factor may have been that relations with the other *Follies* had become too strained to bear. For whatever reason, Fay's touring with Harry was now at an end. From this point on, their correspondence resumes. That spring he

was required to undertake yet another gruelling tour, beginning in March in Portsmouth, then on to Manchester, Sheffield and Glasgow and many other provincial towns and cities. It is little wonder that on his constant diet of heavy drinking, cigar smoking and Gargantuan meals that the 15-stone Harry Pélissier was becoming increasingly ill under the pressure of this relentless regime. In March 1913, from the Totterdells Hotel in Portsmouth, he wrote what appears to be to be his final letter to his young wife, or at least the last to have survived. It was composed at 1.30 on a Friday night, and it makes clear that illness had necessitated his missing shows and that he was not feeling himself. From the outset there is a pleading tone, verging on desperate. The handwriting has become erratic and more of a scrawl and it is clear that his volatile temper is getting out of control. A fight has actually taken place on stage between himself and Douglas 'Boy' Maclaren:

My dear you must really come & look after me – I am so sick of everything just the same as you are –

I went to the thought reading lady this afternoon – she told many extraordinary things, saw your forecast & told me more extraordinary things about you – I am to do as you tell me! - & I really do want looking after – one thing she said was I wasn't to lose my temper – I made an enormous resolution not to do so – result – a big row with Douglas after the show! –

Disgraceful affair –

Facts as follows –

I pushed him in the coster number a bit harder than he appeared to like – he made some remark to me – under his breath – which I am sorry to say I forget – but I told Ben [Ben Lawes, now employed as Harry's stand-in] to give him a nasty punch as he shoved him off the stage (simply in fun, & remember the bruises he has given me – one of which I am wearing now. I never retaliate as I am afraid that my enormous weight might hurt him) – he was very annoyed and after the curtain came down he came up to me cross & wanted an explanation, he was very impertinent so I hit him not to hurt him but just a slap on the head. He then employed a very clever trick which took me entirely by surprise & landed me slap on my back on the stage! Before most of the company & the stage hands – I then very nearly lost my temper with him & caught him by the legs & threw him down on his back – & when he got up I went for him with I expect the villainous expression on my face which you have observed occasionally – he appeared extremely frightened & said it was only a joke – Fortunately his father was upstairs in my dressing room & I said to him "I shall kill your bloody son one of these days" he was very annoyed & has promised to talk to him about it - & as I pointed out to Dr. Mac [Douglas McClaren's father] it wasn't as if it was on the lawn at Finchley; which wouldn't have mattered – but what sort of story will be going about Southsea tomorrow when one of my troupe assaults me – & as I pointed out if it had been by any new member they would have been dead by now – a monkey mustn't excite an Elephant. I have not retaliated because I feel that once I let myself go I should kill him. – & after all I have done for him I told the Doctor to talk to him & he said I will certainly but why not talk yourself – I say if I do I shall lose my temper again – Charlie Vincent is obviously very annoyed & held a long observation on his family tonight. – I am simply furious –

I hope you can read this effusion as I can hardly do so myself.

You dear darling I wish I was with you & no worries to attend to –

Sunday Me

Love Harry[13]

His final performances were given at the Theatre Royal Plymouth between 21 and 31 May 1913 and, by June, Pélissier was so ill that he was obliged to cancel the engagements that were booked in for the next three months.[14] After a brief and unhappy respite at a nursing home in Hythe, he returned to Fay and his son Anthony at their family home in Earl's Court; and to Fay's mother, Virginia Compton, who would nurse him in his final weeks.

14

The Ghost

Figure 44. Fay and Harry Anthony in 1914

'In devoted attendance'

Harry Gabriel Pélissier died at 1 Nevern Square on 25 September 1913. The cause of death was given as cirrhosis of the liver and heart failure. He was just 39 years old. The years of high-living, relentless touring, copious brandy drinking and cigar smoking had taken their toll. Compton Mackenzie had already departed England for Italy and was staying with Max Beer-bohm in Rapallo, leaving Fay and Faith to witness his final dénouement. Faith recounts a vivid and haunting description:

> [. . .] in August 1913, Harry was occupying the library on the ground floor at Nevern Square, while Fay and I shared her mother's room. Mrs. Compton was living downstairs in devoted attendance on her son-in-law. Anthony, a year old, was in Fay's nursery above.

Harry's heavy-lashed eyes looked tragically from a shrunken face greatly refined by suffering. Of the stout, genial Folly chief there was not a trace. The wizard of laughter was a victim of that most deadly, depressing disease, cirrhosis of the liver. He would never smile again. Late one night Fay and I were talking quietly in the room above when our eyes met in apprehension. Something had passed through the room. We went out on the landing, and there was one of the nurses on the stairs coming to tell Fay that Harry had died suddenly. Next day I went with Fay to buy mourning. In the streets as we drove along were posters: 'Famous Actor Dead', 'Death of Pélissier', 'Folly Chief Dies'. His wife, aged nineteen, sat beside me in silence, her violet eyes clouded, last night's agonised tangle of red-gold hair smoothed under a small black hat. When the saleswoman asked what depth of mourning the young lady required, I found myself unable to say who she was, but whispered: 'her husband is dead.' There was an incredulous glance at the girl who stood framed in the mirror, and then a restrained eagerness to find her a garment suitable both to the occasion and her youth. She would wear it at the funeral, but I should not be there to see, for my ticket to Capri was booked and next day I was gone.[1]

It seems that even in these circumstances, the tragic Fay Compton was alone and abandoned by most of her closest friends and family. The funeral service took place at Golders Green Crematorium, not far from Harry's house in Finchley. A dedication from the rest of *The Follies* was made to 'the Great White Chief' of a floral tribute of white flowers in the shape of a pierrot cap with black buttons down one side.[2] His final resting place was to be with his mother in her grave at Marylebone Cemetery. With her family origins in the Kentish brewing industry, so closely allied to the music hall, perhaps it was his mother, Jennie Keen, who had been the biggest influence on his life and closest to his heart.

The executors to Harry's will were his brother and the family solicitor, the Honorable Charles Russell. The gross value of his estate was £13,098.14s.4d; again, it is worth emphasizing that this was over a million pounds in today's money.[3] In recent years, his published music had gained him over £1,000 a year, while for the past six years his constant touring and seasons at the Apollo had accumulated an average income of over £6,000 and, in one year alone, reaching the grand sum of £12,000.[4] The will had been drawn up 'immediately after my [Harry's] marriage'[5] on 16 September 1911. This had been a busy day indeed, as the couple had gone straight from their wedding breakfast to perform a matinée and evening show at the Apollo.[6] Did Harry have some forebodings of his imminent death in drawing up the will so hastily after the ceremony? Two years later, almost to the day, as he lay dying, on 9 September 1913, a codicil was added by which an allowance of up to £100 per annum was granted for the maintenance of his young son, Harry Anthony Compton Pélissier. This amendment was witnessed rather poignantly by his nurse, Dorothy Anne Raxe, and the Compton's housekeeper, Constance Weatherhogg.[7] Perhaps Harry felt that it was necessary to protect Harry Anthony's future from any potential lack of thrift on the part of the boy's young mother. In fact, still being technically a minor, Fay Compton would not have had immediate access to her inheritance. The official trustees were now Harry's brother Frederick and the solicitor Charles

Russell, but the question remains as to whether they would have had any strong motivation or interest in maintaining a close scrutiny and control over Fay's financial affairs. It is fair to assume that the young widow remained under the guiding parental influence, not to say firm control, of her mother Virginia. True to the family credo, and far from basking in her new-found wealth, Fay was immediately set to work.

> I was now, through the loss of my husband, one of the many who are 'looking for work'. I wrote to all the managers for interviews. I tried to persuade each one I saw that it would be immensely to his advantage to engage me as a member of his company, but with no success [. . .] My Folly training – invaluable though it was to be in the future – left me at that time rather in the position of the 'tweenie' who feels that neither kitchen work nor housework is her job. I had only been a short time on the stage. I was neither an actress nor a musical comedy artist, nor experienced enough in 'Folly' work to be of any real value in that line.[8]

As we shall see, *The Follies* themselves did in fact continue to put on shows without their former maestro, appearing later that year for a short run at the Palladium. However, rather cruelly one might think – and possibly indicative of their attitude to the young Mrs Pélissier – Fay was not offered any role. Instead, she boldly trooped around the audition circuit, failing to get a part as Gladys Cooper's understudy in the play *Diplomacy*, on the grounds that she was too young. Sir Gerald du Maurier had a hand in this rejection, so one cannot help wondering if some residual bitterness still lingered from Harry's savage send-up of his brother's play *An Englishman's Home*. She then failed in a reading for Jerome's *Robina in Search of a Husband* at the Haymarket. 'I was becoming discouraged,' she explains, 'almost everybody had seen me, but no-one was at all interested in me'.[9]

Yet that indomitable, almost bloody-minded, spirit, which so attracted Harry to her in the first place, still displayed itself. Probably through Compton family connections, she arranged an interview with the established actor and theatre manager Arthur Bourchier, who had been in charge of the Garrick theatre until a year before. He put her in touch with his successor at the Garrick, the producer Louis Meyer. 'Meyer wants a pretty flapper,' he said. 'I think you'll do'.[10] It transpired that the part had to be spoken in German, but, unflappable as ever, Fay got some overnight language coaching and took on the minor role of Anise in *Who's the Lady?* Being seen towards the end of the run by the actor-manager Robert Courtneidge (who had produced *The Arcadians*), she was offered the starring role in *The Pearl Girl* at the Shaftesbury theatre. This was a run-of-the-mill Gaiety style 'girl'-themed musical comedy – but it was Fay's first step into the legitimate theatre beyond the world of pierrot shows and revue.

It was also where she encountered her second husband, her leading co-star, Lauri de Frece. Again, he was a significantly older man, 34 years of age when they married in 1914, barely a year after Harry's death. Perhaps it was a marriage made in haste; single motherhood may not have seemed at the time a state that should persist for too long. In fact, Fay makes very little mention of her second husband in her memoirs save to say that he was a good and patient dance teacher during the run of *The Pearl Girl*. The still 19-year-old Fay must have been reeling from all that had happened to her and hardly in the clearest frame of mind.

Their next engagement took them both to America in *Tonight's the Night* at the Madison Square Theatre in New York. Originally only Lauri de Frece had been cast in the show, but Fay insisted on accompanying him and, when the actress initially cast to play the character of Victorine fell ill, she took on the role. The American tour consisted of a run in Boston and Philadelphia and then a return to New York, as well as an informal trip to Coney Island with Jerome Kern and his English wife. Fay's career was beginning to take off, but she was by her own admission neither a natural singer nor a dancer. Back home in England in 1915 and cast as the lead in Ziegfeld's *The Only Girl*, she turned to the eminent vocal tutor Herman Klein for singing lessons. 'Mr. Klein did not turn me into a marvelous prima donna, but he made it possible for me to sing the songs and fulfill the engagement'.[11] The show got a mixed response, but was not a complete flop. 'After its London run the play went on a tour, and on the halls the joys of playing twice a night and three matinées a week were mine once more'.[12]

Fay and Lauri de Frece together then joined the cast of the musical revue *Follow the Crowd* at the Empire in London. 'Let me say at once I did not like revue and revue did not like me'.[13] For the first time in her life, Fay moved across into the world of straight acting and displayed a strong and natural flair for comedy in the American farce *Fair and Warmer*, which was to run at the Prince of Wales theatre for over a year. It was during this run that she recounts her 'pleasure at seeing my sister Kay back from America, and my father's joy at seeing us back together again, to be followed so soon, alas, by his death; and towards the end of the run the delirious joy of Armistice Day'.[14] It was November 1918 and all this time, including the perilous crossings back and forth to America, the First World War had been raging. Fay was next engaged to perform in Somerset Maugham's *Caesar's Wife* and then in *Summertime*, both at the Royalty theatre, and the light comedy *Tea for Three* at the Haymarket. At 23 years of age, Fay Compton was becoming an established West End star. It was then that her career was to enter a whole new phase through her association with the work of J.M. Barrie, for it was in early 1919 that she was cast alongside the celebrated actor H.B. Irving (Sir Henry Irving's son) in Barrie's *The Professor's Love Story*.

My Barrie Book

Such was the profound importance that Fay attached to her professional relationship with J.M. Barrie that during these formative years of her career, she kept a sort of rehearsal diary, a mixture of scrapbook, photo album and journal that she called *My Barrie Book*. 'The first page is White (*sic*), and across it in bold letters I can trace the name Lucy. The page is a blank one and so was my mind when first entrusted with this part in *The Professor's Love Story*. I was stunned by the honour of being asked to play with H.B. Irving in a Barrie play'.[15] One has to bear in mind the veritable Colossus that J.M. Barrie represented on the West End stage at this time. His fantasy play *Peter Pan,* with its central motif of the 'boy who would never grow up' had struck a deeply resonant chord with audiences who had suffered the terrible, youthful losses of the First World War. Barrie was noted for the regular attendance he gave to his own play rehearsals, as well as for the subsequent revisions he would make to the scripts. In *My Barrie Book,* Fay writes regarding rehearsals for *The Professor's Love Story,* 'How awful I am in this part. I wish Sir James would say something, though I know he would only tell me how bad I am [. . .] He's been in the stalls all to-day again, but not a word from him'.[16] Fay's insecurity regarding her own abilities shines through these passages, but in fact she had no need to fear; her low opinion of herself was unwarranted for not only did she thrive in the part of Lucy, but at the end of the run she received a note from the author. 'I hope you will be able to play Peter. It will be a joy to hear from Mr. Boucicault that it is to come off'.[17]

Figure 45. Fay Compton, 1926

Boucicault was the producer of *Peter Pan* at the Duke of York's, and it did come off and throughout the course of 1919, Fay Compton thrillingly and dashingly delivered the eponymous role with a swashbuckling bravado that sings out from the photographs and notes of her scrapbook. 'The pages are written and re-written with happy memories of learning to speak Peter's words, think Peter's thoughts, sing Peter's songs, fly with Peter's wings, fight Peter's battles, be friends with his friends and take care of Wendy as he did'.[18] At one point in these scrapbook recollections, Fay recounts having been introduced to J.M. Barrie when just a little girl, having been taken to see the original production of Peter Pan in 1904, and having foretold that she would one day play the part. She speculates on inviting all the tiny children who have written her fan letters to the tea-parties that were regularly held for the children in the play and the children of the cast members. 'But perhaps [. . .] they would have been disappointed to find the Peter, of whose small boyhood they apparently had no doubt, with a small boy of his own'.[19]

All this time, the young Harry Anthony, now aged seven, had been in the care of his grandmother Virginia. His existence was no secret, but it seems that he was kept somewhat in the shadows and apart from his mother as she concentrated on building her career. Curiously, as she recounts her son's first visit to the theatre, she mistakes his age; or did she prefer readers not to realise that she had been just seventeen when he was born?

When Anthony came to see me play Peter, he was only five, and when Peter was left alone in the lagoon scene saying, 'To die would be an awfully big adventure' a loud wail rose from the box, and poor Ant had to be carried out crying, 'They've left her alone – left her all alone!'[20]

Mary Rose – Rosemary

Was J.M. Barrie present at the Duke of York's that night to witness this traumatic scene? The figure of the young Fay Compton, in the guise of *Peter Pan*, had been left alone and abandoned on an imaginary island; her distantly held son expressing his painful consciousness of own mother's isolation and distress. There, on stage, a bitter metaphor of Fay's own life story of teenage motherhood and bereavement; all imbued with the tragic fable of the child-in-adult, adult-in-child, of the 'child who would never grow up'. Barrie's next play was to prove his most critically and commercially successful work after *Peter Pan*. It was entitled *Mary Rose* and it was to be written especially for and dedicated to Fay Compton. It tells the story of a young girl who quite literally, both physically and psychologically, never grows up; of a girl deprived of her childhood who disappears on a remote island; a girl who has a son called Harry, whom she scarcely meets; until that is, she returns years later, in the form of a ghost unaltered in age or appearance. In truth, perhaps it was the ghost of Harry Pélissier that was about to return. In her memoir *Rosemary*, Fay writes:

> There is no denying that from the very beginning there was something 'different' about the production of *Mary Rose*. Even before she talked to me from the typed pages of a manuscript, I was wondering about her, wondering if it could really be true that Barrie was going to write a story especially for me, wherein I should find a heroine whose creation on the stage he could entrust to me.[21]

The story outline of *Mary Rose* (one can hardly call it a plot) is that an 11-year-old girl from Sussex is taken on holiday by her parents to a remote Scottish island, a tiny speck of land that bears the mythical name 'The Island That Likes to Be Visited'. She suddenly disappears. The parents search frantically over a period of days until two weeks later the young girl reappears just as suddenly as she had vanished, totally oblivious as to what has occurred. To her, the fortnight's disappearance seemed but a matter of minutes. All of this is recounted in the past, for in Act One of the play we first encounter Mary Rose back home in Sussex, aged 18 and about to be married. As the act closes, Mary Rose insists on being taken back to the island, despite the reservations of her husband-to-be. Move forward three years in time, and we are in Act Two, the young couple are indeed back on 'The Island That Likes to Be Visited', and we learn that their new-born child, Harry, has been left in the care of a nurse. Again, Mary Rose suddenly disappears, only this time for a further 25 years. Act Three finds us back in the family's Sussex cottage, where a reunion is taking place between her parents and her husband, a man who, feeling abandoned and broken-hearted, had taken himself off to sea for the intervening period. Then, suddenly once more Mary Rose makes another reappearance – completely unaltered since she was last seen, still apparently aged just twenty-one, untouched by age or time. In the final scene she is reunited with her son, who has come back to the haunted house in search of his mother's ghost, and it is their reunion that finally sets her spirit at rest.

Barrie had originally conceived the play as a darker, more sinister sequel to *Peter Pan*. 'The Island That Likes To Be Visited' was in fact to be Peter Pan's 'Never Land' and the character of Mary Rose was originally to be called Joanna, another incarnation of Wendy, as Leonee Ormond has pointed out in her study of J.M. Barrie:

> In the first manuscript the island is revealed as a place of perfect happiness, the Never Land, the home of Peter Pan. Behind a gauze curtain the audience was to see the trees through which Peter and the lost boys make their way underground [. . .] By originally locating Mary Rose's two disappearances on Peter's island and by returning her to it at the end, Barrie relied on a direct theatrical reference. He was wise to change the ending, which an audience unfamiliar with *Peter Pan* would find inexplicable and bizarre.[22]

So, Barrie, famous for the continual re-writing of his work, decided to make *Mary Rose* a completely stand-alone play. However, many parallels remain between the two works. As Peter Hollindale writes in the introduction to the Oxford Classic edition, 'they represent a continuing preoccupation in Barrie's work with the tragic interplay between time and timelessness and fantasy-as-reality. In both plays these themes are represented by the child-mother and the death-in-life-tragedy of perpetual youth'.[23]

In the person of Fay Compton, J.M. Barrie had met a real-life Mary Rose, the embodiment of the youthful tragedy that so obsessed him. His decision to name Mary Rose's son 'Harry' (both the name of Fay's deceased husband and the legally given name of her infant son) leads to a truly disturbing reading of some of the lines in the play. Take, for example, the scene where the ghost of Mary Rose, appearing to be just 21 (when in fact she is in her fifties) is reunited with her son Harry. This fully-grown man, now in his thirties, appears to be older than his own youthful mother! In fact, Mary Rose, still unaware that she is a timeless, ageless ghost, either deliberately or innocently takes her son to be her (now deceased) husband Simon, and doggedly refuses to believe otherwise:

MARY ROSE. You – you are not Simon are you?
HARRY. No. My name is Harry.
MARY ROSE. (*stiffening*) I don't think so. I strongly object to your saying that.
HARRY. I'm a queer sort of cove, and I would like to hear you call me Harry.
MARY ROSE. (*firmly)* I decline. I regret, but I absolutely decline.
HARRY. No offence.
MARY ROSE. I think you are sorry for me.
HARRY. I am that.
MARY ROSE. I am sorry for me too.[24]

Many people might have felt sorry for Fay Compton. Her life thus far had been laden with tragedy and instability. The hasty marriage to her second husband, Lauri de Frece, had proved a total disaster. By the time *Mary Rose* opened at the Haymarket theatre on 22 April 1920, they had already been divorced for nearly a year since their decree nisi of 28 May 1921.[25] The dashing actor with the matinée-idol looks had proved to be a faithless and promiscuous cad; having contracted a fatal disease and made his way to Trouville-sur-Mer in Calvados, France, he died on 25 August 1921. At the age of just 26, Fay Compton found herself widowed for the second time.

Barrie was perfectly aware of the tragic aspects of his starring actress's life. Fay was the very embodiment of that youthful innocence combined with a knowing experience that he sought to represent on stage – 'the child-mother and the death-in-life-tragedy of perpetual youth'.[26] And Fay was aware of this herself. So strongly did she identify with the part of Mary Rose that, when in 1926 she published a memoir of her thus far short career, she entitled it *Rosemary*, a subtle but significant inversion of the play's title. What exactly did she mean by this? Surely one likely interpretation is that she considered her own life in many ways to be an inverted reflection of the eponymous heroine. Whereas Mary Rose was the perpetual child, a combination of Peter Pan and Wendy, who 'would never grow up', Fay Compton had been the child star and wife and mother and widow who had conversely, never been granted a real childhood, who had prematurely been required to act the grown-up even in her early adolescence, with a marriage at just 17 years of age to a man 20 years her senior. The fact that she made this allusion in the title of her memoirs; and that, despite Harry's own remonstrances, she retained her youthful correspondence for future years, suggest that, regardless of her family's ignorance or silence on the matter, this was a personal history that Fay wished eventually to be known. As Peter Hollindale writes, '[. . .] it is unstoppable time in the world outside that makes for Mary Rose's tragedy, and she, even more than Peter Pan, is a disturbing version of Barrie's lifelong obsession with child-in-adult and adult-in-child'.[27] Fay Compton was an incarnation in the real world of both these concepts. One might almost feel that Barrie cynically exploited the depths of Fay's own personal experience and emotions to achieve the extraordinary effects that she was, by all accounts, able to convey on stage. The play was a run-away success. In fact, it pays testament to the ruthless dedication of the artist on the parts of both Fay Compton and J.M. Barrie that they were able to so enlist the forces of reality, the tragedy so redolent in their own experience and imagination, into the representation of their art. Both the play and Fay's performance received universally rapturous reviews and Fay's identification with the role did not go un-noticed: 'No actress but Fay Compton could, perhaps, have created the name-part so surely and so delicately';[28] 'An irresistible attraction'.[29]

One must also recall that J.M. Barrie, some ten years prior, had engaged in something of a running battle with Fay's first husband. Harry Pélissier had been such a thorn in the author's side for many years with his parodies of *Peter Pan* and *What Every Woman Knows* and *An Englishman's Home*, that Barrie had even felt constrained at one point to write his own faintly damning review of *The Follies* and their 'potted plays'.[30] By employing Harry's widow to play

Peter Pan, then subsequently in creating a role for her that so closely mirrored her own history and in creating his own 'Harry' on stage, was the playwright perhaps giving himself the final say? It is worth remembering that the young Fay Compton was strikingly beautiful. At this stage in her life, with her pale ivory complexion and a thick mane of wavy red hair, she had come to resemble even more closely the young Ellen Terry, that close family friend who similarly embodied the pre-Raphaelite ideal. Her eyes were equally striking. Faith Mackenzie wrote of her that 'She had a baby face, but her violet eyes were not a baby's eyes'.[31] J.M. Barrie once famously commented with glaring disapproval on seeing Sir George Frampton's statue of Peter Pan in Kensington Gardens, 'It doesn't show the devil in Peter'. One suspects that Fay certainly did.

'Squandermania'

But what a heavy price Fay Compton must have paid for all her hard-won success. When not appearing in the West End or travelling on tour, she spent most of her time in the country house she had bought with Lauri de Frece near Bramley in Surrey. There, she seems to have given most of her attention and affection to her dogs and ponies. Dogs had always played a significant part in her life and had been a running motif in the relationship with her 'Binkie', H.G. Pélissier. She was certainly not paying close attention to their son, Anthony. He had been left in the care of his grandmother Virginia while Fay revelled in the carefree, bohemian lifestyle to which she had been so brusquely introduced by Harry Pélissier himself. Of a return trip from New York, in 1925, she wrote, 'When I had to sail home again my cabin on the *Mauretania* became a sort of super-green room, for I left at one o'clock in the morning, and all my theatrical friends, including Gertrude Lawrence, Beatrice Lillie, Auriol Lee, Ashley Dukes, Dick Barthelmes, Glen Hunter, Clifton Webb, Leslie Howard, Jack Buchanan, Noel Coward, Robert Andrews, and I can't remember how many more, all came along after their work to give me a cheery au revoir'.[32] What comes across is a free living, free loving, independent modern woman with a sharp talent for comedy and a no-nonsense wit that gained her a favoured place among the sophisticated theatrical society of her time. The association with Noel Coward was to prove enduring. It seems that they may have been introduced by Monty's wife, Faith. Andro Linklater writes:

> In London Monty had stayed with Faith at Markham Square. There he met her smart homosexual friends, including the young Ivor Novello and the even younger Noel Coward, and the latest Compton star, his sister Fay, who that summer was appearing in James Barrie's *Mary Rose*. Catching the expansive, spendthrift mood of the moment, he indulged in what he called 'squandermania', or spending lavishly on luxuries.[33]

These, after all, were the 'Roaring Twenties', the jazz age, one great heady, orgiastic, reckless party, a sort of antidote, a search for a kind of oblivion after the hideous nightmare of the First World War. Fay took full advantage of these decadent days, becoming it seems something of a wild child. Following her divorce from Lauri de Frece, she was married again within a year to the actor Leon Quartermaine. In June 1921, they both narrowly survived a car collision[34] and, on one occasion, the wild partying may even have found Fay Compton arrested and cautioned by the police, along with Ivor Novello, for possession of cocaine.[35] Fay's first appearance with Novello was in the London premiere of Ferenc Molnar's melodrama *Liliom*. It was promoted in the most lurid terms, with little regard to restraint: 'Fay Compton and Ivor Novello in a Hungarian Peasant Play (featuring) wife beating [. . .] and brutality'.[36] The image of a free-living, bohemian wild child, a modern woman, is one that Fay Compton seems to have deliberately cultivated. A publicity still for her appearance as Yasmin in Flecker's *Hassan* at the Haymarket in March 1924, displays her unashamedly as a kind of vamp in the mould of the notorious silent film star, Theda Bara.[37]

In 1931, Fay and Novello appeared together in Dodie Smith's first play *Autumn Crocus* and, in 1934, in the film version of the same. At this time, Novello too made no effort to disguise the decadent excesses of his bohemian lifestyle. Wild parties were being thrown at Redroofs, his country house near Maidenhead, to which Fay would have been a regular guest. Cecil Beaton dubbed it 'the Ivor/Noel naughty set'.[38] In Novello's play *The Party*, produced at the Strand theatre in 1932 and intended as something of a celebrity exposé, cocaine is brazenly disported. One critic wrote, 'I feel Mr. Novello did wrong in introducing a tragic note, when a young wife, thinking she has been deceived by her husband, attempts to commit suicide by taking an overdose of cocaine. (Some skeletons, even a dramatist, should leave to moulder in their cupboard)'.[39]

This is the social scene into which the young widow and mother Fay Compton was thrust and into which she seems to have thrown herself quite willingly, indeed with gusto. As a direct consequence perhaps, in July 1936, she was required to take abrupt absence from her West End appearance in *Call It a Day* at the Globe for an emergency nose operation[40] – an ailment that was to trouble her for the rest of her life. Could there perhaps have been some connection to those wild parties? In 1928, Fay was successfully cited in the divorce proceedings brought by Mrs Ronald Alfred Trew against her husband 'on the grounds of misconduct [. . .] with Miss Fay Compton, the actress'. Trew had apparently 'fallen in love with Fay and visited her at her flat in John Street, Adelphi'.[41] Miss Compton had by now become Mrs Leon Quartermaine; they too were divorced, in February 1946. At no time does Fay seem to have attempted to play down her risqué reputation with the public. Perhaps that is why she had to face 'persistent barracking'[42] on the first night of *Autumn Crocus* at the Lyric, for which the critic of the *Nottingham Journal* considered her 'not too well cast in the role of a quiet little school teacher from Eccles'.[43] Even in 1951, Fay was playing up to her image by appearing in the UK premiere of Jean Cocteau's *Intimate Relations,* a study of near-incest banned by the Lord Chamberlain for 12 years and billed as 'The Powerful and Gripping Sex Drama that shook half Europe'.[44]

Andro Linklater writes:

[. . .] much of her disastrous private life since Pélissier's death left her a widow at nineteen can be seen as an attempt to secure some emotional independence. She neglected her young son, Antony [*sic*], and to Virginia's dismay embarked on a succession of love affairs culminating in a failed second marriage. 'I deeply, deeply blame myself for many of her failings and sins,' her mother agonised some years later.[45]

In fact, Virginia Compton herself was in her own way enjoying the reckless abundance of the times. Linklater goes on to point out that, 'Lavish as his [Monty's] squandermania had been, it was soon surpassed by his mother, who was beginning to indulge an urge to extravagance held in check during thirty-five years of marriage. In 1915 she started a small organisation to help unemployed actresses find work and to give them shelter'.[46] This was the Theatre Girls' Club in Soho. Not long after Pélissier's death, Virginia had purchased its headquarters at 59 Greek Street. It ran successfully long into the 1960s and, in later life, provided overnight accommodation for herself and at various times for her actress daughters. Monty became a trustee. It seems quite possible that, while Fay was busily 'in search of work' following Harry's death, Virginia may have found a convenient use for the unexpected inheritance of which she was guardian.

Blithe Spirit

On balance, it is hard to see how the wild child Fay would ever have settled down into the quiet role of motherhood, even if Harry Pélissier had not died so suddenly in 1913. It may have been an ill-fated match from the start. On the other hand, it is possible to see Harry and Fay as somewhat unlikely soulmates who might well have shared years of a blissful, mutual bohemian decadence together had they been granted the opportunity. In 1925, Fay undertook an extraordinary attempt to contact her late husband at a spiritualist séance, held by Herbert Dennis Bradley, a celebrated inter-war medium, in the study of his Kingston house. It was reported thus at the time:

> Several members of the theatrical profession appear to have been converted to spiritualism after taking part in séances at Mr. Bradley's house. Miss Fay Compton writes (quoted from *Wisdom of the Gods* by H. Dennis Bradley), 'I was aware of a great force that seemed to be surging through me. Mr. Bradley thinks I am psychic and that I am able to give the spirits help in coming through. This may account for this strange feeling.' At this sitting, at which Mr. George Valiantine, the American, was the medium, the late Harry Pélissier, Miss Compton's first husband, is said to have spoken to her. Mr. Bradley writes: 'Pélissier is a very virile and determined spirit. He spoke to her in a voice that vibrated with love. He is apparently as much attracted to her now as he was whilst he was on earth. Not only did he speak to her, but he spoke to Leon Quartermain [*sic*] (Miss Compton's present husband) with an understanding of the changes which had occurred in earth conditions. Pélissier told Fay that when she passed over, he would be there to welcome her.[47]

In fact, the medium George Valiantine was later exposed as a fraud, not least by H. Dennis Bradley himself,[48] but the incident surely attests to Fay's strong and genuine bond with her deceased husband that she should have gone to such desperate, even alarming, lengths to 'contact' him. Professionally, of course, Fay went on to become a great star, not just of the West End stage but also of British cinema and television – appearing in over 40 films and in the BBC's legendary *Forsyte Saga* in the 1970s. Along the way, one of her early triumphs was to appear in the premiére of Noel Coward's *Blithe Spirit* at the Piccadilly theatre in July 1941. In this she created the role of Ruth, Charles Condomine's second wife – who fails to see a ghost.

15

The Legacy

Figure 46. Portrait of H.G. Pélissier by Sir John Collier

A lost satirical voice

On 4 August 1914, a little less than a year after Harry Pélissier's death, Great Britain declared war on Germany. In fact, hostilities on the continent had already been raging since July of that year as a result of Austria-Hungary's declaration of war with Serbia. Even before that, for at least a decade, the dreadful, fear-laden shadow of conflict had been steadily growing. With the outbreak of open war, there was little mood for the frivolities of satire. A voice such as Harry Pélissier's would be easily drowned out and forgotten in the nationalistic fervour of the times. The general tenor of opinion was reflected in an even more rigorous censorship and in the heightened jingoism and militarism of many of the popular music hall songs written during the Great War. Even in 1912, as Nicholson points out: '[. . .] playwrights had complained to the King that since the 1909 enquiry the Lord Chamberlain had "exercised his powers of refusing to license plays far more oppressively than before"'.[1] In the climate of gathering hostility, the theatres and music halls would themselves become recruiting grounds for the trenches, a technique that originated in the patriotic war songs of G.H. 'the Great' MacDermott and in the foyer of Wyndham's Theatre in 1909 with its production of *An Englishman's Home*. For example, at the conclusion of *England Expects* by Seymour Hicks and Edward Knoblock, produced in September 1914, a film-reel of marching soldiers was displayed to the accompaniment of patriotic music while 'stooge' volunteers mounted the stage to encourage other members of the audience to recruit.[2]

The subversive element of popular, working-class music hall gave way almost entirely to a nationalistic sentiment that still characterises its memory to this day. Vesta Tilley would become known as the 'best recruiting sergeant' of World War One with songs such as 'The Army of Today's All Right' and 'Jolly Good Luck to the Girl Who Loves a Soldier'. Likewise, Clara Beck had a huge hit with the Arthur Wimperis song 'I'll Make a Man of You!' It was an era in which male impersonators (female artistes cross-dressing into male costume) could mock a 'cowardly' man for not signing up. Not only did the halls ring to the ubiquitous 'It's a Long Way to Tipperary', 'Pack Up Your Troubles' and 'Goodbyee!', there also came a whole legion of new patriotic war songs. Many of these ridiculed the German nation and its leader in particular, such as 'Belgium Put the Kibosh up the Kaiser', 'The Kaiser's Little Walk to France', 'Hoch Hoch Hoch the Kaiser!', and 'The Germans are Coming So They Say', all of 1914. Then came 'I'm Giving up my Job to the Kaiser' and 'Goodbye Kaiser Bill' of 1915, and 'My Old Iron Cross' of the following year.[3]

As the casualties mounted and war conditions worsened, the song lyrics could become more sardonic and bitter, as in 'Oh It's a Lovely War!' and Vesta Tilley's 'A Bit of a One for Blighty', but even here criticism is muted and there is no mention of death or killing.

> It was [. . .] not possible to use on the music hall stage as harsh a level of sarcasm and black humour as is present in many soldier songs, songs which were invented by and for the lower ranks. Soldiers' songs could ironize about violent 'hangin' on the old barbed wire' or expose a wish to kill their military superiors.[4]

This trend towards a more explicit expression was also a feature of the literary material produced by troops at the front, such as the satirical periodical *The Wipers Times*[5] or the bitterly ironic poetry of Siegfried Sassoon.[6] Of course, songs with a theme of war represented only a portion of the music-hall output at this period. There continued the tradition of sentimental ballads and sexual innuendo in pieces such as 'Why Am I Always the Bridesmaid, Never the Blushing Bride?' or 'A Little of What You Fancy Does You Good'. But even here, the hand of the censor remained in firm control and lyrics were never permitted to be explicit, so that dexterous performers such as Marie Lloyd and Florrie Forde would utilise a suggestiveness of gesture and delivery in their performance that often went completely over the censor's head. Compton Mackenzie, however, makes the observation that had Harry Pélissier lived he might well have provided a more bitterly critical viewpoint of the war. In his introduction to his sister's memoir, *Rosemary*, he writes:

> I have always felt thankful that he [Pélissier] did not live to encounter the war, for if his humour had moved much further along the lines he was dragging it he might have lapsed into some tragical error of taste that would have seemed unpardonable in that period of strained emotions.[7]

Taste is often the enemy of truth, and Mackenzie may be right that H.G. Pélissier's characteristic candour would have found it difficult to restrain itself.

Those who sought a more frivolous entertainment away from the patriotic choruses would also have found themselves in the vastly expanding emporia of the moving picture. In December 1913, Charlie Chaplin had signed with Mack Sennett in Hollywood and his first appearance as an actor in *Making a Living* would be released in February 1914; in his second feature of that year, *Mabel's Strange Predicament*, the character of the 'Tramp' was born. In the face of this whole new genre of mass entertainment, the world of live, on-stage musical revue and music hall became less and less fashionable. In 1915, the first custom-built film studios were constructed at Lime Grove. By 1914, there were already around 500 cinemas in London alone and, by the 1920s, some of these were able to accommodate as many as 3,000 patrons.[8] The majority of films being shown were not only sentimental and knockabout in character, but, of course, entirely silent apart from the customary live musical accompaniment. They were thus free of dialogue, offering little scope for verbal wit, save for the occasional bland captions that interspersed the filmed action. It was revolutionary in form, if not content; a new era was coming into being and the likes of Harry Pélissier would seem, on the surface, to have become increasingly outdated. However, from one perspective, the routines of the music hall may indeed have contributed to their own demise, for it has even been argued that burlesque sketches of the Edwardian era 'had their greatest impact in terms of the influence they wrought on early film comedy'.[9]

Similarly, after the war, the taste in popular music itself would move on from the customary march and waltz rhythms, the cakewalk and ragtime of the music hall and concert party and a new craze would develop for the Charleston and for Big Band Jazz, for the dance halls and night clubs of the West End. All of this would be symbolised in the brash and confident musicals of Irving Berlin, George Gershwin and Jerome Kern that were being imported from America. In these escapist diversions, there was also little to be found of satire or even social comment. Throughout the western world there seemed to be an almost all-encompassing desire for social conservatism, sentimental romance and heavy-handed censorship, prevalent not just through the Great War itself, but further enhanced through the Socialist-fearing 1920s, the Depression era of the 1930s, the wearily war-torn years of the 1940s and the subsequent Cold War of the 1950s.

A nurturer of talent

Perhaps, therefore, the most direct artistic legacy of H.G. Pélissier can be traced in the careers of those other actors, writers and composers whose careers he helped nurture and shape. As has already been noted, he discovered and was the formative influence upon the young Fay Compton, who would go on to such a distinguished acting career. Likewise, his influence upon her brother, Compton Mackenzie was significant. When first employed as Harry's script writer and lyricist, Mackenzie had been a struggling actor and unpublished author. Although their principal collaboration on *All Change Here*, the musical revue of 1910, was not a success, his work with Pélissier was to be a major inspiration for no less than five of his early, formative novels. His first critical and commercial success was *Carnival*[10] (the second of his published works). This was very much informed and inspired by Mackenzie's days with *The Follies*. Its leading female character, the dancer Jenny Pearl was closely based on Monty's real-life lover at the time, Chrissie Maude; she had been a member of the chorus line in *All Change Here* at the Alhambra. Indeed, the West End variety theatre of the opening decade of the twentieth century forms the whole backdrop to that particular novel, although Compton Mackenzie never went so far in that work as to create a figure who closely resembled Harry Pélissier himself.

The closest portrayal of the Maestro that Monty ever came up with may have been Henry or Harry Snow, the father of the eponymous heroine of his subsequent work, *The Adventures of Sylvia Scarlett*.[11] Portions of this epic novel, a self-conscious update of the heroine, Becky Sharp, of Thackeray's *Vanity Fair*, also borrow heavily from Mackenzie's experience with *The Follies*. Harry Snow, an alcoholic pierrot performer, dies in mysterious circumstances, falling off a cliff, either in a drunken accident or in a misjudged attempt to murder a young lover, half his age, with whom he is jealously besotted. If it was intended to represent Pélissier in any way, after half a decade's absence (being published in 1918), this was a distinctly bitter and dismissive way to do it. What are more clearly based on his *Follies* experience are the descriptions of the ramshackle and impecunious lifestyle, and the relentless touring of seaside towns by the pierrot troupe – not something that Mackenzie would himself have been a part of, (since *The Follies* were already appearing in the West End when he joined them), but which could clearly have been the fruit of conversations during his year-long association with the members of the cast as they reminisced and recounted their past experiences. Indeed, despite his falling out with Harry Pélissier over the marriage to his young sister, Compton Mackenzie would always maintain that their collaboration on *All Change Here* represented one of the happiest periods of his life. 'The revue was a failure,' he wrote, 'but since it led directly to my writing *Carnival*, I look back at it with an affectionate emotion that no other production ever has evoked, or ever will evoke'.[12]

Something else that Mackenzie may owe to these formative experiences with the great satirist is the candour of sexual expression and social observation that increasingly characterises his serious novels. When his thinly veiled autobiographical novel *Sinister Street* exploded on to the bookstands in 1913, it developed into an immediate cult among schoolboy readers, avid to explore its honest account of youthful sexuality and adolescent relationships. Although banned by many popular outlets, including W.H. Smith, for the very explicit nature of its writing, it remained an influential favourite with such budding talents as Cyril Connolly, George Orwell and Evelyn Waugh. Both in his fiction and in his autobiographical memoirs, Mackenzie displayed a frank approach to his own sexual inclinations and encounters, and an open and supportive disposition towards both the homosexual and sex-worker communities. For its time, this was little short of rare and courageous. It should be remembered that, while the likes of D.H. Lawrence and Virginia Woolf amongst others may have claimed the louder plaudits for their outspoken and pioneering sexual attitudes, Mackenzie too was something of a trailblazer in this regard, and his experiences with H.G. Pélissier may well have encouraged him. It should be borne in mind that when he protested so vociferously against Pélissier's marriage to his young sister, it was not so much on the grounds of Pélissier's lifestyle – which he had to some degree shared – so much as on the basis that his sister was far too young to understand or accommodate them. Today, Mackenzie is probably best remembered for his lighter, comic works such as *Whisky Galore* and *Monarch of the Glen*. This in itself is something of a travesty for his serious novels were extremely groundbreaking and influential in their time and, like Pélissier, he is perhaps worthy of critical re-evaluation.

Arthur Wimperis was another to whom Pélissier gave his first foothold on the ladder to artistic success. As we have seen, their earliest collaboration went back as far as 1893 with the published song 'A Memory of Spain'. However, they would continue to work together throughout the early years of *The Follies* touring days, up to and including their seasons at the Apollo and even occasionally beyond. It is arguable that Wimperis's formative experience with Harry Pélissier during their satirical collaborations on such songs as 'What A Happy Land Is England' (of 1904) and 'What A Very Great Improvement It Would Be' (of 1906) informed the style of his groundbreaking musical success of 1909, *The Arcadians*. It was undoubtedly with *The Follies* that Wimperis had honed his song-lyric and script-writing skills, and it was these that he was able to develop over the subsequent four decades with a successful West End and Hollywood career.

Harry's only child, Anthony, would also go on to forge a distinguished stage and film career, despite his singularly difficult entry into the world. His father had died when he was barely 18 months old, to be followed by near abandonment at the hands of his mother. These early traumas clearly left their mark. As Fay pursued her youthful acting career, either through choice or through family pressure, the young Anthony was left in the care of his grandmother,

Virginia, though even here there seems to have been little love. He was sent to boarding school at five years of age and, by all accounts, grew up in an atmosphere of loneliness and bitter resentment. His outburst at the age of seven, when taken to see his mother's portrayal of Peter Pan, gave testament surely to his own conflicted emotions and his feelings towards her. 'She is all alone! Don't leave her alone!' he is reported to have cried.[13] Nevertheless, upon reaching adulthood, he decided to try his own hand at acting. In 1935, he turned to the family friend Noel Coward, who cast him in his play cycle *Tonight at 8.30.*[14] And it was with this very work that Anthony Pélissier subsequently made his directorial film debut when he transferred it to the screen.[15] In fact, he was at the same time writing some pieces of his own, one of which, *Talk of the Devil,* a short comedy for a West End revue, featured a young John Mills. Out of this collaboration developed a life-long friendship and a professional partnership that spawned some of that actor's finest screen roles. *A History of Mr. Polly,* based on the H.G. Wells novel and directed by Anthony Pélissier in 1949, is counted by Mills as his favourite screen role.[16] In *The Rocking-Horse Winner*[17] of 1950, based on a short story by that youthful friend of Compton Mackenzie's formative years, D.H. Lawrence, John Mills chose to play a more minor role rather than a lead part, (a decision which he subsequently regretted), and the result was critically, though not commercially, successful – perhaps for that very reason.

However, the film is remarkable in other ways. Every scene is exquisitely shot and beautifully, hauntingly framed by the director and his cameraman and editor, John Seaborne. The central motif of the film is a young boy's fatal obsession to raise money to fund the decadent and spendthrift habits of his negligent and distant mother as she slides into penniless ruin. He does so through the ghostly voice of a rocking-horse that is able to predict the winners of races; but, tragically, the stake that he has placed is his very own life. The film offers a chilling echo of Anthony Pélisser's almost orphan-like upbringing and relationship with his own distant and career-focused mother. In its atmospheric telling and its elegant framing, it presages what was to be his own later career – that of a fine artist working on the Mediterranean coast, withdrawn and absent and dislocated from the world of show-business, into which he had been born and to which he had been initially attracted. His son Jaudy Pélissier recalls,

> I think my father was a lot more aware of his [Harry's] success than he ever let on and that this created a lot of pressure on him to live up to. Harry wrote, composed and performed to critical and commercial acclaim, something my father would have been very aware of. As a young man, I'm sure he wanted to live up to that success; and in his own way he was equally multi-talented. Of course, when my grandfather died, it was only two days after Fay's nineteenth birthday. But sadly, she was just a young girl with her whole life to lead and certainly didn't want to be saddled with a little boy and the maternal responsibilities that went with it.[18]

In fact, one of the very first enterprises together of Anthony Pélissier and John Mills was not a film at all, but rather an attempt on stage to revive the songs and sketches of Anthony's own father, Harry Pélissier. The late thirties were an unproductive and rather inactive period in the British film industry. In 1937, the young John Mills and Anthony Pélissier took themselves off to Saenenmoser in the Swiss Alps for a skiing holiday in order to commiserate and recuperate. Mills recalls it thus:

One evening in the bar we were discussing the theatre as usual, and the Pélissier Follies came up in the conversation. After the second bottle of heavy Swiss red wine had been consumed, we decided that London was ready and waiting with bated breath for a revival of the famous Follies. Ant had the rights of several of his father's famous numbers – 'Moon, Moon, serenely shining' [*sic*] and so on – and he could put together rapidly and with little problem a superb show. Fired with enthusiasm, heightened by the wine, we returned to London. Ant contacted a friend of his, Robert Nesbitt, who liked the idea, and together they devised the show. An excellent cast was assembled, including my old friend Doris Hare, Gene Gerrard, and an enchanting young musical comedy actress called Roma Beaumont [. . .] Initially things looked fairly promising. An enthusiastic reception on the first night and a mixed bag of notices, some good, some fair; but unfortunately for us, James Agate, the one critic at the time who was powerful enough to make or break the show, wrote a long brilliantly argued piece in the Sunday Times which I feel sounded the show's death-knell. Agate made the point that 'Pélissier's acting went on up to his death when all genius in his kind was not eclipsed but as far as we can see extinguished forever. The Co-optimists who followed in 1921 were a pale

Figure 47. Pelissier Follies of 1938; Anthony Pélissier at the back, John Mills, second row far left.

182

echo of the Follies and the Pélissier Follies of 1938 are a still paler echo of the Co-optimists.' James Agate was right. Harry Pélissier was the Follies. The shows that followed with his name on the bills, but without his presence on the stage were pale, ghostly creations that never materialized.[19]

In fact, in 1913, *The Follies* had every intention of attempting to keep the show on the road after Harry's death. With professional courage and determination, they continued to fulfill the bookings that had already been made; those which had not already been cancelled at any rate. The forward dates in Harry's diary of 1912–14 for July to September 1913 are rather poignantly penciled through as 'cancelled'.[20] However, under the new stewardship of Dan Everard, *The Follies* were back at the Coliseum on 3 November 1913 for a run that lasted through till 6 February 1914. In March of that year, they had a short season at the Palladium and then were on tour through the summer throughout the country from Peterborough to Cheltenham and Wolverhampton. A photograph in *The Bystander* of 29 October 1913 portrays *The Follies* with the caption 'Heading for Bristol under Dan Everard'.[21] In November 1914 they were once again back at the Coliseum for a short season, this time until 10 December. They then continued touring the provinces throughout the Great War.

Providing entertainment for wounded soldiers became a staple of their activities and helped keep the public aware of their continued activity after Harry's demise. In February 1916, they were cheerily photographed in the presence of Lady Douglas Haig, as they entertained the injured at the Third London General Hospital in Wandsworth.[22] Dan Everard was the natural successor to take over the management of *The Follies*. He had always been Harry's administrative second-in-command and his marriage to Dollis Brooke thrust his wife into a starring role in the company, although in truth she required little encouragement, having already played the female lead in *Aladdin* at the Alhambra. However, the bookings began to grow thinner and more sporadic as the years passed. The critical reception was lukewarm at best. In 1919 the impresario Ernest C. Rolls attempted to revive their fortunes with a series of matinées at the Strand theatre. He even went so far as to employ a lookalike 'H.G. Pélissier' in the form of actor-comedian Ben Lawes, but the Maestro's shoes proved too big to fill:

[. . .] in Mr. Ben Lawes, they have achieved a figure in bulk, features and voice quite uncannily like the Founder. Yet despite this species of incantation, despite the enlistment of clever people whom he would have made brilliant, and the production of sketches that he would have made uproarious, the Founder refuses to come to the feast [. . .] You can now see all that Pélissier was to the Follies. It was not simply his songs and impersonations, or those amazing audacious chats with the audience before the curtain. It was just by being present on the stage, jovial, cynical, self-confident [. . .] like Falstaff transfiguring mean taverns into palaces.[23]

And thus, *The London Mail* of 30 August 1919:

> Ben Lawes, who is commendably stout, hasn't Pélissier's sense of humour as a personality, and he was wise I think to curtail the famous curtain lectures [. . .] Dan Everard gives an excellent impersonation of himself as he was under the Pélissier régime, and Dollis Brooke is the only other 'old contemptible' [. . .] In short, the present company should always be accepted.[24]

Only Dan and Dollis seemed up to the task. The original cast members had moved on. Ben Lawes was brusquely dropped from the show as the troupe staggered on, touring intermittently and with ever-shorter seasons. In February 1921, yet another attempt was made to revamp *The Follies* revues. Lauri Wylie scripted the book, intended as a series of reminiscences along with songs and potted plays in the Pélissier style. 'Novelty will be the main feature of the performance,' reported the *Sunday Sportsman*, 'the Follies' will be presented on new lines, with a new "book", new dresses, and new scenes'.[25] It was reported in the *Empire News* of 13 February 1921:

> Once more the famous and some-time incomparable troupe of pierrots known as The Follies is to be revived [. . .] Item in the programme:– A Grand Spectacular Cinematographical Super Six-and-Six Production Tarzan of the Shapes; a Children's Play for Grown-ups [. . .] Lauri Wylie is the guilty man who has perpetrated this atrocity.[26]

The show ran for just two weeks until 13 March 1921. Lamely, the company returned to sporadic summer tours until their final appearance on 29 September 1923 at the Pump Rooms in Bath. Finally, it was the end for *The Follies*. Dan Everard had kept very clear and precise financial accounts, much more comprehensive than the hastily scribbled and idiosyncratic records of his deceased former leader. That week beginning 24 September, the company made the disappointing sum of £128.6s.4d. He wrote in his diary:

> This week is a between seasons date being neither summer nor winter. Town very empty of visitors. Residents don't support very strongly and won't come out if wet. Strong attraction against us at theatre. Musical comedy.[27]

In fact, the takings were fairly average for them by now and far from their worst. At Great Yarmouth in August 1920, they had amassed just £25.19s.5d.[28] But both the bookings and the income were in a general decline. In 1915 *The Follies* had made over £240 in their Christmas week and nearly £270 in Edinburgh in a single week in May 2016.[29] The writing had truly been on the wall since Harry Pélissier's demise. Nobody could replace his personality and wit. John Mills's comment on James Agate's assessment had surely been right: 'Harry Pélissier was the Follies'.[30]

In 1939, the BBC wrote to Dollis Brooke requesting a memoir of her years with *The Follies* for possible use in a radio broadcast. Dollis replied:

The show restarted under my husband's management only two weeks after his death (Harry Pélissier's) and played a record time of 19 weeks on end at the Coliseum and from then until 1920 my husband managed it in trust for Harry's son Anthony and then purchased it from the trustees and it continued until 1923 when we both gave up the stage owing to the arrival of our own son.[31].

In the late twenties, some popular interest began to be rekindled in the music hall years prior to the Great War. At 8pm on Friday 12 October 1928, the BBC broadcast a one-hour programme of *Folllies'* songs and sketches featuring Dan Everard, Dollis Brooke and Lewis Sydney among others. It was re-broadcast twice the following evening at 8pm and then again at 9.35pm. The total fee received by the company was £190.[32] On 25 and 26 January 1929, between 8pm and 9pm and again between 9.35pm and 10.35pm, *The Follies* performed a live retrospective broadcast for the BBC. Ten years later in 1939, the producer Leslie Bailey put together *The Scrapbook for 1910*, another reminiscence of *Follies'* songs and sketches. It was recorded on 9 November and broadcast on 3 December of that year between 9.15pm and 10.15pm. On that occasion Dollis Brooke received £6.60 for her contribution.[33] Another altogether different show was compiled for January 1958, again by Leslie Bailey, but this time a nostalgic representation of the year 1908 on its fiftieth anniversary. This was entitled a *Scrapbook for 1908* and as well as encompassing Ford Motor Cars and Collins Music Hall, unemployment legislation and Baden-Powell, it featured a short contribution from Dollis Brooke relating memories of *The Follies* as the orchestra played Harry's songs 'My Moon' and 'Under the Weeping Willow'. The cast included Deryck Guyler and Andrew Faulds among others' but apart from Dollis, none of the surviving *Follies* took part.[34]

An obituary to Dan Everard appeared in the *Worthing Herald* of 19 December 1936 relating that he had passed away in a local nursing home.[35] His widow, Dollis, continued living at their home in Worthing, until later that year she moved back to London, where she resided in Golders Green – not far from their previous residence during the 1920s. Despite their valiant efforts, *The Follies* rather faded away against the competition of emerging forms of entertainment and without the presence of their guiding spirit.

The creator of English musical revue

What did live on of course in one form or another was *The Follies* as a name and title. The original company was never billed during Harry Pélissier's lifetime as *Pélissier's Follies*. They were known quite simply as *The Follies* and were familiar to theatrical circles under that name, not only throughout Britain, but also in America by way of the reports and reviews they had received in the New York press. Indeed, according to Compton Mackenzie, *The Follies* had been invited to perform in the United States on several occasions – opportunities that Pélissier declined on the grounds that he doubted his brand of humour would be understood on that side of the Atlantic.[36] When Ziegfeld unashamedly began using the name for his own productions in 1907, Harry Pélissier had already been using the title for over a decade and it was of course necessary for Ziegfeld to distinguish his works by inserting his own surname into the bill. However, these shows had none of the satirical, improvised edge or intimate confessional style of Harry Pélissier's revues. They owed more to the *tableau vivants* of the *Folies Bergère*, vaudeville and variety and the chorus lines of the Gaiety girl-themed musical comedies. There can be little doubt that the originator of *The Follies* in the Anglophone world, both as the theatrical concept of a satirical musical revue and as a company title, was Harry Pélissier.

Certainly, after Pélissier had introduced the concept of a longer, theme-linked, comic routine with original songs in his *Bill Bailey* sketch of 1903, the fashion took off more widely in the West End. His style was immediately adopted at the Oxford, Pavilion and Tivoli music halls[37] and thereafter by Albert de Courville at the Alhambra from 1912 and Charles Cochrane at the Ambassadors in 1914.[38] The way was now ready for the influx of American style musical comedy and variety acts led by Alfred Butt at the Palace Theatre in that same year. As has been noted, in the 1920s *The Co-optimists* offered up a rather tame version of *The Follies* with their own pierrot-costumed revue, while the full fruition of variety and musical comedy during this inter-war period might be said to have completed the music-hallisation of theatre as anticipated by Albert Chevalier. It seems clear that H.G. Pélissier left the legacy in Britain of a genre that we now call musical revue. From that perspective, Pélissier's influence persisted, even thrived, in the succeeding decades. According to Maggie B. Gale: 'A singular characteristic of the London stage between the wars was the growth of musical comedies, variety shows and revues [that] drew on the Victorian and Edwardian world of music hall'. She goes on to point out, however that it was only: 'From the mid-1930s a more politically astute form of revue developed. Intimate rather than spectacular, *This Year, Next Year* at the Gate Theatre was the first of the "topical, witty and satirical" revues which became especially popular'.[39] In style, if not entirely in substance, Pélissier's notion of the musical revue lived on, with its essential elements of topicality, wit and intimacy.

Another pretender to Harry Pélissier's claim to be the originator of musical revue is André Charlot, on whose behalf it is sometimes argued that he introduced musical revue on to the London stage. Charlot himself, in an essay of 1934, defined revue as a 'medley of spectacle, topicalities, sketches, songs etc. with a full cast consistent with the size of theatre where it is being produced, and no attempt at a plot of any kind'.[40] In fact, Harry Pélissier had been offering precisely this to the London public throughout the entire decade before Charlot arrived from France as a talent hunter at the Alhambra in 1912. And when James Ross Moore claims that: 'For several years the portly, ingenious Pélisser had run this enlarged version of a "concert party"',[41] he rather misses the point that the founder of *The Follies* had never in fact presented a conventional concert party, enlarged or otherwise, but on the contrary, had always deliberately sought to bring precisely that notion of French revue to British audiences years ahead of its presumed innovator, André Charlot. This, of course, had always been quite explicit in the very name of the troupe. By comparison, Charlot's early revues at the Alhambra, such as *Kill That Fly!* and *Eight Pence A Mile* were in effect rather tame variety spectacles, while his later grander works such as *The Revue of 1924*, which transferred to Broadway, owed as much to Ziegfeld as they did to Paris.

As already noted, *The Follies* without Pélissier continued into the 1920s and their work was remembered by many, including the likes of John Mills at the end of the 1930s, as still being familiar to the general public. Their memory staggered on with the pale imitation of their style presented by *The Co-optimists* at the Royalty and Palace theatres until 1927, while those prominent literary visitors to *The Follies* at the Apollo, including Bernard Shaw, J.M. Barrie, G.K. Chesterton, a young Robert Graves and many others, would have retained the memory of their anarchic style. However, if there was a direct successor to H.G. Pélissier, it was surely Noel Coward, who was to become such a firm friend of Harry's widow Fay and his son Anthony. With his subtly transgressive songs such as 'Mad About the Boy' and in his satirical numbers like 'There is Bad News Just Around the Corner' and 'Mad Dogs and Englishmen', he closely reflects that intimate, witty, cabaret style first originated by H.G. Pélissier. However, Coward's songs and musical comedies were on the whole of an altogether more restrained and polite nature than Pélissier's anarchic revels. The wilder satirical musical revue would enjoy a brief post-war revival in the private clubs of Soho, such as Elsa Lanchester's 'Cave of Harmony'. Opened in Charlotte Street in 1924, this venue would become a favourite haunt of Arnold Bennett and Evelyn Waugh amongst others.[42] By contrast, the music halls and variety theatres continued their decline, maintaining a sanitary and 'respectable' inoffensiveness, whilst simultaneously degenerating into an innocuous poor relation to the dance halls and cinemas, as portrayed in John Osborne's *The Entertainer*.

A pioneer of the absurdist spirit

The heady spirit of absurdist and satirical creativity that so typified *The Follies* was to a large extent effectively buried by the censorial powers of the Lord Chamberlain's office. However, from the late 1950s onwards, it was to re-emerge in a whole new generation inspired by the anarchic nonsense of *The Goon Show* and the sardonic social commentary of *Beyond the Fringe*. It is surely no coincidence that the sixties and seventies, those decades which saw the full bur-

Figure 48. At home in Elm House, Finchley

geoning of this free-spirited creativity, would make direct reference to the Edwardian era, not only in their theatrical and literary forms but also in their style of fashion and music. Revamped ruff collared shirts and smoking jackets and dandified rakish haircuts became once more in vogue, echoing the style of Oscar Wilde, particularly among the so-called 'Mods' – a term that itself borrowed from 'Modernists' of the early twentieth century. So too, John Lennon and *The Beatles* drew heavily on the British music hall style in their revolutionary album *Sergeant Pepper's Lonely Hearts Club Band.*

The long-skirted Biba look mimicked the turn-of-the-century freedom and elegance of the Gibson Girl and the Bloomsbury Group. Graphic artists drew inspiration from the likes of Aubrey Beardsley and the late pre-Raphaelites with their psychedelic swirls and hypnotic patterns. Even the drugs of choice in the 1960s echoed the alcohol, laudanum, opium and hashish of pre-Great-War Britain, while Mary Quant made the pillbox, fringe hair-cut and skinny physique of the 'flapper' once again *à la mode*. All of this seemed refreshingly 'new' at the time, of course, the music itself being electrified in a technologically revolutionary way. However, in style and substance, it was as though the nation was engaging in the artistic and cultural reawakening of a lost pre-1914 generation; in a collective demonstration of what the world might have become had the hand of militaristic, censorial authoritarianism not dragged it into the apocalyptic conflict of 1914–18. It was a world into which H.G. Pélissier and his pioneering Follies would have fitted quite seamlessly.

However, immediately following the Great War, it was on the Continent, rather than in Britain, in the clubs and cabarets of Berlin, Paris and Vienna that the more potent and

Figure 49. The Follies, 'Flying Matinee', 1906 postcard

sharper-edged breed of satirical revue was to enjoy its most celebrated heyday. Such places and their risk-taking style would be admired and copied and re-introduced to English shores by the likes of British performers including Peter Cook and John Wells, ironically unaware that a British forerunner, in the person of H.G. Pélissier, had done exactly the same a half century before. To all intents and purposes the subversive, fearless and anarchic wit of H.G. Pélissier had lain dormant until the emergence of Spike Milligan and *The Goon Show* in the 1950s, followed swiftly by the satirical boom of the 1960s and all that it represented.

Milligan was a popular entertainer, not part of the established mainstream, but it would be a mistake to dismiss or downplay the enormity of his influence upon the broader culture. That would surely be to repeat the fatuous error of the Edwardian establishment, that of cultural snobbery, of falsely distinguishing the mainstream, legitimate theatre from its popular counterpart. In February 1962, reviewing *The Bedsitting Room* (the play Milligan co-wrote with John Antrobus), Kenneth Tynan observed: 'We are deep in Goon country where the fifth and basic freedom is that of free association [. . .] Yet it is capable of finesse, at least as practised by Messrs Milligan and Antrobus [. . .] It would be well worth a trial at the Royal Court'.[43] Similarly, Michael Palin appears in no doubt as to Milligan's originality and impact. In his television biography *A Life on Screen* he recalls his first childhood encounters with those pioneeringly inventive radio broadcasts of *The Goon Show*:

These were something that I knew I could never explain to my father. And I just hoped and prayed that my father would never come in. But he did come in. And it was in one of those extreme moments where Minnie and Henry Crumb were talking [he mimics the voices] and he said to me 'Is the set broken, old boy?' I said, 'No, no, no, that's the way it's supposed to be', and he could never understand there wasn't something wrong with the sound system causing these falsettos.[44]

Like Pélissier, Spike Milligan in his own time represented a connection between what Jeff Nuttall in *Bomb Culture* refers to as the distinct social groupings of; 'pop [. . .] the prerogative of working class teenagers, protest [. . .] the prerogative of middle class students and art [. . .] the prerogative of the lunatic fringe. He goes on to say:

> Perhaps the most important bridge [. . .] was 'The Goon Show', a radio programme that ran throughout the late fifties and went a long way to preparing the ground for the current hybrid sub-culture. [. . .] The Goon Show was protest. The Goon Show was surrealist and therefore art, and the Goon Show was every National Serviceman's defence mechanism, was therefore [*sic*] art.[45]

This was all something that John Lennon and *The Beatles* would embrace and develop and through which they and others would ultimately transform Western culture. However, one might equally argue that this phenomenon had deeper roots. For Humphrey Carpenter, the origins of *The Goon Show* can be found in the sometimes brutal and destructive nonsense of Edward Lear or Lewis Carroll.[46] And, indeed, it was this anarchic comedic tradition, developed in a theatrical setting by Pélissier, that was to spontaneously re-ignite in the work of these later twentieth century absurdists, including Peter Sellers, Peter Cook, Michael Palin, Terry Jones and Terry Gilliam amongst a myriad of others. The further influence of this tradition can clearly be seen in the works of John Antrobus, John Arden, Tom Stoppard, Harold Pinter, Ken Russell and Richard Lester and in the anarchic creations of *The People Show*, *The Living Theater of New York* and avante-garde 'happenings' of the latter part of the twentieth century.

In a musical context, the subversive, satirical style found its revival in the works of Joan Littlewood at The Theatre Workshop, in productions like *Oh! What A Lovely War* and *Fings Ain't Wot They Used T'Be*. His invention of the 'potted play' as a form of comedy sketch has become almost ubiquitous in the repertoire of entertainers from Morecambe and Wise to French and Saunders, while his skilful parodic piano playing has been echoed in the routines of Victor Borge and Dudley Moore.

In contemporary cinema, the influence of these latter-day satirists and absurdists can be seen in the work of Mel Brooks, the Coen Brothers and Charlie Kauffman and Wes Andersen, as well as in a wide range of surreally subversive British and American comedy from Woody Allen to *The Young Ones*, *Little Britain*, *The Flight of the Condor* and, indeed, that whole post-Thatcher phenomenon of stand-up, 'alternative' comedy and pop-up theatre. As a songwriter, one might count among his successors not only Noel Coward, but also Cole Porter, Flanders and Swann, Tom Lehrer, Victoria Wood and Tim Minchin.

Perhaps it is arguable that a whole fabric of British nonsense, absurdity and satire has woven its own tradition from Dean Swift and Laurence Sterne to Lewis Carroll and Edward Lear and on into *The Goon Show*, *Monty Python's Flying Circus* and the work of Armando Iannucci, and that *The Follies*, in a theatrical context, were just one more extraordinary thread in this vast canvas.

Perhaps ultimately, too, it is the case that so maverick a spirit as H.G. Pélissier, offering so varied and unpredictable an output, was too hard to label. The commercially organized world demands a label, and it is very hard to pin one on Pélissier, which may be why he loved so much to lampoon the world of commercial theatre and advertising. History too loves a linear narrative and Pélissier does not fall easily into any of the accepted narratives of modern times. In many ways, for the reasons stated, his career represents an abrupt cul-de-sac, having no immediate and obvious contemporary successor or line of inheritance – except in the manner already suggested in which he may have influenced burgeoning talents such as Ivor Novello, Noel Coward and Compton Mackenzie. He emerges untidily from a host of cultural traditions, including the music hall, the seaside pierrot and minstrel shows, the concert party, classical operetta, burlesque and French revue. He was an impresario, a comedian, a composer and a satirist, impossible to pigeon-hole, almost amateur rather than professional in spirit, although that would be a distinction he would hardly recognise. Above all he lived his life and created and performed his works in an impromptu, ad hoc manner which leaves historical study in something of a quandary. Displaying very little regard for either the past or the future, or even to his own written scripts and compositions, which were readily discarded and improvised, where exactly does one place a figure like H. G. Pélissier? One senses that everything he did, he did on impulse, and that he lived almost entirely in the present tense. So perhaps in that sense he represents the very essence of a true narrative history, albeit an unquantifiable one, in which our human story is the sum total of our collective momentary impulses. Perhaps, rather than developing in straight lines, history moves in waves and cycles of progression and regression, and Pélissier's life and work represent a disruptive ripple, or swell even, of the former. On the other hand, if history is indeed a constant, singular narrative, then, like Pélissier's life-story itself, like his romances and his revels, his improvised skits and songs, his ad-libs, his 'potted plays' and his signature extemporary chats to the audience before the curtain call, perhaps it is all simply made up as we go along, an impromptu and absurd, if entertaining chaos.

Afterword

This book was conceived, researched and completed between the years 2016 and 2022. That same period has witnessed the increasing spread of authoritarian attitudes and activity across the globe from China's suppression of the Uyghur minority in Xinjiang to Burma's devastation of the Myanmar people and Bolsonaro's wanton exploitation of the Amazon. At the same time, there has arisen a whole panoply of controversial issues from the Brexit referendum and the election of Donald Trump as US president to the efficacy of covid vaccinations, the validity or otherwise of climate change and the place of 'cancel culture' in our own society.

On the day I write, the Russian dissident Alexei Navalny faces a sentence of 13 years in a high security prison simply for daring to criticize his government while a former comedian and satirist turned politician called Volodymyr Zelensky sits besieged in his own capital for daring to defy the authority of a neighbouring state. Surely nobody who has lived through these events could fail to have appreciated the pivotal role that freedom of expression and access (or lack of) to reliable information has played, alongside the concomitant dissemination of 'fake news'.

The reader will be relieved to hear that this is not an appropriate space in which to discuss all those momentous events at any length. However, it is perhaps worth underlining how the authoritarian censorship that dogged H.G. Pélissier and *The Follies* foreshadowed in many ways our own contemporary experience.

When the minister of foreign affairs of the Russian Federation, Sergey Lavrov, addressed the UN Assembly on 19 February 2022 (from which scores of diplomats walked out), he railed against not only the liberal and democratic values of the West, but also its 'permissiveness'. There is surely no coincidence that an autocratic regime, as well as being the most censorial in terms of freedom of expression, can equally reveal itself as the most sexually and culturally repressive, homophobic, racist and misogynistic; to which we might add that such powers are the most likely to execute and incarcerate their own citizens, while militarily assaulting those of their neighbours. Never is this tendency more chillingly effective than when a nation is either drowsily unaware or selectively fails to appreciate that it is being manipulated, repressed, censored and misinformed.

As has been outlined in these pages, the censorial regime of Edwardian Britain became even more repressive with the advent of open military hostilities in 1914 – an outcome that persisted and even deepened over the course of the following half century. The collective amnesia that in many ways seems to have shrouded these events is made stark by the largely forgotten and neglected history of *The Follies*.

'Repeat a lie often enough and it becomes the truth' was the mantra of one Joseph Goebbels, perhaps his most long-lasting contribution to uncivilization, for it has since become one of the hallmarks of our 'fake news', cypher-war, dark web, troll and bot age. By way of contrast, 'eternal vigilance is the price of liberty' (a remark attributed to Thomas Jefferson) might be considered the counter aphorism.

Among the eternally vigilant dissenting voices and disruptive activists of late Victorian and early twentieth century Britain, H.G. Pélissier, like his modern equivalents, paid little heed to 'echo chambers' or 'fake news'. He told it as he saw it to as wide-ranging an audience as possible, unafraid of the disapproval he might draw or the powers he might offend. Indeed, as has been pointed out by Compton Mackenzie among others who worked with and knew him, his sketches finally became so daring and radical that he gradually lost the sympathy and favour of his regular audiences and ultimately his place in the West End. Arguably, it is this very kind of spirit that is required the world over in our own time and the story of *The Follies* is a salutary one.

Freedom of speech is a fraught subject where there are conflicting rights and varying notions of tolerance, made even more complex by the increasing role of social media and the Internet, so immediate, influential and easily accessible in the free world. However, as has been forcefully and convincingly argued by Jacob Mchangama in his *Free Speech: a Global History from Socrates to Social Media* (Basic Books. 2022), the dangers that can ensue from undue limitations placed on free speech are all too stark and it should always be borne in mind that any 'legal' restrictions one seeks to impose on others may in time be used to justify similar impositions upon oneself. History is full of such lessons.

In my imagination, amid the criminally insane missile strikes and murder of Ukraine, amid the dense and suffocating smog of ashen dust and nuclear fallout that may eventually engulf us all, I can somehow already hear the voice of H.G. Pélissier and *The Follies* ringing out their tragi-comic satire 'What A Happy Land is England!' . . . and Russia . . . and China . . . and . . .

Anthony Binns
March 2022.

Appendix A

The Songs and Other Compositions of H.G. Pélissier

The Lyricists: A.D.= Arthur Davenport; C.M. = Compton Mackenzie; D.M. = Douglas Maclaren; H.G.P.= H.G. Pélissier; A.W.= Arthur Wimperis

The Style: [AM] = American Minstrel; [CP] = Classical Parody; [MH] = Music Hall; [N] =Nonsense/Comedy; [RB] = Romantic Ballad; [RC] = Romantic Comedy; [S] = Satire

Published either by Francis, Day & Hunter, by Reynolds & Co. or by Joseph Williams Ltd unless otherwise stated and on date given (where known)

Title	Lyricist (where known)	Style	Publisher and date (where known)
All Change Here: A Revue	Instrumental piano score		Enoch & Sons 1911
All on the Road to Brighton	B.B. Redwood + H.G.P.	[S]	Reynolds & Co.
Alone	H. Heine	[S]	Joseph Williams Ltd (London); Schubert & Co. (New York)1902
Antiques		[MH]	Not known
Awake!	W. Davenant	[R]	Robert Cocks & Co. 1897
Back to the Land	A.D.	[S.]	Joseph Williams Ltd 1909
The Banyon Tree		[N]	Unpublished
Before the Flood	Morris Harvey	[S]	Joseph Williams Ltd 1910
The Big Bamboo	C.M.	[RC]	Joseph Williams Ltd 1911
A Burglar's View of Life	H.G.P.	[S]	Reynolds & Co. 1893
Chubby Little Cherub	A.D.	[MH]	Joseph Williams Ltd 1909
The Cigarette Song	A.D.		Unpublished
Contrary Mary	A.D. + H.G.	[MH]	Joseph Williams Ltd 1908
Coronation Day	Hugh E. Wright	[MH]	Joseph Williams Ltd 1911
The Dandy One Step	Fitz-Patrick Lewis	[AM]	Joseph Williams Ltd 1912
Dear Little Children of the Slums		[S]	Unpublished

Derry Down Dey!	A.D.	[S]	Mills & Boon 1910
A Dog Song	H.G.	[N/S]	Reynolds & Co. 1893
Down by the Wangaroo	A.D.	[AM]	Joseph Williams Ltd 1910
Down in Idaho	Not known		Not known
Dreaming	Hugh E. Wright	[R]	Joseph Williams Ltd 1911
Dreams of Rest	P.T. Ingram	[R]	Reynolds & Co.
The Drone of the Bumblebee	H.G.P.		Lost
Echoes	A.D.	[MH]	Joseph Williams Ltd 1909
Entente Cordiale	H.G.P.	[S]	Unpublished
The Flower Girl	A.D.	[MH]	Joseph Williams Ltd 1907
The Follies Chorus	H.G.P.	[MH]	Mills & Boon 1910
The Garden Beautiful	Not known		Not known
A Garden of Roses	A.W.	[RB]	Joseph Williams Ltd 1909
Girls	Walter Davidson	[M]	Joseph Williams Ltd 1909
Give Me the Morn	Herbert Fordwych	[RB]	E. Ascherberg & Co. 1902
Give My Love to Mother	H.G.P.	[S]	Unpublished
Gold		[S]	Unpublished
The Hooligan Song	A.D.		Unpublished
Hope on Hope Forever!	Morris Harvey	[S]	Joseph Williams Ltd 1910
In Santa Fé	A.D.	[AM]	Joseph Williams Ltd 1910
In the Springtime	A.D.	[RB]	Joseph Williams Ltd 1907
I Love Thee Dear	H.G.P.	[RB]	Joseph Williams Ltd 1906
It's Just The Same Now	Will C. Pepper	[RC]	Reynolds & Co. 1902
It isn't Love, it's Bacchus	A.D.	[RC]	Joseph Williams Ltd 1908
I Want Somebody to Love Me	H.G.P. + A.D	[RB]	Joseph Williams Ltd 1906
I Want the Moon	Will C. Pepper	[RB]	Reynolds & Co.
I Wanted To Marry A Hero	A.D.	[RC]	Joseph Williams Ltd 1909
I Want to Tell You how I Love You	A.D. + H.G.P.	[RC]	Joseph Williams Ltd 1910
I Worship the Ground	A.D.+ H.G.P.	[RB]	Joseph Williams Ltd 1909
Jane!	H.G.P.	[MH]	Reynolds & Co.
Jane from Maiden Lane	A.D [D.M. – verses]	[S]	Joseph Williams Ltd 1910
Kismet	Hugh E. Wright	[AM]	Joseph Williams Ltd 1911
Li Ti Ti Ti	A.D.	[N]	Joseph Williams Ltd 1909
Little Mandarin	P.T. Ingram + H.G.P.	[MH]	Reynolds & Co.
Love Is A Merry-Go-Round	A.D.	[RC]	Joseph Williams Ltd 1908
Love Me in the Land of Dreams!	P.T. Ingram	[RB]	Reynolds & Co. 1897
Love Me Long	A.D.	[RC]	Joseph Williams Ltd 1910
Lover's Laughter	Hugh E. Wright	[RC]	Joseph Williams Ltd 1911

Love's a Bore	A.D.	[S]	Joseph Williams Ltd 1908
Love's Cradle Song	Not known		Not known
Love's Garden	Instrumental		Not known 1908
Mandy	H.G.P.	[AM]	Joseph Williams Ltd 1907
Mein Faderland	F.S. Pélissier	[S]	Reynolds & Co. 1893
A Memory of Spain	A.W.	[RB]	Gould &Co.
Memory's Garden	Herbert Fordwych	[RB]	E. Ascherberg & Co 1902
The Mole And The Butterfly	Hugh E. Wright	[N]	Reynolds & Co. 1911
Mother's Maxims	H.G.P. + A.D.	[MH]	Joseph Williams Ltd 1908
My Boy from Barbary	A.D.	[RC]	Joseph Williams Ltd 1909
My Canaries	H.G.P.	[AM]	Joseph Williams Ltd 1906
My Lodestar	A.W.	[RB]	Francis Day & Hunter1893
My Moon	A.D.	[RB]	Joseph Williams Ltd 1908
Ohio Boat Song	Percy T. Ingram		Unpublished (signed 1893)
Old Cronies	Edward Oxenford	[MH]	Reynolds & Co. 1898
Our Canadian Canoe	A.D.	[AM]	Joseph Williams Ltd 1904
Pansy of Pennsylvania	Morris Harvey	[S]	Joseph Williams Ltd 1910
A Piano Medley [The Follies]	Piano score Arr. W. Heller		Joseph Williams Ltd 1910
A Piano Medley [Pélissiana]	Piano score Arr. Herman Finck		Joseph Williams Ltd 1910
The Pleasant Countryside		[S]	Not known
Return to the Simple Life	C.M.+ A.D.	[S]	Joseph Williams Ltd 1911
A Salutation	Not Known		Not known
The Seven Sleepers of Ephesus		[MH]	
Since I Walked Out with a Soldier	A.D.	[MH]	Joseph Williams Ltd 1909
The Sun Song	Hugh E. Wright	[AM]	Joseph Williams Ltd 1912
Stalwart Inspectors	A.D.	[S]	Joseph Williams Ltd 1908
Take-Offski	Instrumental piano score	[CP]	Unpublished
Teddy Bear	A.D.	[MH]	Joseph Williams Ltd 1909
Tell Me Why?	Not known		Not known
There's Still a Sun Shining	A.D.	[MH]	Joseph Williams Ltd 1908
The Tiddle-y-pom	A.D.	[N]	Joseph Williams Ltd 1909
Tipperary Millionaire	A.D.	[MH]	Reynolds & Co. 1906
The Toothbrush And The Sponge	A.D.	[N]	Joseph Williams Ltd 1908
Under the Weeping Willow	A.W.	[RB]	Joseph Williams Ltd 1907
Very Refined	A.D.	[S]	Joseph Williams Ltd 1908
Wagner (A Parody)		[CP]	Lost

A Waster's Waltz	H.G.P.	[RC]	Not known
What A Funny World We Live In	A.D. + H.G.P.	[S]	Joseph Williams Ltd 1908
What a Happy Land is England	A.W.	[S]	Joseph Williams Ltd 1904
What a Very Great Improvement	A.W.	[S]	Joseph Williams Ltd 1906
When Roses Bloom	Not known		Not known
Where is a Maid like You?	A.D.	[RC]	Joseph Williams Ltd 1908
A World of My Own	Not known		Not known
Yes, I Don't Think	A.D. + H.G.P.	[S]	Joseph Williams Ltd 1908
You Must Hear What I Say	A.D.	[S]	Joseph Williams Ltd 1908
Ypsilanti	A.D.	[AM]	Joseph Williams Ltd 1908
Zulu Lulu	A.W.	[AM]	Joseph Williams Ltd 1908

Appendix B

The 'potted plays' and sketches of H.G. Pélissier and *The Follies*

Title	First performance	
	Year	Venue
Aladdin	1912	Empire Music Hall
All Change Here	1910	Alhambra Music Hall
An Englishman's Home	1909	Apollo Theatre
Baffles, a Peter-Pantomime	1907	New Royalty Theatre
The Beauty of Bath	1906	Tivoli Theatre
The Beverage Quartettes	1908	Apollo Theatre
Bill Bailey	1904	Palace Theatre
Count Hannibal	1911	Apollo Theatre
The Christian	1908	Apollo Theatre
A Christmas Panto	1907	Palace Theatre
Everybody's Benefit	1908	Apollo Theatre
Faust	1908	Apollo Theatre
Fires of Fate	1909	Apollo Theatre
The Girls from Gottenberg	1908	Apollo Theatre
Grand Opera Skit	1903	Aberystwyth
Hamlet	1905	Palace Theatre
Henry of Navarre	1908	Apollo Theatre
King of Cadonia	1909	Apollo Theatre
Love's Garden	1908	Apollo Theatre
Macbeth	1912	Apollo Theatre
The Merry Widow	1908	Apollo Theatre
Music Hall/Wild West Burlesque	1908	New Royalty Theatre
Nicotine Quartet	1907	New Royalty Theatre

Salomé	1910	Apollo Theatre
Samson	1909	Apollo Theatre
Self-Consciousness or The Fourth Wall	1911	Apollo Theatre
Take-offski/1912	1907	Terry's Theatre
The Voice Trial	Not known	
Wagner: A Parody	1903(?)	Not known
What Every Woman Knows	1908	Apollo Theatre
The Whip	1909	Apollo Theatre
The White Man	1908	Apollo Theatre

Appendix C

A Note on the Sound Recordings

The following listed sound recordings from the British Library and Pélissier Family Archive are all available to listen to on www.pelissiersfollies.com

There are 13 recordings still extant of *The Follies* in performance. They feature 12 of their original songs, plus impersonations by Morris Harvey, and are in some ways revealing of how they might have sounded live, although of course they do not capture the improvised nature of much of what they did. They were recorded on disc and released for sale in or around 1909–10 by the *Odeon* label. This company was founded in 1903 by the Berlin-based Max Strauss and Heinrich Zuntz and took its name from the Paris Odeon Theatre. One wonders whether Pélissier's continental connections might have played a part in their subsequent collaboration. *Odeon* was a ground-breaking company, producing the first double-sided disc (all *The Follies* recordings were released in this format) and in 1909 the first full-length recording of an orchestral work. This was Tchaikovsky's *Nutcracker Suite,* performed by the London Palace Orchestra under the baton of Herman Finck – Pélissier's very own arranger and conductor at the Apollo Theatre. These recordings give further testimony to the forward-looking nature of Harry Pélissier's management, always alert to new opportunities. In 1909–10, the gramophone disc (then made from a brittle shellac material) had only just replaced the cylinder as a form of sound recording and these discs represent some of the earliest ever made in the music-hall genre. This pioneering innovation may owe something to the influence of their then sketch and lyric writer Compton Mackenzie, since both he and his father Edward were avid collectors of gramophone records. In 1923, Mackenzie (along with his brother-in-law (Christopher Stone) went on to found and edit *Gramophone* magazine, the pre-eminent such periodical of its time. The recordings are listed below, along with the performers credited, their catalogue listing in the British Library and some observations by the author on what they seem to reveal.

Listing	Title	Performer(s)
1CL0006151 S1	**Dutch Pipe**	*The Follies*

This a song that featured in the sketch entitled *Nicotine Quartets*. It is a celebration of the joys of pipe-smoking, so typical of their libertarian, gender role breaking (both men and women are smoking) and bohemian lifestyle. It also displays the harmonic range and power of the *The Follies'* voices when arranged for chorus. Aside from the humour, it is clear that the audience was treated to a fully professional musical event.

1CL0006151 S2   **Hookah Song**   *The Follies*

This too is a song that featured in the sketch entitled *Nicotine Quartets*. It is amusing to note how the voices begin to slow and slur on the chorus line 'hubble-bubble'. One may draw whatever inference one wishes. It concludes with an abrupt discord.

1CL0006152 S1   **A Garden of Roses**   **Effie Cook and** *The Follies*

This is an example of *The Follies* in their light operatic mode. Cast members were chosen for a variety of skills. Effie Cook was a trained classical singer and often took a lead role in such numbers. Its striking melody anticipates the works of Ivor Novello and Noel Coward a decade and more later.

1CL0006152 S2   **My Moon**   **Muriel George and** *The Follies*

Likewise, Muriel George was a trained singer and went on to a successful radio career after the First World War. This evocative ballad with its graceful backing harmonies was one that John Mills would recall in the thirties when he and Anthony Pélissier embarked on their revival of *The Follies*.

1CL0006153 S1   **Cigarette Song**   *The Follies*

Another in the trilogy of songs from *Nicotine Quartets*, a serenade to tobacco that is a typical *Follies'* satire on the sentimental romance of the Gaiety 'Girl' themed musicals so popular at the time.

1CL0006153 S2   **Mother's Maxims**   **Ethel Allandale and** *The Follies*

Though not classically trained, Ethel Allandale brought years of concert-party experience to this music-hall style number. Her enunciation is crystal clear from all those *al fresco* and promenade performances. Intriguingly, she sings in the *sprechgesang* style that later typified the performances of Bertolt Brecht, Lotte Lenya and others in the Berlin cabarets of the twenties and thirties, mixing the melody with half-spoken phrases. Thus, the full satirical weight of the lyrics is dramatically presented, while simultaneously perhaps the natural shortcomings of her singing voice are cleverly disguised. The subject matter of the song would have been close to Ethel's heart – a sexually precocious young woman deliberately misinterpreting her mother's austere advise.

1CL0006154 S1   **Back to the Land**   **H.G. Pélissier and** *The Follies*

This is the only recording that seems to feature the voice of H.G. Pélissier himself, certainly in the lead role. What is immediately striking is his crystal-clear enunciation, projected effortlessly one imagines across the beaches of all those coastal resorts, as well as across the stalls and balconies of the Apollo in Shaftesbury Avenue. Again, the lyrics are presented in a half-spoken, half-sung style, in tones reminiscent of the later Michael Flanders. He is accompanied by rich, graceful harmonies in the backing chorus and by a solo piano. It is probable that the piano playing that features on all these recorded pieces as the sole instrumental accompaniment (aside from the occasional percussion) is his own handiwork. The lyrics, by Arthur Davenport, are laced with topical puns and satirise the contemporary fashion, encouraged by the Asquith government, for a return to rural life.

1CL0006154 S2   Indulges in the Sincerest Form of Flattery Morris Harvey

This is the only piece to be recorded that does not feature compositions by Pélissier himself. 'Put Me Among the Girls' was written by the prolific and popular song-writers Clarence Murphy and Dan Lipton for the Australian music-hall entertainer Billy Williams. His was a rough and ready, no-nonsense, man of the common people style that made him a great favourite in the halls. However, Morris Harvey performs the song in the manner of G.P. Huntley, a distinguished and rather aristocratic actor of the straight theatre and light musicals. The joke here is to juxtapose this popular, one might say 'plebeian' number with Huntley's patrician timbre. Impersonation was a regular feature of *The Follies* shows, and the explicit naming of the butt of this joke on the recording further underlines Pélissier's brazen disregard of the Lord Chamberlain's regulations regarding the prohibition of any reference on stage to living public figures. Before joining *The Follies*, Morris Harvey had himself been both a straight actor and a music-hall entertainer and went on to a successful film career in the subsequent decades. As though to underscore the striking echoes of this era with the 'Swinging Sixties', this particular song was itself covered by Davy Jones of *The Monkeys* in 1965. For good measure, we are then provided on this recording with a song by Harry Lauder (another music hall star) in the style of the classical actor Lewis Waller. This suggests that *The Follies'* audience was indeed very mixed and would have been familiar enough with all these genres to 'get the joke'. The breaking down of barriers between popular and more 'high-brow' entertainment was one of Pélissier's constant struggles with the Lord Chamberlain.

1CL0006155 S1   Echoes   Muriel George and *The Follies*

Another performance by Muriel George, this time in a light operatic style. That this is a tongue-in-cheek satire on the Gaiety-style musical ballads of the time is highlighted by the over-the-top, lugubrious delivery and the odd piano phrase that undercuts the pathos.

1CL0006155 S2   Ypsilanti   Gwennie Mars and *The Follies*

How very ahead of its time this melody sounds – as though it might be at home in a Rogers and Hammerstein musical of a later age. The lead voice is that of Gwennie Mars, performing with a richly sounding male backing chorus. It is in fact a parody of the lavishly sentimental 'black-face' minstrel songs of the period. Typical of *The Follies*, the lyrics undercut the beauty of the score. Gwennie is singing as a male character. Such gender-swapping was a regular feature of their shows. The suitor represented has failed to make enough money to bring his American lover back to Scotland. 'Money's scanty,' he/she opines, 'I'm dilettante, and so Amante has to wait in Ypsilanti!'. He/she 'never dreamt a pile took so much makin''.

1CL0006156 S1 **I Worship the Ground** **Gwennie Mars and *The Follies***

Gwennie Mars performs a mock romantic ballad with a male backing chorus, and once again the result seems strikingly prescient of Ivor Novello and the 'torch songs' of the twenties and thirties.

1CL0006156 S2 **Down by the Wangaroo** **Gwennie Mars and *The Follies***

Another comic parody of the sentimental minstrel style, again with rich and melodious backing harmonies in the chorus.

Private Collection **Contrary Mary** **Ethel Allandale and *The Follies***

This is much more of a classic music-hall number performed by the experienced Ethel Allandale with a male backing chorus. It gives testimony to the range of *The Follies'* targets. In this bright and sparky number Ethel is somehow mysteriously producing magnificent vegetables and flowers in her modest inner-city garden. Intrigued and bemused, her husband discovers 'some dozens of tins and pots' of Phospherine and Tatcho discarded about the place. These were in fact popular herbal medicines and hair treatments generously laced with alcohol and quinine. As with so much of *The Follies* work, nothing is quite what it seems. 'Contrary Mary' is an illicit drinker and the strength of her discarded 'tonics' has produced miraculous results.

Illustrations

PFA – Pelissier Family Archive

AB – Private collection of Anthony Binns

23   H.G. Pélissier in his customized Metallurgique. PFA.

24   *The Follies* at the Apollo Theatre. Courtesy of the V&A Museum.

25   H.G. Pélissier at the piano by Norman Murrow from 'Pure Folly' by Fitzroy Gardner, 1906. PFA.

26   The double keyboard caricatured in *The Sketch*, 2 Dec. 1908. PFA.

27   Compton Mackenzie c. 1911. Photo by Faith Mackenzie. PFA.

28   Self-caricature by H.G. Pélissier from *Granta Magazine* 10 Feb. 1912. PFA.

29   Pélixir cartoon by Arthur Wimperis from 'Pure Folly' by Fitzroy Gardner, 1906. PFA

30   Caricature of H.G.P. by by E.T. Reed. PFA.

31   H.G. Pélissier as Bacchus in the musical fantasy *Love's Garden*, 1911. AB.

32   Facsimile of Mr Pélissier's Invaluable Map. PFA.

33   'The Follies Sunday at Home' by Norman Murrow. PFA.

34   H.G. Pélissier as Maud Allan's *Salomé*. PFA.

35   Douglas 'Boy' Maclaren. Photo by Hana. PFA.

36   'A Follies' Outing'. from 'Pure Folly' by Fitzroy Gardner, 1906. PFA.

37   *The Nicotine Quartets*. Photo by Hana. Courtesy of the V&A Museum.

38   H.G. Pélissier as May de Colté. Photo by Hana. from 'Pure Folly' by Fitzroy Gardner, 1906. PFA.

39   Fay Compton aged 22. Enamel. PFA.

40   Wedding photo from *The Daily Graphic* 18 Sept. 1911. PFA.

41   Letter from Harry to Fay dated 9 July 1909. PFA.

42   Fay Compton as a member of *The Follies* aged 18. PFA.

43   H.G. Pélissier photo by Hana from 'Pure Folly' by Fitzroy Gardner, 1906. PFA.

44   Fay Compton with her son, Harry Anthony 1914. PFA.

45   Fay Compton, 1926. PFA.

46   Portrait of H.G. Pélissier by Sir John Collier. PFA.

47   *Pélissier Follies* of 1938. **PFA.**

48   H.G. Pélissier at home in Elm House, Finchley. PFA.

49   *The Follies*, 'Flying Matinee' 1906 postcard. PFA.

Back cover: H.G. Pélissier. From 'Melodious Memories' by Herman Finck. AB

Books and Collections Cited

Anstey, F. 'London Music Hall' *Hayes Monthly Magazine,* Vol. 91 (1891): 190–202.

Arthur Lloyd. The Music Hall and Theatre History Site Dedicated to Arthur Lloyd, 1839–1904 Online (www.arthurlloyd.co.uk).

Bailey, Peter (ed.) *Music Hall: The Business of Pleasure.* Oxford University Press, 1986.

Bailey, Peter. '"Naughty but nice": Musical Comedy and the Rhetoric of the Girl, 1892–1914' in *Edwardian Theatre: Essays on Performance and the Stage.* ed. Michael R. Booth and Joel H. Kaplan. Cambridge University Press, 1996: 36–60.

Baker, Richard Anthony. *British Music Hall.* Pen &Sword, 2014.

Barker, Felix. *Edwardian London.* Laurence King, 1995.

Barrie, J.M. *Mary Rose.* Oxford University Press, 1995.

Barrie, J.M. *Peter Pan and Other Plays.* Oxford University Press, 1995.

BBC Proms. A Listing of Historical Performances. Online (www.bbc.co.uk/proms/events/by/date/2021).

BNA – British Newspaper Archive. Online (www.britishnewspaperarchive.co.uk).

Booth, J.B. *Pink Parade.* Thornton Butterworth, 1933.

Caputi, Anthony. *Buffo: The Genius of Vulgar Comedy.* Wayne State University Press, 1978.

Carpenter, Humphrey. *That Was Satire That Was.* Phoenix, 2002.

Carpenter, Humphrey. *Spike Milligan: The Biography.* Coronet, 2004.

Collection of the Public General Statutes, passed in the Sixth and Seventh Year of the Reign of Her Majesty Queen Victoria. Eyre and Spottiswoode, 1843.

Compton, Fay. *Rosemary: Some Remembrances.* Alston Rivers Ltd, 1926.

Cook, Matt. *London and the Culture of Homosexuality 1885–1914.* Cambridge University Press, 2003.

Daly, Brian. *Albert Chevalier: A Record by Himself.* Nabu Press, 2011.

De Jongh, Nicholas. *Politics, Prudery and Perversions.* Methuen, 2000.

DNB – *Dictionary of National Biography 1912–1921.* Oxford University Press. 1927.

Donohue, Joseph. 'What is Edwardian Theatre?' in *Edwardian Theatre: Essays on Performance and the Stage.* ed. Michael R.Booth and Joel H. Kaplan. Cambridge University Press, 1996: 10–35.

Finck, Herman. *My Melodious Memories.* Hutchinson & Company, 1937.

Findlater, Richard. *Banned.* MacGibbon & Kee, 1967.

Gale, Maggie B. 'The London Stage 1918–1945' in *The Cambridge History of the British Theatre,* Vol. 3: *Since 1895,* ed. Baz Kershaw. Cambridge University Press, 2004: 143–167.

Ganzl, Kurt. *The British Musical Theatre,* Vol. 1: *1865–1914.* Macmillan, 1986.

Gardner, Fitzroy. *Pure Folly.* Mills and Boon, 1910.

Gardner, Fitzroy. *Reminiscences of an Old Bohemian.* Hutchinson, 1926.

Hiley, Nicholas. 'The Play, the Parody, the Censor and the Film' *Intelligence & National Security,* Vol. 6(1) (1991): 218–228.

Holroyd, Michael. *Bernard Shaw,* Vol. 2. *1898–1918.* Chatto & Windus, 1989.

Holroyd, Michael. *A Strange and Eventful History: The Dramatic Lives of Ellen Terry, Henry I and Irving and their Remarkable Families.* Chatto & Windus, 2008.

Howard, Diana. *London Theatres and Music Halls 1850–1950.* American Library Association, 1970.

Kilburn and Willesden History. Dick Weindling and Marianne Colloms's Website for History Stories about this Area of London. Online (https://kilburnandwillesdenhistory.blogspot.com/).

LCP – Lord Chamberlain's Portfolio Collection, British Library, London

Linklater, Andro. *Compton Mackenzie: A Life.* Chatto & Windus, 1987.

Mackenzie, Compton. *My Life & Times,* Octaves 2, 3 & 4. Chatto & Windus, 1963–65.

Mackenzie, Faith Compton. *As Much As I Dare.* Collins, 1938.

Maurier, Guy du. *An Englishman's Home.* Harper & Brothers, 1909.

McQueen Pope, W. *The Melodies Linger On.* W.H. Allen, 1950.

Monrós-Gaspar, Laura. *Victorian Classical Burlesques: A Critical Anthology.* Bloomsbury Academic, 2015.

Moon, Howard. *The Invasion of the United Kingdom.* Unpublished PhD Thesis. University of London, 1968.

Moore, James Ross. *Musical Revue: A Digest of an Intimate Understanding: the Rise of British Musical Revue 1890–1920*. Unpublished PhD Thesis. University of Warwick, 2000.

Morrison, Matthew. *The Soho Theatre 1968–1981;* Society for Theatre Research, 2017.

Mulla, John. 'You Can't Help Laughing, Can You? Humour and Symbolic Empowerment in British Music Hall During the Great War' in *Humor, Entertainment, and Popular Culture during World War I*; eds Clementine Tholas-Disset and Karen A. Rizenhoff. Palgrave Macmillan, 2015.

Nicholson, Steve. *The Censorship of British Drama 1900–1968*. University of Exeter, 1999.

Nield, Sophie. 'Popular Theatre 1895–1940' in *The Cambridge History of the British Theatre Vol. 3: Since 1895*, ed. Baz Kershaw. Cambridge University Press, 2004: 86–109.

Nuttall, Jeff. *Bomb Culture*. MacGibbon & Kee Ltd, 1968.

Oxford Handbook of the British Musical, eds Robert Gordon & Olaf Jubin. Oxford University Press, 2017.

Pearson, Hesketh. *Gilbert and Sullivan*. Hamish Hamilton, 1935.

Pélissier, H.G. *Potted Pélissier*. Martin Secker, 1913.

PFA – Pélissier Family Archive, in private ownership.

Pick, John. *The West End; Mismanagement and Snobbery*. John Offord, 1983.

Pickering, Michael. *Blackface Minstrelsy in Britain*. Ashgate, 2008.

Report of Joint Select Committee on the Stage Plays Censorship, 1909. Online (https://www.bestfile-book.com/pdf/report-from-the-joint-select-committee-on-stage-plays-censorship-with-the-proceedings-evidence-and-appendices-and-index-theatres-stage-plays-censorship/).

Russell, Dave. 'Varieties of Life: The Making of the Edwardian Music Hall' in *The Edwardian Theatre: Essays on Performance and the Stage,* ed. Michael R. Booth and Joel H. Kaplan. Cambridge University Press. 1996.

Russell, Dave. 'Popular Entertainment, 1776–1895' in *The Cambridge History of British Theatre,* Vol. 2: *1660 to 1895*, ed. Joseph Donohue. Cambridge University Press, 2004: 369–387.

Russell, Dave. *Popular Song in England, 1840–1914*. Manchester University Press, 1997.

Rutherford, Lois. '"Harmless nonsense": The Comic Sketch and the Development of Music Hall Entertainment', in J.S. Bratton (ed.) *Music Hall: Performance and Style*. Open University Press, 1986: 131–151.

Schoch, R.W. *Victorian Theatrical Burlesques*. Ashgate, 2003.

Shaw, G.B. *Pygmalion*. Penguin, 2003.

Shaw G.B. *The Shewing Up of Blanco Posnet.* Privately printed, 1909. Pengin Books, 1965.

Thompson, David. *England in the Nineteenth Century.* Penguin, 1950.

Thomson, Peter. 'The New Drama and the Old Theatre' in *The Cambridge History of British Theatre* Vol. 2, ed. Joseph Donohue. Cambridge University Press, 2004: 405–422.

Victoria & Albert Theatre Museum. H.G. Pélissier Archive RF 2006/69 THM 345; uncatalogued collection.

Wood, Harry. 'The Play All London Is Discussing: The Great Success of Guy du Maurier's *A Englishman's Home,* 1909' *Theatre Notebook*, Vol 70(3), 2016: 184–214.

Notes

*PFA = Pélissier Family Archive; LCP = Lord Chamberlain's Portfolio Collection;
V&A = Victoria & Albert Theatre Museum H.G. Pélissier Archive*

Chapter 1: The Mystery

1   Mackenzie. Octave 4: pp. 118–119.
2   *The Tatler* 4 Dec. 1907.
3   *New Age* 29 Feb. 1908.
4   *The New York Times* 26 May 1909.
5   *Dictionary of National Biography:* pp. 30–31.
6   *The Times* 19 Jul. 1907.
7   *The Daily Telegraph* 19 Jul. 1907.
8   *The Spectator* 13· Feb. 1909.
9   *The Sunday Saturday Review* 9 May 1908.
10 Gardner. *Pure Folly:* p. 3.
11 *The Sunday Times* 20 Feb. 1910.
12 Carpenter. *That Was Satire That Was.* Phoenix, 2002 (quoted on front cover).
13 *Ibid* p.130.
14 *Dictionary of National Biography:* pp. 430–431.
15 *Dictionary of National Biography Twentieth Century Digest.* Oxford University Press, 1967.
16 *Who Was Who (1897–1915).* Bloomsbury, 2014.
17 Robert Gordon & Olaf Jubin. *The Oxford Handbook of the British Musical.* Oxford University Press, 2017.
18 Gardner. *Pure Folly:* p. 26.
19 *The Sketch* 9 Oct. 1907.
20 Gardner. *Pure Folly:* pp. 25–27.
21 PFA. 'A Dog Song' by H.G. Pélissier (composed 1893). Francis, Day & Hunter.
22 PFA. 'The Tiddle-y-Pom' by H.G. Pélissier & Arthur Davenport. Francis, Day & Hunter, 1909.
23 LCP 1905. *Hamlet.*
24 Gardner. *Pure Folly:* p. 2.
25 LCP 1907. *Baffles.*
26 PFA. 'The Toothbrush and the Sponge' by H.G. Pelissier & Arthur Davenport. Francis, Day & Hunter, 1908.
27 *The Daily Telegraph* 2 Mar. 1909.
28 Mackenzie. Octave 4: p. 119.

29 Pélissier: pp. 19–20.

30 *BBC Proms;* entry for 11, 20, 26 Sept. and for 11 Oct. 1901; and 24 Oct. 1902; Online (www.bbc.co.uk/proms/events/works).

31 In 1940, Arthur Wimperis was awarded the Oscar for best screenplay for *Mrs. Miniver.*

Chapter 2: The Alien

1 *Certificate of Naturalization* Jean Frederic Antoine Pélissier; dated 14 Aug. 1854.

2 *Greater London, Inner London & Outer London Population & Density History Census:* p. 513.

3 Robert W. Longee. *Mid-century Revolution 1848; Society and Revolution in France and Germany.* D.C. Heath & Company, 1972: p. 105. And Wolfram Siemann. *The German Revolution of 1848–49.* Macmillan Press, 1998: pp. 56–57.

4 *Population Census 1901.*

5 J.W. Hulse. *Revolutionists in London: A Study of Five Unorthodox Socialists.* Clarendon Press, 1970.

6 Pélissier: p. 19.

7 *Certificate of Naturalization* Jean Frederic Antoine Pélissier; dated 14 Aug. 1854.

8 Gardner. *Pure Folly:* Foreword.

9 *The Directory of Gold & Silversmiths, Jewellers & Allied Traders 1838–1914;* entry under Pélissier.

10 *The Globe* 25 Sep. 1913; obituary.

11 *The Directory of Gold & Silversmiths, Jewellers & Allied Traders 1838–1914;* entry under Pélissier.

12 Joseph Conrad. *The Secret Agent.* Penguin Books edition, 2007. *Introduction* by Michael Newton, p. xix.

13 Hermia Oliver. *The International Anarchist Movement in Late Victorian London.* 1983. (quoted in the preface). Republished by Routledge, 2015.

14 J.W. Hulse. *Revolutionists in London: A Study of Five Unorthodox Socialists.* Clarendon Press, 1970.

15 Henry James. 'The Princess Casamassima' *The Atlantic Monthly.* 1885–86.

16 Joseph Conrad. *The Secret Agent.* Methuen, 1907.

17 The Metropolitan Guide (1893).

18 Stephen Wade. *Spies in the Empire.* Anthem Press, 2007: p. 30.

19 See Chapter 7. The Rebel.

20 *Migrations in the German Lands 1500–2000* ed. Jason Coy, , Chapter 4. Ulrich Niggeman, 2016: p. 96; quotes *Histoire de l'etablissement des Francais refugiez* by Charles Ancillon.

21 *Ibid.* p. 96.

22 Stephanie J. Snow. 'Commentary: Sutherland, Snow and Water: The Transmission of Cholera in the Nineteenth Century'. *The International Journal of Epidemiology,* Vol. 31(5) (2002): pp. 908–911.

23 John Snow. *On the Mode of Communication of Cholera.* John Churchill, 1855.

24 *Certificate of Naturalization* Jean Frederic Antoine Pélissier; dated 14 Aug. 1854.

25 PFA. *Wedding Certificate of J.F.A. Pélissier & Jennie Keen.*

26 PFA. *Birth Certificate of Frederick Pélissier.*

27 London Borough of Barnet Archives.

28 *The Globe.* Obituary. Sept. 1913.

29 *M.A.P. Magazine (Mostly About People);* an article entitled 'In the Days of My Youth'. 9 Jun. 1906.

30 The Highgate School Registry 1885.

31 *Ibid.*

32 Pélissier: p. 13.

33 *M.A.P. Magazine (Mostly About People);* an article entitled 'In the Days of My Youth'. 9 Jun. 1906.

Chapter 3: The Amateur

1 *Era* 2 Apr. 1896.

2 *Ibid.*

3 *Ibid.*

4 *Ibid.*

5 *Ibid.*

6 *M.A.P. Magazine (Mostly About People);* an article entitled 'In the Days of My Youth'. 9 Jun. 1906.

7 *The Waterloo Directory of English Newspapers and Periodicals 1800–1900.*

8 McQueen Pope: pp. 274–275.

9 See Chapter 8, The Bohemian.

10 Laura Ormiston Chant. *Why We Attacked the Empire;* quoted in Baker: p. 42.

11 See Chapter 7, The Rebel.

12 *Era* 26 April 1890.

13 Anstey, p. 190.

14 See Chapter 6, The Satirist.

15 Gardner. *Pure Folly:* p. 32. Gardner refers to Pélissier as having been educated 'both here and in France'.

16 PFA. Hand-written on the score of the unpublished *Ohio Boat Song.*

17 Gardner. *Pure Folly*: p.34.

18 *M.A.P. Magazine (Mostly About People);* an article entitled 'In the Days of My Youth'. 9 Jun. 1906.

19 Colney Hatch Lunatic Asylum was founded in the 15th Century in the Borough of Barnet. It became Friern Hospital and was finally closed down in 1993.

20 Felix Barker. *Edwardian London.* Laurence King, 1995: p. 103.

21 *M.A.P. Magazine (Mostly About People);* an article entitled 'In the Days of My Youth'. 9 Jun. 1906.

22 Frederick Willis. *Peace and Dripping Toast, Memories of the 1890's.* Phoenix House, 1950.

23 *M.A.P. Magazine (Mostly About People);* an article entitled 'In the Days of My Youth'. 9 Jun. 1906.

24 Baker: p. 13.

25 *Entr'acte* 18 Sept. 1886.

26 *General Theatre Programme.* 2 Feb. 1884.

27 *M.A.P. Magazine (Mostly About People);* an article entitled 'In the Days of My Youth'. 9 Jun. 1906.

28 PFA. 'Mein Faderland' by H.G. & F. Pélissier. Reynolds & Co., 1903.

29 *M.A.P. Magazine (Mostly About People);* an article entitled 'In the Days of My Youth'. 9 Jun. 1906.

30 'If It Wasn't For The Likes O' Huss (A Burglar's Song)' by H.G. Pélissier. Reynolds & Co., 1902.

31 Brecht & Weill. *Die Dreigroschenoper.* First produced in Berlin in 1928.

32 G.B. Shaw. *Pygmalion.* Penguin. 2003: pp. 45–46. First produced in New York and London in 1914.

33 Compton, p. 19.

34 *M.A.P. Magazine (Mostly About People);* an article entitled 'In the Days of My Youth'. 9 Jun. 1906.

Chapter 4: The Pierrot

1 *M.A.P. Magazine (Mostly About People);* an article entitled 'In the Days of My Youth'. 9 Jun. 1906.

2 Gardner. *Pure Folly:* p. 34.

3 Pickering: p. 23.

4 *Ibid.*

5 *Ibid.*

6 *Ibid.*

7 J. Abbot. *The Story of Francis, Day & Hunter;* quoted by Pickering: p. 23.

8 Pickering: p. 19.

9 Online (jeffreygreen.co.uk/137-minstrel-shows-in-britain).

10 *Ibid.*

11 Pickering: p. 23.

12 *Ibid.*

13 *Ibid.*

14 *The St. James' Magazine* n.s.1. Apr.–Sep. 1868.

15 James Greenwood. *The Wilds of London.* 1874. Republished by Taylor & Francis, 1985.

16 Pickering: p. 23.

17 *The Strand Magazine* Jun. 1909: pp. 866-893.

18 G.R. Searle. *A New England?* Clarendon Press, 2004: p. 553.

19 *Ibid.*

20 Kathlyn Ferry. *The British Seaside Holiday.* Shire, 2009: p. 9.

21 *Ibid.* p. 21.

22 *Booth & Rowntree Surveys* 1899 and 1935; quoted in F.M.L. Thompson. *The Rise of Respectable Society.* Fontana, 1998: p. 291.

23 P.J. Waller. *Town, City and Nation.* Oxford University Press, 1992: p. 131.

24 G.R. Searle. *A New England?* Clarendon Press, 2004: p. 555.

25 Kathlyn Ferry. *The British Seaside Holiday.* Shire, 2009: p. 35.

26 Compton Mackenzie. *The Adventures of Sylvia Scarlett.* John Murray, 1918: p. 61.

27 *Ibid.* pp. 59–60.

28 *The Daily Telegraph.* 12 Feb.1910; an interview with H.G. Pélissier.

29 *Globe* 25 Sept. 1913. Obituary.

30 Lee Jackson. *Dirty Old London.* Yale University Press, 2015.

31 V&A. Tour Diaries.

32 Kathlyn Ferry. *The British Seaside Holiday;* Shire, 2009 p. 101.

33 *Ibid.* p. 65.

34 'I Do Like to be Beside the Seaside' by John A. Glover-Kind. 1907; recorded by Mark Sheridan 1909.

35 Matthew Lloyd, Online (http://www.arthurlloyd.co.uk/PrinceOfWalesTheatre/LEnfant.htm). I am alos indebted to Dr Tony Lidington of Exeter University for his informative guidance regarding *L'Enfant Prodigue* and Clifford Essex.

36 BNA. *The Spectator* 4 April 1891: p. 15.

37 Bill Pertwee. *Pertwee's Promenades and Pierrots.* Westbridge Books. 1979: pp. 21-35.

38 *M.A.P. Magazine (Mostly About People);* an article entitled 'In the Days of My Youth'. 9 Jun. 1906.

39 See Chapter 6, The Satirist

40 Gardner. *Pure* Folly: p. 1.

41 *Wilfrid Baddeley: Stats.* Tennis Archives. Online (www.tennisarchives.com).

42 *The Bud Collins History of Tennis,* 2nd edition. New Chapter Press, 2010: pp. 415–435.

43 Gardner. *Pure Folly:* p. 2.

44 V&A. Tour Diaries.

45 *Worthing Intelligencer* 8 Aug. 1896.

46 *Ibid.*

47 *Ibid.*

48 *Ibid.*

49 *Folkestone Herald* 29 Aug. 1896.

50 *Barnet Times* 30 Oct. 1896.

51 *Southampton Times* 24 Apr. 1897.

52 *Sussex Coast Mercury* 12 June 1897.

53 Nield: p. 102.

54 Pickering: p. 23.

55 Nield: p. 102.

56 Russell. *Popular Song in England*: p. 94.

57 *The Times* 27 Sept. 1933: p. 11.

58 *Hastings Argus* 14 July 1897.

59 *The Worthing Intelligencer* 8 Aug. 1896.

60 *Folkestone Herald* 29 Aug. 1896.

61 *Ibid.*

62 PFA. 'A Dog Song' by H.G. Pélissier. 1893. My friend, the pianist Paul Smith, has perceptively likened this song to the dry-witted, sardonic and sesquipedalian style of the Yorkshire-born singer-songwriter Jake Thackray (1938–2002), also much influenced by French *chansons réalistes*.

Chapter 5: The Folly

1   *Worthing Intelligencer* 5 Aug. 1896.

2   *Finchley Times* 30 Oct. 1896.

3   *Coventry Times* 6 Jan. 1897.

4   *The Morning Post* 2 Nov. 1904.

5   *Barnet Press* 31 Oct. 1896.

6   Carpenter. *Spike Milligan*: p. 12.

7   *Ibid.* p. 5.

8   *Ibid.* p. 5.

9   *Ibid.* p. 2.

10 *Ibid* p. 27.

11 *Stage* 4 Apr. 1898.

12 Gardner. *Pure Folly*: p. 2.

13 Moore, James Ross. *Musical Revue: A Digest of an Intimate Understanding: the Rise of British Musical Revue 1890–1920*. A Thesis Submitted for the Degree of PhD at the University of Warwick; Online (http://wrap.warwick.ac.uk/4012/).

14 Gardner. *Pure Folly*: p. 2.

15 *Croydon Advertiser* 6 Dec. 1896.

16 *Croydon Guardian* 7 Dec. 1896.

17 *The Brighton Herald* 30 Jan. 1897.

18 *The Brighton Guardian* 27 Jan. 1897.

19 *The Newcastle Daily Leader* 9 Mar. 1897.

20 *The Newcastle Chronicle* 8 Mar. 1897.

21 *Isle Of Wight Observer* 2 Oct. 1899.

22 Tommy Parsons. 'Remembering Ron Bagnall' in *Call Boy* ed. Geoff Bowden, Vol. 53(2): p. 29.

23 Gardner. *Pure Folly*: p. 2.

24 V&A. Tour Diary (1904).

25 V&A. Cuttings Album.

26 Russell. 'Popular Entertainment, 1776–1895': p. 383.

27 For details on the life of Albert Chevalier, I am grateful to Richard Anthony Baker's *British Music Hall;* Pen &Sword, 2014 and *Albert Chevalier: A Record by Himself* by Brian Daly; Nabu Press, 2011.

28 Russell. *Popular Song in England*: pp. 94–96.

29 V&A Programmes. On 24 Jan.1908, *The Follies* presented a private performance at a reception and soirée held by Winston Churchill in the Royal Midland Hotel, Manchester. This venue was to become something of a northern base for *The Follies,* and for their sister company *The Ragamuffins* or *Follies Two* as Pélissier preferred to call it.

30 Gardner. *Pure Folly*: p. 3.

31 *Love's Garden: A Fantasy* by H.G. Pélissier & Arthur Davenport. Joseph Williams Ltd, 1908.

32 Gardner. *Pure* Folly: p. 4.

Chapter 6: The Satirist

1 LCP 1905/17. *Bill Bailey*.

2 Gardner. *Pure Folly*: p. 2.

3 *Ibid.*

4 *The Daily Telegraph* 1 Nov. 1904.

5 Russell. 'Popular Entertainment, 1776–1895': pp. 379–380.

6 Caputi: p. 20.

7 Rutherford: p. 146.

8 Rutherford: p. 150.

9 Baker: p. 30. And Russell. 'Popular Entertainment, 1776–1895': p. 384.

10 Russell. *Popular Song in England*: p. 94.

11 British Library. *Collection of the Public Statutes*: pp. 677–683; para. 16.

12 *Ibid.* para. 22.

13 Baker: pp. 1–7.

14 Russell. 'Popular Entertainment, 1776–1895': pp. 377–380.

15 Ganzl: pp. 946–947.

16 *Lady's Pictorial* 11 Dec. 1905.

17 *The Morning Post* 18 Jan. 1905.

18 *The Sun* 11 Jan. 1905.

19 *Bystanders* 15 Feb. 1905.

20 Dave Russell points out that: 'By 1914 even the profoundly respectable Illustrated London News could include a picture of Marie Lloyd. (Russell. *Popular Song in England*: p. 98). Pélissier had in fact achieved a similar, if not greater, status a decade before.

21 *Tatler* 4 Dec. 1907.

22 Schoch: p. xx.

23 *The Illustrated London News* 18 Apr. 1868.

24 Schoch: p. xxvii.

25 Monrós-Gaspar: p. 72; *Antigone Travestie* by Edward L. Blanchard 1845: line 134; For historical background detail on burlesque, I am grateful to *Victorian Classical Burlesques (A Critical Anthology)* by Laura Monrós-Gaspar, 2015.

26 William Archer. *English Dramatists of Today*. S. Low, Marston, Searle & Rivington, 1882: p. 113. Online (https://ounasvaara.net/pdf/english-dramatists-of-to-day-1882-by-william-archer).

27 Schoch: p. 233; quotes *Fraser's Magazine 57* (Feb. 1858).

28 *Ibid.* p. 12.

29 *Ibid.* p. xxviii; from an unattributed press cutting.

30 Moore: pp. 44–45.

31 Mackenzie. Octave 4: p. 110.

32 LCP 1905/17.

33 LCP 1905/17.

34 LCP 1907/17.

35 *Ibid.*

36 LCP 1907/17.

37 LCP 1905/17.

38 Carpenter. *That Was Satire That Was*: p. 121.

39 *The Morning Post* 18 Jan. 1905.

40 *The Complete Beyond the Fringe;* ed. Roger Wilmut. Methuen, 1987.

41 *The Tatler* 9 Oct. 1907; an article entitled 'Hamletitis'.

42 *The Circle* 18 Jan. 1905.

43 *Morning Post* 18 Jan. 1905.

44 LCP 1905/1917.

45 PFA. 'What A Happy Land Is England' by H.G. Pélissier & Arthur Wimperis. 1904.

46 PFA. 'What A Funny World We Live In' by H.G. Pélissier & Arthur Davenport. 1908.

47 LCP 1907/17.

48 LCP 1909/22.

49 LCP 1908/2.

50 Howard: entry under 'Royalty'.

51 *The Times* 19 Jun. 1907.

52 Howard: entry under 'Terry's'.

53 *The Stage* 21 Feb.1901.

54 Howard: entry under 'Apollo'.

55 LCP 1907/6.

56 *Ibid.*

57 *Ibid.*

58 *Sphere* 30 Mar. 1907.

59 Carpenter. *That Was Satire That Was*: pp. 91–115.

60 J.M. Barrie. *What Every Woman Knows;* first produced 1908.

61 J.M. Barrie. *Mary Rose*; first produced 1920.

62 Hall Caine. *The Christian*; first produced 1908.

63 *The Complete Beyond the Fringe;* ed. Roger Wilmut. Methuen, 1987.

64 Franz Lehar, Franz. *The Merry Widow*; first produced 1905.

65 LCP Vol 12. 1907.

66 LCP Vol 25. 1908.

67 William Devereux. *Henry of Navarre: A Romantic Play in Four Acts;* first produced 1907.

68 Oscar Wilde. *Salomé*; first produced 1891.

69 *The Complete Beyond the Fringe;* ed. Roger Wilmut. Methuen, 1987.

70 Gardner. *Pure Folly*: p. 37.

71 PFA. *The Toothbrush and The Sponge* by H.G. Pélissier & Arthur Davenport. 1908.

72 *Ibid. Li-Ti-Ti-Ti* by H.G. Pélissier & Arthur Davenport. 1909.

73 *Ibid. Back To The Land* by H.G. Pélissier and Arthur Davenport. 1909.

74 *Ibid.* 'What A Very Great Improvement It Would Be' by H.G. Pélissier and Arthur Wimperis. 1906.

75 Carpenter. *That Was Satire That Was*: p. 109.

76 Carpenter. *That Was Satire That Was*: p. 103.

77 *Punch* 9 Jun. 1906. The caption reads: "DON'T WORRY ABOUT THIS GO AND SEE THE FOLLIES" [. . .] (On Thursday night Mr. Asquith attempted to shake off the cares of state by a visit to 'The Follies' at the Apollo Theatre.)'

78 Carpenter. *That Was Satire That Was*: p. 107.

Chapter 7: The Rebel

1 *Report of Joint Select Committee; 1909*: para. 194.

2 Findlater: p. 105. Henry James was in fact a longstanding associate and collaborator of the actor-manager Edward Compton, Harry Pélissier's future father-in-law. So, James' opinion may give some indication as to the general attitude in the Compton household into which H.G. Pélissier would marry.

3 De Jongh: pp. 35–43.

4 Macqueen Pope: pp. 274–275.

5   De Jongh: pp. 35–43.

6   *Report of Joint Select Committee; 1909*: para. 3421.

7   *The Observer* 14 Feb. 1909.

8   *The Evening Standard* 19 Feb. 1909.

9   *The Pelican* 26 Feb. 1909.

10   *The Stage* 25 Feb. 1909.

11   *Referee* 21 Feb. 1909.

12   *Reynolds* 21 Feb. 1909.

13   *The Irish Times* 20 Feb. 1909.

14   *The Daily Mail* 20 Feb. 1909.

15   *The Observer* 28 Feb. 1909.

16   *The Winning Post* 27 Feb. 1909

17   *The Daily Mirror* 25 Feb. 1909.

18   *The Daily News* 26 Feb. 1909.

19   *The Times,* 27 Feb. 1909.

20   *The Daily Chronicle* 25 Feb. 1909.

21   V&A. Press Cuttings.

22   Thomson, David: p. 195.

23   *Ibid.* p. 199

24   Moon: pp. 379–428.

25   Du Maurier: p. 5.

26   Hiley: p. 223.

27   Du Maurier: p. 5.

28   Wood: p. 193.

29   *The Daily Mail* 25 Feb. 1909. The Reader or Examiner of Plays from 1885 to 1911 was George Alexander Redford. His immediate superior was the Comptroller, Sir Douglas Dawson, who held office from 1907 to 1920. One consequence of the fall-out from the Report of the Joint Committee of 1909 was that Redford had a co-examiner somewhat forced upon him in the reactionary figure of Charles Brookfield, thus prompting his resignation. The clear implication was that Redford was being made a scapegoat for the scandal and confusion that had surrounded the ban on *The Follies* sketch and the subsequent enquiry.

30   Wood: p. 31.

31   *The Times* 15 Feb. 1909.

32   Wood: pp. 184–208.

33   *Ibid.*

34   *Ibid.*

35   Nicholson: p. 36.

36   *The Morning Post* 1 Mar. 1909.

37 *The Daily Graphic* 26 Feb. 1909.

38 *The Daily Mail* 25 Feb. 1909. The

39 Gardner. *Pure Folly:* p. 43.

40 *The New York Sun* 14 Mar. 1909.

41 *The Daily Telegraph* 2 Mar. 1909.

42 *The Daily News* 2 Mar. 1909.

43 Hiley: p. 223.

44 *The Daily Chronicle* 25 Feb. 1909.

45 Carpenter. *That Was Satire That* Was; pp. 183–187. (Interesting to note also that 'The Establishment' was a private club and thus evaded the Lord Chamberlain's censorship, rather as Pélissier in his earlier career had evaded the censor by playing music halls and private concerts.)

46 *The Star* 27 Feb. 1909.

47 *The Star* 2 Mar. 1909.

48 *The Illustrated London News* 6 Mar. 1909.

49 Nicholson: p. 45.

50 G.B. Shaw. *The Shewing Up of Blanco Posnet.* London. 1911. Penguin edition, 1965: p.36. I am grateful to Professor Leonard Conolly, former President of the Shaw Society, for drawing my attention to this.

51 *Ibid.* p14.

52 Nicholson: pp. 45–46.

53 *The Daily Mail* 25 Feb. 1909.

54 *Report of Joint Select Committee,* 1909.

55 *Ibid.*

56 *Ibid.*

57 *Ibid.*

58 *Ibid.*

59 PFA. 'What A Very Great Improvement It Would Be' by H.G.Pélissier & A.Davenport.

60 V&A. Programmes.

61 Virginia Woolf; 'Notes on the Exhibition of Manet and Post-Impressionism in London'. In *Mr Bennett and Mrs Brown.* Hogarth Press, 1924. This is an essay reflecting on the post-impressionist exhibition mounted by Roger Fry in 1910.

62 Hiley: p.223.

63 *Ibid.*

64 *Era* 13 Jan. 1912.

65 Holroyd. *Bernard Shaw. Vol.2*: p. 237.

66 *Ibid.*

67 Mackenzie. Octave 4: pp. 118–119

68 See Chapter 8, note 26. *Sunday Times* 6 Dec. 1908.

Chapter 8: The Impresario

1   Gardner. *Pure Folly*: p. 43.
2   The cast of *The Whip* attended a special matinée performance of Pélissier's parody of their play, where they provided 'an endless accompaniment of laughter', although the author, who had taken the legal action was not invited. Reported in *The Daily Mail* 10 Nov. 1909.
3   V&A. Letters, Diaries & Tour Date Books.
4   *The Daily Mail* 18 Feb. 1910.
5   Pick: p. 31.
6   Booth: p. 172.
7   V&A. Programmes.
8   Bailey. *Music* Hall: p. 87.
9   Pick: p. 99.
10 Anstey: p. 190.
11 V&A. Programmes.
12 *Globe* 27 Sep. 1913.
13 Matthew Lloyd, Online (www.arthurlloyd.co.uk): entry for 'Savoy Theatre'.
14 *Tribune* 17 Apr. 1907.
15 V&A. Letters, Diaries & Tour Date Books.
16 Gardner. *Pure Folly*: p. 8.
17 Nield: p. 91.
18 Finck: pp. 31–32.
19 Gardner. *Pure Folly:* pp. 91–96.
20 PFA.
21 V&A. Programmes.
22 *Clarion* 22 Mar. 1907.
23 Gardner. *Pure Folly:* Foreword.
24 Russell. 'Popular Entertainment, 1776–1895': p. 381.
25 Russell. *Varieties of Life*: p. 65.
26 *The Sunday Times* 6 Dec. 1908.
27 Thomson, Peter: p. 415.
28 V&A. Photographs.
29 Gardner. *Pure Folly*: pp. 126–131.
30 V&A. Photographs.

Chapter 9: The Composer

1   Mackenzie: Octave 4: p. 104.
2   *The Times* 23 Sep. 1933: p. 11.
3   V&A. An unpublished hand-written score.
4   Compton: pp. 96–100.

5   *New Dictionary of National Biography*: contribution by N.T.P. Murphy. Oxford University Press, 2004.

6   PFA. 'I Want Somebody To Love Me' by H.G. Pélissier & Arthur Davenport. 1906.

7   PFA. 'My Boy from Barbary' by H.G. Pélissier & Arthur Davenport. 1909.

8   Russell. *Popular Song in England*: p. 136.

9   LCP 1907/17.

10 Russell. *Popular Song in England*: pp. 125–135.

11 Donohue: p. 16; Russell, *Popular Song in England*: p. 96; Russell, 'Popular Entertainment, 1776–1895' pp. 72–75; Nield: p. 91.

12 Nield: p. 92.

13 Russell. *Varieties of Life:* p. 62.

14 *The Strand Magazine* June 1909: p. 689.

15 PFA. 'The Dandy One-Step' by H.G. Pélissier and Fitz-Patrick Lewis. 1912.

16 PFA. Musical Scores. 'Pansy of Pennsylvania' by H.G. Pélissier and Morris Harvey. 1912.

17 PFA. 'The Toothbrush and the Sponge' by H.G. Pélissier and Arthur Davenport. 1906.

18 Andrew Lamb. *Jerome Kern in Edwardian London*. Institute for Studies in American Music, 1985

19 'How D'You Like to Spoon with Me?' 1905. Lyrics Edward Laska, music Jerome Kern. In the 1991 revival of *Showboat* at London's Adelphi Theatre, this song was especially included for performance by the very wonderful Jan Hunt in the character of Ellie May Chipley, Ms Hunt's *piece doe resistance* being to both sing and dance, as well as play the spoons.

20 LCP 26/3/1906.

21 Compton: p. 138.

22 Gardner. *Pure Folly*: p. 2.

23 Aristide Bruant. Editions Salabert, 1910

24 V&A Programmes.

25 'There Are Bad Times Just Around the Corner' by Noel Coward. 1928.

26 PFA. 'Back to the Land' by H.G. Pélissier & Arthur Davenport. 1909.

27 *Le Français* Jun. 1909.

28 Christophe Ghristi. Sleeve notes to audio CD, *Opium, Mélodies françaises*. Performed by Phillipe Jarousky and Jerome Ducrois. Erato, 2009.

29 *Ibid.*

30 *The Daily Telegraph* 12 Feb. 1910.

31 Pearson: pp. 41–91.

32 PFA. 'Alone' by H.G. Pélissier; words from Heinrich Heine. 1906.

33 PFA. 'Awake' by H.G. Pélissier; words by Sir William Davenant. 1897.

34 *BBC Proms;* entry for Prom 16 on 11 Sep. 1901. Online (www.bbc.co.uk/proms/events/by/date/1901).

35 PFA. Correspondence.

36 *Ibid.*

37 *Ibid.*

38 *Ibid.*

39 Barker: p. 121.

40 The Gibson Girl was an idealized feminine image of the 1890s and early twentieth century; see *Beyond the Gibson Girl* by Martha H. Patterson. University of Illinois Press, 2005

41 Bailey, 'Naughty but nice': pp. 36–60

42 V&A. Scrapbooks.

43 PFA. 'My Boy From Barbary' by H.G. Pélissier & Arthur Davenport. 1909.

44 Nield: p. 105.

45 *Love's Garden* by H.G. Pélissier & Arthur Davenport. Joseph Williams Ltd, 1910: pp. 8–10.

46 Bailey. 'Naughty but nice': p. 54.

47 PFA. 'Dreaming' by H.G. H.G. Pélissier & Hugh E. Wright. 1911.

48 PFA. 'I Want the Moon' by H.G. Pélissier & Will C. Pepper. Reynolds & Co.

49 *New Dictionary of National Biography;* contribution by N.T.P. Murphy. Oxford University Press, 2004.

50 *All Change Here* by H.G. Pélissier & Compton Mackenzie. Unpublished. Performed in 1910.

51 Paul Webb. *Ivor Novello: Portrait of a Star.* Haus Publishing, 2005.

52 'Thoughts of You' by Ivor Novello.

53 'Mad About the Boy' by Noel Coward. 1932.

54 PFA. 'My Boy From Barbary' by H.G. Pélissier & Arthur Davenport. 1909.

55 PFA. 'My Lodestar' by H.G. Pélissier & Arthur Wimperis. 1893.

56 PFA. 'What A Very Great Improvement It Would Be' by H.G. Pélissier & Arthur Wimperis. 1906.

57 PFA. 'Under The Weeping Willow' by H.G. Pélissier & Arthur Wimperis. 1907.

58 PFA. 'Zulu Lulu' by H.G. Pélissier & Arthur Wimperis. 1908.

59 PFA. 'A Garden of Roses' by H.G. Pélissier & Arthur Wimperis. 1907.

60 *The Dairymaids.* 1906.

61 *Mrs. Miniver.* 1942.

62 PFA. 'Our Canadian Canoe' by H.G. Pélissier & Arthur Davenport. 1904.

63 PFA. 'Jane From Maiden Lane' by H.G. Pélissier & Arthur Davenport. 1910.

64 PFA. 'What A Funny World We Live In' by H.G. Pélissier & Arthur Davenport. 1908.

65 PFA. 'Mother's Maxims' by H.G. Pélissier & Arthur Davenport. 1908.

66 PFA. 'Contrary Mary' by H.G. Pélissier & Arthur Davenport. 1908.

67 Gardner. *Pure Folly:* p. 82

68 *The Arcadians;* music by Lionel Monckton & Howard Talbot, lyrics by Arthur Wimperis. 1909.

69 Compton Mackenzie. *Carnival.* Martin Secker, 1912.

70 PFA. 'The Big Bamboo' by H.G. Pélissier & Compton Mackenzie. 1911.

71 PFA. 'Return To The Simple Life' by H.G. Pélissier & Compton Mackenzie. 1911.

72 Gardner. *Pure Folly:* p. 97.

73 V&A. Documents: letter dated 17 Jan. 1913.

74 V&A. Documents: letter dated Nov. 1913.

75 V&A. Documents: letter dated Aug. 1914.

76 V&A. Documents: document dated 8 Jun. 1904.

77 V&A. Documents: letter dated 20 Oct. 1908.

Chapter 10: The Caricaturist

1   *The Manchester Chronicle* 19 May 1907.

2   V&A. Programmes

3   *Ibid.*

4   *Ibid.*

5   *Punch* 23 Feb. 1910.

6   V&A Cuttings Album. 'Opera Hat, Stage and Stalls' (no date given).

7   PFA. *The Granta* 10 Feb. 1912.

8   Gardner. *Pure Folly*: p. 11.

9   *Ibid.*

10 *The Collected Drawings of Aubrey Beardsley;* ed. Bruce S. Harris. Bounty Books; New York, 1967: p. 89.

11 *Ibid.* p. 127.

12 V&A. Cuttings Album: *The Times;* article by Denis Mackail (no date given).

13 Morrison: p. 47.

Chapter 11: The Bohemian

1   V&A. Programmes.

2   Gardner. *Pure Folly:* p.104.

3   *Love's Garden* by H.G. Pélissier & Arthur Davenport. London. Joseph Williams Ltd, 1910.

4   *Ibid.*

5   Gardner, *Pure Folly*: p. 52.

6   Linklater: p.109.

7   Interview with Jaudy Pélissier; conducted by the author in 2019.

8   Cook: pp. 42–46.

9   Nicholson: p. 126.

10 Cook: pp. 44–56.

11 V&A. Tour Date Diaries.

12 E.M. Forster. *Maurice.* Edward Arnold, 1971. Penguin edition, 1972: p. 51.

13 *Ibid.* pp.57–61.

14 Bram Stoker. *Dracula*.1897; Penguin edition, 1993. Preface by Maurice Hindle: p. xx.

15 Cook: pp. 4–23.

16 Mackenzie: Octave 2: pp. 253–257.

17 Arthur Ransome. *Bohemia in London.* Chapman and Hall, 1907. Republished by Isha Books, 2013: p.128.

18 Gardner. *Pure Folly*: p. 84.

19 LCP 1907/17. *The Nicotine Quartets.*

20 Gardner. *Pure Folly*: p.47.

21 *The Daily Mirror* 9 Sep. 1909.

22 *The Evening News* 9 Sep. 1909.

23 *Ibid.*

24 Gardner. *Pure Folly*: p. 55.

25 *The Globe* 25 Nov. 1909.

26 *The American Review of Reviews* Sep. 1910: p. 368.

27 Compton: p.27.

28 Gardner. *Reminiscences of a Bohemian*: p.66.

29 *Ibid.*

30 *Ibid.*

31 *The Times* 25 Sep. 1913; funeral notice of H.G. Pélissier.

32 Gardner. *Reminiscences of an Old Bohemian*: p. 80.

33 *Southampton Times* Apr. 1897.

34 V&A Photographs & LCP *The Nicotine Quartets.*

35 Gardner. *Pure* Folly: p. 57.

36 V&A. Advance Date Book. July 1908 to July 1910.

37 *Ibid.*

38 Compton: pp. 34–35

Chapter 12: The Romantic

1   *The Daily Mirror* 19 Sep. 1911.

2   Holroyd. *A Strange and Eventful History*: p. 182.

3   Mackenzie. Octave 1: p. 142.

4   Mackenzie. Octave 2: p. 227.

5   Linklater: p. 17.

6   *Ibid.* pp. 29– 30.

7   Nicholson: pp. 128–140.

8   Mackenzie, F. C.: pp. 235–236.

9   The Willesden and Kilburn Historical Archive. Online (https://kilburnandwillesdenhistory.blogspot.com/).

10 Mackenzie: Octave 4: p. 63.

11 Linklater: p. 101

12 Mackenzie. Octave 4: pp. 100–102.

13 *Ibid.* p. 257. The Theatre Girls Club was founded in 1914 by Virginia Compton. It replaced and continued the work of The Soho Club and Home founded by Maud Stanley in 1880. It provided reasonably priced accommodation for young actresses in the West End, particularly during rehearsal periods. There is an extensive archive at the V&A still to be researched.

14 *Ibid.* p. 197.

15 Mackenzie. Octave 4: p. 128.

16 *Ibid.* p. 101.

17 *Ibid.* p. 102.

18 *Ibid.* p. 103.

19 *Ibid.* p. 128.

20 PFA. Correspondence.

21 *Ibid.*

22 Mackenzie. Octave. 3: pp. 224–226.

23 Compton: p. 91.

24 PFA. Correspondence.

25 *Ibid.*

26 Virginia Compton, an unpublished memoir. Virginia Compton wrote a comprehensive memoir detailing her childhood experiences and family history. It is unpublished and resides with the Literary Collection of Compton Mackenzie at Texas State University in Austin. Andro Linklater draws on it extensively in his biography *Compton Mackenzie: A Life.*

27 Linklater: p. 19.

28 *Ibid.* p. 20.

29 *The Kissed Mouth.* Online (http://kilburnandwillesdenhistory.blogspot.com/2015/01/the-famous-folly-from-kilburn.html).

30 Linklater: pp. 17–30.

31 *Ibid.* p. 16.

32 *Ibid.* pp. 17–30.

33 Mackenzie: Octave 4: p. 132.

34 Linklater: p. 22.

35 Mackenzie, F.C.: p. 220.

36 Compton: pp. 96–97.

37 Mackenzie. Octave 4: p. 132.

38 Compton: p. 99.

Chapter 13: The Shadow

1 Compton: pp. 95–99.
2 *Ibid.* p. 105.
3 *Era* 4 Dec.1913. I am grateful to learn from Catherine Mortimer Hart – whose grandfather's brother was married to Gwennie or Gwenllean Mars – that she actually 'came from a very talented and respected musical family' and died of food poisoning in India, shortly after having left *The Follies* in 1914 and having had a baby son called John.
4 Compton: pp. 31–32.
5 V&A. Cuttings Album. *The Times* article by Denis Mackail (no date given).
6 V&A. Diaries 1912–1914.
7 *Ibid.*
8 *Ibid.*
9 PFA. Correspondence.
10 Compton: p.111.
11 *Ibid.*
12 *Ibid.* p. 113.
13 PFA. Correspondence.
14 V&A. Letters, Diaries & Tour Date Books.

Chapter 14: The Ghost

1 Mackenzie, F.C.: p. 236
2 Reported in Kilburn and Willesden History Archive. Online.
3 PFA. *The Last Will & Testament of H.G. Pélissier.*
4 Reported in the Kilburn and Willesden History Archive. Online (https://kilburnandwillesdenhistory.blogspot.com/).
5 PFA. *The Last Will & Testament of H.G. Pélissier.*
6 *The Daily Mirror* 19 Sep. 1911.
7 PFA. *The Last Will & Testament of H.G. Pélissier.*
8 Compton: p. 115.
9 *Ibid.* p. 117.
10 *Ibid.* p. 117.
11 *Ibid.* p. 146.
12 *Ibid.* p. 149.
13 *Ibid.* p. 150.
14 *Ibid.* p. 171.
15 *Ibid.* p. 185.
16 *Ibid.* p. 185.
17 *Ibid.* p. 188.
18 *Ibid.* p. 187.

19 *Ibid.* p. 190.

20 *Ibid.*

21 *Ibid.* p. 196

22 J.M. Barrie. *Peter Pan and Other Plays.* Oxford University Press, 1995; Introduction by Peter Hollindale: p. xiv.

23 Ibid.

24 J.M. Barrie. *Mary Rose.* Oxford University Press, 1995: p. 294; Lines 510–522.

25 Reported in *The Western Morning News* 30 May 1921.

26 J.M. Barrie. *Peter Pan and Other Plays.* Oxford University Press, 1995; Introduction by Peter Hollindale: p. xiv.

27 Ibid.

28 *The Sketch* 25 Aug. 1920.

29 *Portsmouth Evening News* 23 Aug. 1928.

30 *Sphere* 30 Mar. 1907.

31 Linklater: p. 108.

32 Compton: pp. 257–258.

33 Linklater: p. 196.

34 *The Tewkesbury Register and Agricultural Gazette* 18 June 1921.

35 A Pélissier family anecdote as related to me by Jaudy Pélissier, Fay's grandson.

36 *The Illustrated Sporting and Dramatic News* 15 Jan. 1927.

37 V&A. Photographs.

38 Philip Hoare. *Noel Coward: A Biography.* Sinclair-Stevenson/Simon & Schuster USA/ Recorda Distrubuda, Brazil, 1995: p. 123.

39 *The Illustrated London News* 4 Jun. 1932.

40 *Era* 22 Jul. 1936.

41 *The Daily Herald* 5 Dec. 1928.

42 *Nottingham Journal* 7 Apr. 1931.

43 Ibid.

44 *Portsmouth Evening News* 16 Jun. 1951.

45 Linklater: p. 197.

46 Ibid.

47 Reported in *Portsmouth Evening News* 4 Dec. 1925; quotes *Wisdom of the Gods* by H. Dennis Bradley. Werner Laurie, 1929.

48 H. Dennis Bradley. *And After.* Werner Laurie, 1931.

Chapter 15: The Legacy

1 Nicholson: p. 114.

2 *Ibid.* p. 119.

3 Mulla: p. 181.

4   *Ibid.* p. 186.

5   *The Wipers Times.* (First published 1916–1918). Osprey. 2018.

6   Siegfried Sassoon. *The War Poems.* Faber and Faber Ltd., 1983.

7   Compton: p. 34.

8   Online (www.londonsilentcinemas.com).

9   Russell. "Popular Entertainment, 1776–1895": p. 380.

10   Compton Mackenzie. *Carnival.* Society of Authors, London, 1912.

11   Compton Mackenzie. *The Adventures of Sylvia Scarlett.* Society of Authors. London, 1918.

12   Compton: p. 24.

13   *Ibid.* p. 190.

14   Noel Coward. *Tonight at 8.30;* first produced Manchester 1935.

15   *Tonight at 8.30;* film directed by Anthony Pélissier, 1952.

16   John Mills. *Up in the Clouds:* Weidenfeld & Nicholson, 1980: pp. 136–139.

17   *The Rocking-Horse Winner;* a film directed by Anthony Pélissier, 1950.

18   Interview with Jaudy Pélissier conducted by the author, 2019.

19   John Mills. *Up in the Clouds.* Weidenfeld & Nicholson, 1980: p.136.

20   V&A. Diaries 1912–1914.

21   *The Bystander* 29 Oct. 1913.

22   *Daily Sketch* 12 Feb. 1916.

23   *Athenaeum* 29 Aug. 1919.

24   *London Mail* 30 Aug. 1919.

25   *Sunday Sportsman* 13 Feb. 1921.

26   *Empire News* Feb.1921.

27   V&A. Diaries 1912–1914.

28   *Ibid.*

29   *Ibid.*

30   John Mills. *Up in the Clouds.* Weidenfeld & Nicholson, 1980: p. 136.

31   V&A. Documents

32   *Ibid.*

33   *Ibid.*

34   *Ibid.*

35   *Worthing Herald* 19 Dec. 1936.

36   Compton: p. 33.

37   Ganzl: pp. 946–947.

38   Nield: p. 104.

39   Gale: pp. 155–157.

40   Quoted in *Charlot: The Genius of Intimate Revue* by J.M. Moore. McFarland & Co., 2005: p. 15.

41   *Ibid.*

42 Elsa Lanchester. *Herself: An Autobiography.* St Martin's Press, 1983: pp. 54–63.
43 Carpenter: *Spike Milligan:* pp. 223–226.
44 *Michael Palin: A Life on Screen.* BBC documentary, 2018.
45 Nuttall: pp. 114–125.
46 Carpenter. *Spike Milligan:* p. 150

Index

*Anthony Binns (right) and Jaudy Pélissier (left) share a
tipple with H.G.P. at the family grave in Marylebone
cemetery*

Anthony Binns is a graduate in history from King's College, London University. He has contributed articles and reviews to various historical and theatrical magazines, including items on H.G. Pélissier and Ronald Bagnall to *The Call Boy,* the quarterly magazine of the British Music Hall Society. He has written several plays and musicals under the names of Mitch Binns and Mitch Feral. These include *Barnstormers*, produced by Century Theatre and based on the memoirs of the eighteenth-century travelling actress, Charlotte Lowes – the first contemporary work to be taken on a tour of the Indian sub-continent by the British Council; and *Sweet Engineering of the Lucid Mind* – which won the 'Offcuts Short Play Award' in 2010. He is the lead singer/songwriter of the world music band *Moveable Feast* and, as Tommy Parsons, he has performed in music hall and variety throughout the UK. He is a member of the Society for Theatre Research.

E: anthony.binns@outlook.com

Despite coming from a theatrical family that goes back 200 years, **Jaudy Pélissier**, grandson of H.G. Péllissier**,** does not tread the boards. After a short career in the film industry, he now runs his own branding and digital media consultancy. *The Funniest Man in London* is the unlocking of the first of many theatrical stories from the Compton, Bateman and Compton Mackenzie family archives.

E: joe@pelissier.co.uk

The Book of Syn

Russell Thorndike, Dr Syn and the Romney Marsh

By Keith Swallow

The Reverend Christopher Syn, Doctor of Divinity, was a man of many parts: Vicar of Dymchurch; swordsman and duellist; ruthless pirate; smuggler; and murderer. His exploits are so embedded in the culture of Dymchurch and the wider Romney Marsh that many people are unaware that he was a fictional character, the creation of Russell Thorndike.

Thorndike himself lived a life almost as full as that of his chief character; he was a Shakespearian actor, raconteur and bon viveur, as well as a prolific writer and historian. That many believe that Syn once walked the earth is down to Thorndike's ability to weave so much reality into his tales.

However, Syn's existence extends beyond Thorndike's seven novels. There have been three films (including versions by both Disney and Hammer) and Syn has appeared on the stage, in musicals and in comics. There is also a bi-annual 'Day of Syn' held in Dymchurch – the largest free festival in the South of England.

This book explores the life, times and influences of author Russell Thorndike; the Syn novels, films and plays; the realities of smuggling at the time that the novels were set; and the places on Romney Marsh that captivated and inspired Thorndike.

ISBN: 978-0-9548390-9-3
Price: £16 from any good bookshop
(or see www.edgertonpublishing.co.uk)

Destiny Defined

Dante Gabriel Rossetti and Elizabeth Siddal in Hasting

By Jenny Ridd

For several years Jenny Ridd lived at 5 High Street, Hastings, a house visited by the Pre-Raphaelite poets and painters Dante Gabriel Rossetti and Elizabeth (Lizzie) Siddal. With her husband, Peter Marsden, Jenny uncovered the true story of the couple's happy visit in 1854, using the architecture of the house, an excavation of the garden and local documents.

This book sets these new discoveries into the context of the later Rossetti/Siddal relationship, which was destined to descend into jealousy, illness, depression, infant mortality, accidental death and eventual exhumation.

Included in the book are copies of letters relating to Lizzie's visits to Hastings and, for the first time together, the three drawings of Lizzie made on the same day by Gabriel, Barbara Leigh Smith and Anna Mary Howitt at Scalands, the farmhouse owned by Barbara's family.

ISBN: 978-9548390-4-8

Price: £10 from any good bookshop
(or see www.edgertonpublishing.co.uk)

Nanny Goat Island

Dungeness Then and Now

By Keith Swallow

To the uninitiated, the stark beauty of Dungeness is totally unexpected only two hours from central London. 'Unique'; 'magical'; 'a special place' – all these descriptions hold true, but all this would have been totally different had a vast new ferry terminal, offering the shortest route from London to Paris, been built. This is the story of the development of this special corner of Kent, from the early settlers, whose only source of milk was the animals that they kept untethered on the shingle, to the current day. It explores the hardships of those who have earned a living from fishing the waters here, the coming of the railway, wartime fortification, nature conservation, lifeboat and rescue services, the construction of the power stations – and exploding goats!

ISBN: 978-0-9933203-4-7
Price: £15 from any good bookshop
(or see www.edgertonpublishing.co.uk)